IN SEARCH OF *TUNGA*

T0373416

AFRICAN PERSPECTIVES
Kelly Askew and Anne Pitcher
Series Editors

A complete list of titles in the series can be found at www.press.umich.edu

In Search of *Tunga*

Prosperity, Almighty God, and Lives in Motion in a Malian Provincial Town

André Chappatte

University of Michigan Press
Ann Arbor

For questions or permissions, please contact um.press.perms@umich.edu

Published in the United States of America by the
University of Michigan Press
Printed and bound by CPI Group (UK) Ltd, Croydon, CR0 4YY

First published November 2022

A CIP catalog record for this book is available from the British Library.

Library of Congress Cataloging-in-Publication Data

Names: Chappatte, André, author. | Michigan Publishing (University of Michigan),
    publisher.
Title: In search of Tunga : prosperity, Almighty God, and lives in motion in a Malian
    provincial town / André Chappatte.
Other titles: Prosperity, Almighty God, and lives in motion in a Malian provincial
    town | African perspectives (University of Michigan. Press)
Description: Ann Arbor : University of Michigan Press, 2022. | Series: African
    perspectives | "Glossary and Orthographic Conventions" (pages xi–xiii) includes
    "Concise Glossary of Bamanan Terms". | Includes bibliographical references (pages 197–
    217) and index.
Identifiers: LCCN 2022023738 (print) | LCCN 2022023739 (ebook) | ISBN 9780472075652
    (hardcover) | ISBN 9780472055654 (paperback) | ISBN 9780472220748 (ebook)
Subjects: LCSH: Islam—Mali—Bougouni (Sikasso) | Muslim men—Religious life—
    Mali—Bougouni (Sikasso) | Male immigrants—Mali—Bougouni (Sikasso) | Piety. |
    Bougouni (Sikasso, Mali)—Religion. | Bougouni (Sikasso, Mali)—Social life and
    customs. | Bougouni (Sikasso, Mali)—Emigration and immigration. | Bougouni
    (Sikasso, Mali)—Description and travel.
Classification: LCC BP64.M29 C43 2022 (print) | LCC BP64.M29 (ebook) |
    DDC 297.096623—dc23/eng/20220622
LC record available at https://lccn.loc.gov/2022023738
LC ebook record available at https://lccn.loc.gov/2022023739

Publication of this volume has been partially funded by the African Studies Center,
University of Michigan.

Cover photograph © André Chappatte; reprinted courtesy of the author.

In memory of my father

CONTENTS

CHAPTER 8

Digital materials related to this title can be found on
the Fulcrum platform via the following citable URL:
https://doi.org/10.3998/mpub.12122503

ACKNOWLEDGMENTS

The development of this book has been a kind of *tunga* that started fourteen years ago. Many things have happened since. How could I make it short but powerful? This book owes a primary debt to my host family in Bougouni, Mali, and the *aventuriers* I met in town. Four months into my fieldwork, the head of my host family, Kader Traoré, passed away. Kader was the first person of Bougouni who introduced me to local Muslim life through the prism of a constructive sincerity. *In ni baara* Kader; *Ala ka hinɛ e la.* Riding across Bougouni on a bicycle, I met warm and generous people, especially the *aventuriers*. They accepted me as I was—naïve and curious—showed patience with my efforts in speaking Bambara, and let me enter into their lives. Unfortunately, I lost touch with most of them. I missed them and wholeheartedly hope their lives and families have flourished since. Before going to Bougouni, I spent two months in Bamako, where I lived with and took intensive Bambara classes given by Mohamed Larabi Diallo. *Nin karamɔgɔ, a ka farin dè!* I praise the strictness of his teaching. *In ni baara* Mohamed; *Ala ka hinɛ e la.* This book also owes a big debt to the intellectual freedom I enjoyed at ZMO Berlin between 2014 and 2019; special thanks to Anandita Bajpai, Svenja Becherer, Katrin Bromber, Joseph Désiré Som I, Ulrike Freitag, Paolo Gaibazzi, Claudia Ghrawi, Sonja Hegasy, Kai Kresse, Peter Lambertz, Silke Nagel, Saadi Nikro, Samuli Schielke, Michael Schutz, Abdoulaye Sounaye, and İlkay Yilmaz for all the joyful moments and inspiring discussions we shared together.

Close to home, I thank my mother and my brothers who visited me in Bougouni. Special thanks to my twin brother, who, during his first job, sent me 250 Swiss francs (about US$267) each month while I was without much money in the field. Special thanks also to my wife for her love, patience, and generosity; she has taught me over the years to be more aware of the forces of egoism that arise in academia and its highly individualistic career path. Finally, this book owes a special debt to my father, who passed away a few years ago. As his son, I more and more realize that his indefatigable commitment to the values of love, knowledge, and social justice paved the way to my becoming as a fieldworker. *Merci, papa.*

GLOSSARY AND ORTHOGRAPHIC CONVENTIONS

ORTHOGRAPHIC CONVENTIONS

ŋ = [ng]
ɲ = [ny]
ɛ = [è]
ɔ = [ò]
c = [ch]
aa, ee, ii (. . .) = long vowels
an, en, in (. . .) = nasalized vowels

Words in plural are written with a "*w*" at the end. The structure of compound words may be stressed by a period (".") to indicate their composite linguistic structure.

CONCISE GLOSSARY OF BAMANAN TERMS

adamaden	human being
adamadenya	human condition
baara	work
Bamanankan	bambara language
Bamanaya	to be Bamanan, Bamanan religious practices
baraji	divine award
barika	physical strength, blessing
bonya	respect
cɛkɔrɔba	old man
dabali	evil spell
dakan	destiny
danaya	trust
danbe	honor

danga	curse
danga den	cursed child
diinɛ	religion
djinɛ	jinn, spirit
dubabu	blessing
dusu	heart, courage, anger
facɛ	legacy of the father
garijɛgɛ	luck
gwa	extended family
hɔrɔn	noble
hɔrɔnya	nobleness
jamu	family name
janfa	treachery
jɛli	praise singer and bard (people of castes)
jon	slave
juguman	bad, nasty, evil
juguya	badness, nastiness, evilness
jurumu	sin
kamalen	young unmarried man
karamɔgɔ	teacher, master, scholar
kɛlɛya	jealousy
ko	problem, difficulty, affair
kɔrɔtɛ	magic poison
kuma	speaking
kunbenyɛrɛ	crossroads
laada	custom
limanyia	faith
maloya	shame
mɔrikɛ	Muslim scholar in occult sciences (marabout)
musokɔrɔba	old woman
nataba	cupidity, greed
nkalon	lie
numu	blacksmith
ɲamakala	artisan
ɲɛgoya	selfish, selfishness
ɲɔgɔndɛmɛ	solidarity
sababu/sabu	cause, reason, motive
saraka	offering, sacrifice
silamɛ	Muslim

silamɛya	Islam
sɛli	Muslim prayer
sɛnɛkɛla	farmer
soma	sorcerer, diviner
somaya	sorcery
subaga	witch
sunguru	young unmarried woman
tɛriya	friendship
tɔgɔ	name
tɔɔrɔ	suffering, harm, pain
tunga	adventure, journey, foreign country
wari	money
wurudi	Islamic rosary
zana	proverb

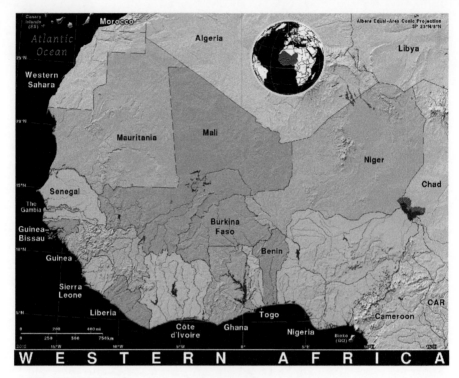

Fig. 1. Map of West Africa. (Copyright d-maps.com)

Fig. 2. Map of Mali.
(Copyright d-maps.com)

CHAPTER 1

Tunga

"Tomorrow Is in God's Hands"

During my 17-month stay (December 2008–April 2010) in the Malian provincial town of Bougouni (60,000 inhabitants), I used to visit a *grin* (informal male meeting spot) located at the threshold of a noisy and dusty gasoline-powered mechanical mill. I sat there with two of my friends, the owner of the mill and a civil servant. Soon after we started chatting and joking about various issues, a sweating hefty man, whose torn clothes were covered with flour and grease, would come out of the mill to silently prepare tea for us. This man in the prime of his life would then swiftly move within the mill when people brought bags of grain on carts or on their backs for grinding. An increasing number of (mostly better-off) urban households paid a few hundred francs to grind their harvested grain in such modern mills rather than continuing to grind with the traditional but tiring pestle and mortar.[1] In early 2009 the owner of the mill introduced me to this mill worker when he was serving us tea. Kassim was a single man in his mid-thirties who struck me with his reverential and diligent attitude.[2] I wished to converse with him, but at first he was reserved. After all, I was the friend of Kassim's patron. In this context, respect could also require a self-effacing presence. Slowly but surely, we became acquainted during the course of my visits to this *grin*. Kassim later opened a small street food shop in Bougouni as a night activity supplementing his day work in the mill. A friendship arose when I regularly visited Kassim in his shop.

In our conversations, Kassim often shared with me the ups and downs of his life trajectory since he had left his native village in northern Côte d'Ivoire for the coastal town of San Pedro a few years ago. Thanks to his efforts, however, Kassim's economic situation had improved during my stay. In early 2010 he left the mill to run a cement-built shop servicing mobile phones. A wedding project even hatched in his mind. The burgeoning prosperity he was achieving by the end of my stay, however, had been preceded by years of hardships. Once, while fixing a mobile phone in the evening, he told me how he came to Bougouni:

> I grew up in a village in northern Côte d'Ivoire [. . .]. Then, I moved to San Pedro to seek money. I found a job as a dockworker in San Pedro harbor, where I stayed for a couple of years. . . . However, I lost everything in the civil war. I could not return home with empty hands! Then I decided to go off on adventure to Mali, where there is nobody from my family. At that time, Côte d'Ivoire was dangerous! From Bouaké to Zégoua, our bus had to cross more than 30 roadblocks set up by the rebels. A policewoman from the same town as me helped me to cross them safely. . . . The bus reached Sikasso [in southern Mali]. Nobody helped me there except someone who previously lived in Côte d'Ivoire. I told him my story. He then replied, "You will suffer, mate. It's harsh here!" Indeed, I suffered. I slept outdoors for one month and did not manage to eat properly. But the problem was where to store my only bag in a safe place during the day. I lied to *touts* ['*coxers*' or transport organizing personnel] by telling them that I was expecting money from my big brother in order to go to Bamako [the capital of Mali]. They kept my bag for four days. After that it was too much! I did the same trick with a street vendor sitting next to the bus station, but she started to refuse me after a couple of days. Then I moved out of the bus station and stayed a couple of days around a mosque, where I stored my bag and prayed regularly. Eventually, someone noticed my comings and goings and offered me a job as a gardener for his eldest brother. I accepted and lied to him that I already did such a job in Abidjan [*laughs*]. I was willing and the wage was correct, but the patron did not give us enough food. I watered the plants for three months. My co-worker then convinced me to go to Bamako, where, he told me, job opportunities are better. Then we traveled together to Bamako. However, Bamako turned out to be too harsh! The only work I found there was as a *wɔtɔrɔtigi* [cart driver]. I did not accept it. It is too shameful and physical [*laughs*]. After a couple of weeks in Bamako, we moved to Ouéléssébougou to greet the eldest sister

of my friend. I did not manage to find a job there either. Then we moved to Bougouni to greet a relative of my friend. I fortunately met my Ivorian aunt there.[3] She helped me a lot. She found me a job as a houseboy and handyman with her younger brother's family in Bougouni.[4]

Kassim fled San Pedro in late 2002 when the Ivorian crisis hit this town. His northern identity put him in danger at that time in southern Côte d'Ivoire (Marshall-Fratani 2006). He traveled to southern Mali, most likely for its cultural similarity to his home region. Kassim had the advantage of speaking Dyula, a Mande language close to Bambara.[5] His journey, which unexpectedly reached Bougouni, illustrates how such a life away from home is often shaped by hardships, specific ethics, and encounters. His regional identity and Muslim devotion concurrently helped him to move forward on this tortuous search for a livelihood but also dignity. The manifold steps of his journey (village—big town one—big town two—capital of Mali—big village—provincial town), coupled with their fortuitous dimension, do not capture a mere rural-urban migration. As he stated, "I am an *aventurier*."[6]

In this part of the West African savanna, people often employ the Bambara term *tunga* and the French term *aventure* (adventure) in an interchangeable way.[7] *Aventure* in a West African context, however, does not equate with the French term *aventure*. The word *tunga* does not connote the bourgeois attitude of exploring wild regions and facing extraordinary encounters of all kinds that the term *aventure* meant during colonial times in the novel genre (e.g., Defoe 2021 [1719]; Verne 2005 [1866]) and still does in its popular sense.[8] It neither expresses voluntarily going off on *aventure*, nor a privilege due to economic power, nor a casual fling. As for *tunga*, its pragmatic translation is "foreign country" (Bailleul 1996, 413).[9] In practice, however, *aventuriers* understand such migration as a specific field of experiences that goes beyond the fact of crossing national boundaries. For them, *tunga* starts as soon as one leaves home in both spatial and relational terms (Gugler 2002, 23–24). Home represents the familiar sphere, itself composed of ties (relatives, neighbors, friends), spaces (villages and lands), and traditions (custom, norms, roles). Neither voluntary nor pure constraint, going off on *tunga* is, above all, a customary search for money and more via a migration far from home that dates back to colonial times.

FROM THE GOLD COAST TO BOUGOUNI: BECOMING "CIVILIZED"

Ils sont venus en Gold Coast ou en Côte d'Ivoire pour chercher de l'argent sans doute, mais aussi pour chercher de l'aventure (Rouch 1967)[10]

Labor migration in search for improved life conditions is a long-standing form of economic mobility in West Africa (Manchuelle 1997); still, colonial policy reinforced the necessary nature of this mobility. Soon after the conquest of Afrique Occidentale Française (AOF), the colonial administration started levying a head tax in francs.[11] Towns and roads of AOF became inevitably thronged with rural migrants in search of francs. This tax compelled local inhabitants to work for a colonial economy far from home. Between 1910 and 1950, migrant peanut farmers (*nawétaans*) from the territory of French Sudan, for instance, moved to the western region of Senegal during the rainy season (David 1980). Others worked on the construction of the railroad line Thiès-Kayes (J. Jones 2002). The origin of these economic migrations was coercive. Families sent young members to earn money to pay colonial taxes. With the monetarization of the economy, others migrated to pay bride price. Yet, these migrations opened up new horizons. Over time, some started to journey on their own accord. As Jean Rouch commented in *Jaguar* (1967), a documentary film based on the migration of three men from Niger to the Gold Coast during the 1950s, these migrants also sought *l'aventure*. Often, economic migrants were also motivated by a spirit of *tunga*; they wanted to discover new places, to see new technologies, and to acquire new consumer objects (such as hats, sunglasses, jewelry, umbrellas, clothes) and the status and social distinctions they connoted (David 1980, 113–26). In other words, "the general message was that to prove their manhood, men had to go on adventure in Senegal" (Peterson 2011, 144). After 1950, young men from southern Mali went on *tunga* in Côte d'Ivoire for similar reasons (Gary-Tounkara 2008). To make the documentary film *Moi, un noir* (1957), for six months Rouch followed the daily life of young inhabitants of Niger who migrated to the Treichville district of Abidjan to seek money. Fifty years ago, these young Nigeriens understood money as the main road to marriage, buying a vehicle, building a house, and enjoying a modern life. But their little song "Abidjan when we say your name, Abidjan of lagoon, nice sojourn" turned out to be a fleeting "waking dream" contrasting with the gloomy reality of daily struggles, tiredness, and sadness (Gary-Tounkara 2008). They reached Abidjan but only its site. Few achieved prosperity there.[12] What became of this customary search for money and more in contemporary Mali?

In the context of today's focus on the global world, numerous studies explore South-North migration—for example, Paul Stoller's (2010) study of the lives of West African street vendors in the 1990s in New York. Thomas Fouquet demonstrates how young urbanites in Dakar aspire to travel north for economic emancipation as well as to touch the "fantasized elsewhere,"[13] as the Western world has come to be imagined in West Africa since the colonial period (2007). Jean Schmitz speaks of a "crisis of African migration" (2006, 97); political and economic deterioration in former African destinations (e.g., Côte d'Ivoire, Gabon) compelled migrants to head north. In 2008 Schmitz edited a special issue of the journal *Politique Africaine* titled *Migrants ouest-africans: miséreux, aventuriers ou notables?* Notably, its contributors explore the history of South-North migratory networks and their ramifications along the channels toward Europe. Pointing to the extreme media attention and political failure to stop the tragic South-North migration across the Mediter-ranean (de Haas 2008a, 2008b), however, Sylvie Bredeloup reminds us that in 2017 "more than 70% of African migrations occur within the [African] continent."[14] In her study of the linkages between migration and becoming a "proper person" among people of Fouta Djallon (Middle Guinea), Susanna Fioratta explores hardships in their search for money in Dakar (2020, chapter 4). In his study of West African migration to Brazzaville (the capital of Congo Republic), Bruce Whitehouse further stresses that intra-African migration "has gone nearly unnoticed by the rest of the world" (2012, 5). This mono-graph adds that such migration does not involve only big coastal towns.

Up-market neighborhoods, and hence money and products of foreign manufacture, can also be found in small towns, not to mention the grow-ing mobile internet access found in provincial Africa since the 2010s. The way migrants assess their destinations also depends on where they grew up. Numerous studies of transnational migration involve Senegal, a coastal country that has forged privileged networks with the Western world (espe-cially France) since the colonial period. By contrast, Mali is a landlocked country that suffers from remoteness and had remained on the fringe of colonial policy in terms of investments, compared with forested and coastal West Africa. While a person from Dakar depicts his country as an eco-nomic blind alley, for instance, a Malian sees Dakar as a possible migratory destination. For *aventuriers* of rural inland West Africa (Sahel, savanna), small towns of landlocked countries are already opening doors to wider trends coming from *là où çest évolué* (where it is developed) or *là où çest civilisé* (where civilization is), such as African capitals, Europe, the United States, Mecca, Dubai (since the early 2000s), and now China. Provincial towns also shape an urban network that is often closer to villages and in rapid growth across contemporary Africa.

The term *civilisé*, which was widely used among *aventuriers* in southwest Mali, originates from a French imperial discourse of *civilisation* that initially spread among Africans from colonial posts, such as Bougouni.[15] In the aftermath of the conquest of AOF, the colonial administration settled in a network of existing localities that were strategically located along trade roads. Powerful infrastructures and products of foreign origin (e.g., cement buildings, water tanks, electricity), as well as new economic opportunities, progressively shaped and accelerated the growth of these new colonial posts, which became spearheads of the French *mission civilisatrice* under the Third Republic (1870–1940) within the African continent (Conklin 1997). To the eyes of locals, these colonial posts forcibly became the first "urban" localities of West Africa from where the so-called *civilisation* flows. Such linkages between civilized and urban spaces still shape modernity as a political project (Comaroff and Comaroff 1993) of the self in contemporary French West Africa, however, in a less coercive way. In present-day Mali, the term *civilisé* refers to a more recent conception of modernity as "the new, the diverse, the forward-looking" and an urban lifestyle characterized by "change and movement" (Thomassen 2012, 172). In practice, it refers to "creative adaptation" insofar as these *aventuriers* "'make' themselves modern" (Gaonkar 2001, 18) by attempting to move forward in life. Building upon earlier discourses on the (colonial) urban as crossroads of *civilisation*, this monograph illustrates that an economic migration imbued with a spirit of *tunga* has participated in the rapid growth of provincial towns in the savanna of contemporary West Africa.

TUNGA: "TOMORROW IS IN GOD'S HANDS"

Numerous studies of migration among Africans engage with the concept of *aventure* and the category of male *aventurier*. Taking *tunga* as a field of experience that migrants enter as soon as they leave home, *tunga* should not be exclusively male. In Bougouni, for instance, young women of rural origin moved to town to work as "housemaids" (*baarakaloden musow*) for better-off families.[16] These housemaids, however, neither called themselves *aventurières* nor were called as such; they worked away from home for a precise reason: to help their future husband to finance their wedding. *Tunga* as an open-ended economic undertaking away from home was reserved for men.[17] On the other hand, not all *aventuriers* were single; many were in *tunga* with their wife and children. What is the place for women in this study? In Bougouni men and women traditionally did not intermingle closely beyond family ties. Moreover, my existential approach to *tunga* (see below) asked for a shared intimacy that is tricky to build with the opposite sex outside a sentimental relationship. This monograph consequently narrates male *aventuriers' tunga* in Bougouni while acknowledging the considerable support (cash income, morale, affection) of their wives in their struggle for a better life.

Like the characters in the book *Eaters of the Dry Season* (Rain 1999),[18] certain *aventuriers* in Bougouni went off on *tunga* after first helping their families during *les mois de suture*, the difficult months before the new harvest when granaries are emptying, by providing remittances as seasonal workers. Their temporary economic mobility echoed works on the coexistence of capitalist and domestic economies in West Africa (e.g., Meillassoux 1981; Wooten 2005). Others went off on *tunga* to avoid the weight of "traditional customs" (*laada*) in village life (e.g., gerontocracy); they wanted to gain more freedom and autonomy from home. In this regard, *tunga* can involve an emancipatory rupture (Bardem 1993). Similar to the "economic runaways" explored by Jennifer Diggins on Sierra Leone's southern coast, the *aventuriers'* decision to go off on *tunga* is also motivated by the "webs of debt, obligation and dependency of the kind that characterized their lives under 'parental care' in the family villages" (2015, 328), but they do not run away from home, a point explored further below.

Aventuriers used to say that "*tunga* is a school,"[19] because moving elsewhere widens people's horizons and opens their minds.[20] Returnees brought home prestigious knowledge and took pride in their past sojourns in the wider world. They considered themselves *civilisés* or *évolués* compared with those who never traveled. But first, *tunga* is demanding and hence transforms the *aventurier* into a grown person. As a path to maturity, *tunga* was especially favored by young men of rural origin who left school prematurely because they had to tend the farm and their aging parents. In the *région* of Sikasso, many elders traveled to Côte d'Ivoire during their youth to work in cocoa and coffee plantations. Going off on *tunga* was still regarded as a *rite de passage* (Riccio 2001) to manhood. Whitehouse (2012) explains that the Bamanan proverb *tunga tɛ danbe don* (exile knows no dignity) encapsulates the manifold dimensions of belonging and "strangehood" he encountered in his ethnography. In Bougouni honor (*danbe*) was also a place-bound value (21, 88) insofar as *aventuriers*, away from home, were less reluctant to be engaged in degrading forms of labor.[21] Whitehouse adds that "emigration" is one of the three main ways to escape the weight of people's obligations to their kin (78–83). In a similar vein, *aventuriers* spoke about *tunga* as a way to move away from *le poids du social* (the weight of kin) linked to life at home. *Aventuriers* aimed for a better life forged away from home. However, their move was not cut off from their home communities, on the contrary.

Salif the tailor, for instance, went off on *tunga* because he wanted "to obtain a [respectable] position" (*ka position sɔrɔ*) within his home community. He often compared himself with his big brother, who was settled in the village. For him, this big brother—married, a father, a head of family, a cattle trader, and an owner of cement houses—had already acquired this respectable position. But he, as "unmarried" (*cɛgana*) and still dependent of his family, had not achieved such a position yet. For Salif, building up this position meant "getting a good job" (*ka baara ɲuman sɔrɔ*), "getting married" (*ka muso furu*), "having children" (*ka denw sɔrɔ*), "taking care of the family" (*ka nasɔngɔ di*) and "building a house" (*ka so jo*).[22] Consequently, Salif moved to Bougouni in search of money.

Marriage and parenthood were both conventional gates to adulthood in contemporary Mali. However, heads of family and fathers also went off on *tunga* because they did not enjoy a full respectable status in their home community. When *aventuriers* return home, what happens then?

> I cannot come back home with empty hands. This is shameful. My parents, my brothers, and my friends would be angry about that. If I come home and I see my friends married with kids, living in houses, driving cars and motorbikes . . . and me with nothing, I would be very angry and I would bring shame on my family. I need at least to start something here and to get married before returning home. (Kassim the handyman and mill worker)

Ideally, *aventuriers* who return home wealthy acquire the status of "big man." *Tunga* can transform wealthy returnees into "heroes of modern times," as Rouch (1967) claimed in *Jaguar*.[23] Above, Kassim hinted that *aventuriers* struggle not to return home with empty hands. By going off on *tunga*, they may physically escape home but only momentarily; while away, they carry the prospect of return in mind. *Aventuriers* never fully disjoin themselves from home insofar as the path of *tunga* ends at home, where they must display and achieve concrete achievements.

In contexts of transnational migration among young Soninke men in

Kounda (*région* of Kaye, Mali), a migrant aspires to *realiser quelque chose* (achieve something) in the village (Jónsson 2008, 24). *Aventuriers* should hence think "in terms of 'Walking on Two Legs' as [they] pursue urban along-side rural interests" (Gugler 2002, 31). The narrative of autonomy coexists with the narrative of solidarity (Riccio 2005) because *aventuriers'* prosper-ity is assessed primarily by their home community. *Aventuriers* who settle abroad never sever their origins completely. They most often seek to invest in their village by building a cement house for their parents. *Tunga* is certainly about learning and maturing; however, it ultimately cannot escape being assessed locally in terms of material and social prosperity. With the prospect of return in mind, *tunga* is thus perceived as a circular movement, spun with a boomerang effect, which ideally comes back where it began.

In 2010, one item in particular embodied unsuccessful *tunga* in Mali: the so-called *tunga man jan* bag, which means "*tunga* did not go far away." Thin, rectangular, and decorated with kitsch drawings (e.g., Eiffel tower, flowers), this cheap plastic bag could be found in most local markets. I bought two *tunga man jan* bags because of their big capacity. I used them as a storage cabinet in my room in Bougouni. Salif the tailor laughed at me when he saw them. He told me that when an *aventurier* returns home with a *tunga man jan* bag, people will suspect that its contents are worthless: "If an *aventurier* can afford only such a cheap bag, people think he must surely be poor." An *aventurier* should instead return home with ostentatious bags (e.g., leather bags) because they prefigure prestigious items, hence prosperity on the path of *tunga*. An *aventurier* who returns home with empty hands and goes back to farming in his village was usually despised as *danga den* (cursed child), a point explored in chapter 6. Failure on the path of *tunga* was a recurring source of anxiety for *aventuriers* in Bougouni. Most of them preferred to stay away for years than to return home with empty hands. *Aventuriers* struggled to "become someone" (*e kera mɔgɔ yé*) rather than to be a *mɔgɔ.ba* (literally, big man), a status achieved by only a few of them.

While I recognize the relevance of migration studies that stress the jour-ney to manhood for the background of this monograph, the latter explores above all the fact that *tunga*, as a step into the unknown, puts forward a spe-cific religiosity. In *Migration d'Aventures*, Sylvie Bredeloup (2014) offers an insightful review of the literature of the field of *aventure* among Africans. *Aventure* comes from the Latin *adventura*, which means to break with "the regular, calm, and foreseeable succession of instants" so as to introduce sharp moments of surprise; in this regard, "the *aventure* would be less about event than advent" . . . like "the 'Avent' of a 'mystery'" (22). What I observed among *aventuriers* in Bougouni resonates with the invitation in Bredeloup's book to take *tunga* as an analytical framework that stresses the existential dimension of migration. *Tunga* certainly encapsulates the novelty and hope of migration. When a young man of rural origin leaves home, however, he also finds himself walking on a path toward a better life that is lived as a transformative encounter with the unknown. The unknown, as a semantic field, refers to elusive themes such as tomorrow, destiny, hope, the invisible, and the occult. When speaking about what will come next in his life, Kassim used to utter a local proverb, the title of this introductory chapter, which becomes even more telling for those like him who are on an unpredictable journey away from the security of home: "Tomorrow is in God's hands."[24] For these *aventuriers*, coping with the unknown was about relating to what lies beyond human reach: the occult. As Muslims, they stated that the sovereign of the occult is "Almighty God." In anthropology, how can we explore this specific field of religious experiences? How do *aventuriers* act in the presence of Almighty God when seeking a prosperous Muslim life? What does *tunga* mean in terms of ethical (or moral) life for these *aventuriers*, who describe themselves as "simply Muslims"?[25]

"SIMPLY MUSLIMS" IN WEST AFRICA

Until the turn of this century, an influential body of scholarly tradition in the social sciences of Islam in West Africa focused on religious elites (Muslim scholars, *marabouts*,[26] saints) as the main actors in the Islamic sphere (see Cruise O'Brien 2003; Otayek 1993). Their aim was to study the relations of domination that have shaped Islamic orthodoxy, itself seen as plural, as represented by the classic dichotomy between "traditional African Islam" or "Sufi orders," on the one hand, and "Reformists" or "Islamists," on the other. In this regard, the impact of the colonial period on the religious elite encouraged a historical approach to the question of Islamic orthodoxy in AOF (Launay 1992; Mamdani 1996; Soares 2005). Consider, for instance, the French creation of *la politique musulmane* out of fear of pan-Islamism. Benjamin Soares stipulates that this policy was part of a broader *politique des races* elaborated under the leadership of the governor general of AOF, William Ponty (1908–15). This *politique* "promulgated the idea that each 'race,' recognised as having its own 'particular mentality,' should be freed from 'the religious and political influence of neighbouring groups'" (Soares 2005, 53). This political approach to Islam emanating from a colonial imagination was turned into the notion of *Islam noir* (Black Islam) by French scholar-administrators such as Maurice Delafosse and Paul Marty.[27] For them, West African Islam was different from Maghrebian and Middle Eastern Islam and had to be protected from their influences. In this way, the French intervention with religious authorities was, in fact, an attempt to define what "true" or legitimate (in the sense of obedient) Islam was. This is why numerous scholars say it has been difficult to understand shifts of Islamic authority in AOF without relating these shifts to the actions of the French colonial authorities.[28] With the exception of a new generation of historians who have recently published monographs exploring Muslims "from below" (e.g., Hall 2011; Peterson 2011; Ware 2014), the historiography of Islam in West Africa has therefore been marked by the implicit development over time of a "teleological view of Islam" (Soares 2014, 32). Focuses on religious elites, Islamic orthodoxy, and state control over Islamic authority therefore promoted a "top-down" research perspective in the study of Muslim life in West Africa. This long-standing tendency to analyze the politics of religious movements and their elites has sidelined studies of forms of religiosity associated with the majority of Muslims.

The post–Cold War era, the period of the "second [African] independence" (Clark 2000), promoted activism in numerous West African countries (not all) via political shifts that granted new civic liberties.[29] This civil change increased the visibility of Muslim activism in public life. Most of these shifts were triggered by democratic grassroots movements but thereafter supported by neoliberal interests. In Mali a coup d'état overthrew the military regime of Moussa Traoré (1968–1991) on March 26, 1991, paving the way for the first democratic and liberal era the country has known since it became independent in 1960 (Soares 2006). Officially cutting the link with a socialist conception of the state and its control of economic institutions, the newly established Third Republic of Mali sanctioned the right to property and freedom of enterprise (Rawson 2000), abolished state price controls, and abandoned state control of trade (Lyons and Brown 2010). Since 1991, the Malian society has been characterized by an increasingly lively public sphere, abetted by the new freedom of the press and of association (Perret 2005). These two civil liberties have allowed Muslims to create religious associations and to make religious claims in public via ways of dress, celebrations, and media.[30] Numerous anthropologists have explored activism of leaders and members of Sufi orders (Soares 2005), reformist piety movements (Janson 2014), and new Muslim associations (Schulz 2012). The Islamic renewal (or revival),[31] boosted by the associative opening found in contemporary West Africa, has again sidelined studies of forms of religiosity associated with the majority of Muslims.

Like most Muslims, *aventuriers* whom I encountered during the course of my research in Bougouni were affiliated neither with Sufi orders nor with reformist groups, nor were they members of new Muslim associations, an observation that prevails over the whole sub-Saharan region (Otayek and Soares 2007). Most of these Muslims just told me, "I am Muslim."[32] When I asked them whether they could define more precisely their Islamic affiliations, they just stressed that they were "simply Muslim."[33] Such Muslims, who do not associate themselves with sharply distinct religious affiliations, are difficult to categorize because (1) they constitute the overwhelming majority of Muslims; (2) they are heterogeneous in terms of socioeconomic status; (3) they are not affiliated with a specific religious order, movement, association, or leader; and (4) the so-called experts and their funders do not study "simply Muslims" because they perceive them as politically not (or less) problematic in relation to the formation of the modern (secular, democratic, neoliberal) state.[34] These Muslims, who remain religiously undefined beyond a mere Muslim identity, shape the eclectic masses of the "community of Muslims" (*Ummah*) at large. Despite this heterogeneity, a focus on "simply Muslims" allows me to position this monograph vis-à-vis recent anthropological debates on Islam in which scholars have attempted to transcend the reductionist dichotomy between "traditional African Islam" and "Reformists" (Osella and Osella 2008; Otayek and Soares 2007), a resilient legacy of colonialism. Following the events of September 11, 2001, Western public discourses have further tended to essentialize Islam as the sign of a dangerous "other."[35] With regard to Mali, moreover, the state and its northern territory have been characterized since 2012 in mainstream international media by instability provoked by the so-called Islamic terrorism. This armed violence has boosted funds to finance studies of terroristic forms of political Islam and programs of "deradicalization." Translated into academic, political, and journalistic discourses, emotional shortcuts with Islam often take the form of a simplistic dichotomy between "good" and "bad" Islam (Mamdani 2004) and of the fear of pan-Islamism (Miles 2004b; Miles 2004a).[36] This focus on simply Muslims thus eschews the idea of a Muslim essence, the dichotomies around Muslim identities, and belief in the unity of the Islamic world. It further shows how such reductions impoverish our understanding of the religiosity of the majority of Muslims as a plural, dynamic, and contested field of experiences.

In anthropology the preeminent term that expresses religious experiences is "piety." In ethnographies of Muslim life, piety often comprises the religious experiences of those who claim to be observant: members of Muslim organizations and their religious leaders. This tendency is especially pronounced among anthropologists who base their analysis on conversational materials (including interviews). As anthropologists we apply an elementary rule of thumb: start from the local perspective. This is relevant as long as we explore this perspective through more than just discourses. Otherwise, the scope of our analysis risks being marked out by those who occupy the debate in a given field. In this regard, this monograph explores the field of Islamic piety beyond claims of religious observance. On the other hand, Muslims in Bougouni took the presence of God in their lives seriously. The existence of God is unquestionable among Muslims in West Africa, whether they are observant or not, as Liza Debevec illustrates in her study of "postponing [observant] piety" among Muslims in Bobo Dioulasso (2012, 44). This seriousness becomes especially alive and active when stepping into the unknown, such as in the context of *tunga*. Inspired by Joseph Hill's monograph about women Sufi leaders in Dakar, I therefore explore Muslim *aventuriers'* relation with God as a genuine "spiritual pursuit" in itself (2018, 13). Instead of focusing on the politics of religiosity (e.g., religious identity and policy, dogmatic debate), Hill's primary concern was these Sufi leaders' spiritual religiosity in terms of practice and experience. So I ask, What might piety involve for these *aventuriers*? Do they not have pious concerns?

Opening piety up to "simply Muslims" introduces piety as an open, plural, and complex notion that goes beyond sharply defined religious affiliations and Islamic scholarship. This democratization of piety is ethnographic evidence because, although the religious elites have always claimed authority and legitimacy over piety, it is not their exclusive experiential preserve. My focus on these *aventuriers* who describe themselves as "simply Muslims" is a deliberate attempt to explore Muslim life in West Africa beyond a classical (political) entry point from "above."

In Bobo Dioulasso (Burkina Faso), Debevec noticed that the majority of Muslims refer to themselves as "moderate Muslims" when they critically think of their Muslim identity in relation to the "Wahhabi" (various local groups of reformist Muslims) (2012, 34). While I observed analogous self-designations in Mali (see chapter 3), this monograph does not explore the politics of naming per se. Focusing also on religious experiences in Mali, Dorothea E. Schulz coined the term "observant Muslims" for Muslims who are both unaffiliated and practicing Muslims (2012, xiv, 6). In this monograph, these self-described "simply Muslims" include observant as well as partial and non-observant Muslims, because I consider religious experiences beyond the framework of classic Islamic precepts, as I address in the following sections. From now on I will use "Muslims" and "simply Muslims" interchangeably.

ADAMADENYA: ISLAM WITHIN ETHICAL LIFE

In his influential paper "The Idea of an Anthropology of Islam," Talal Asad (1986) proposes to define Islam as a discursive tradition that includes the founding texts of the Qur'an and oral traditions relating to the words and deeds of the Prophet Muhammad (Hadith). Asad invites scholars to study the social and historical modalities of the relationships of power that frame the enactment of these traditions and the resistances they encounter (16). This approach, which has since been frequently applied in the social sciences, is well illustrated by Saba Mahmood (2005) in her book *Politics of Piety: The Islamic Revival and the Feminist Subject*, in which she explores a grassroots women's piety movement in the mosques of Cairo. Such study of reformist piety movements' ethical self-cultivation projects is relevant because it covers ethnographic realities.

At the same time, how we tackle Muslim life is also framed by our empathy in the field: "We stand in different places, facing different powers, and need different approaches" (Schielke 2015, 92). Veena Das similarly asks, "How does our mode of living with others affect the way we render our experiences in our fieldwork knowable?" (2018, 547). My exploration of street life in Bougouni (see chapter 2) asks for an approach that examines how religiosity is shaped by and inserted into worldly matters. By stressing the concept of discursive tradition, Samuli Schielke rightly notes that the analysts study the continuity of Islamic traditions (2006).[37] Moreover, arguing for a shared "space of discussion" instead of a separate "disciplinary subfield" (Lambek 2000, 310), I consider the study of Muslim life as part of the anthropology of religion. Recent anthropological studies have demonstrated the multiplicity of ways of being Muslim and the contested area of norms of piety (Deeb and Harb 2013; Marsden 2005; Masquelier 2007; Stewart 2016) and Muslims' non-Western and regional intellectual practices (Kresse 2018). Others have stressed phenomena of "new Muslims" as the outcome of a process whereby the growth of secular education and the expansion of a public sphere and new mediums of communication have resulted in a change in the sociology of Islamic knowledge, hence reducing the dependence of Muslims on religious leaders' moral authority (Eickelman and Anderson 2003; Schulz 2003; Soares 2005). Starting from their findings, I assert that piety, as a lived experience, is heterogeneous. It comprises different living conditions implemented in different cultural contexts and is therefore shaped by different religious orientations. I have doubts about Islam-related categories as *transparent analytical categories in terms of causality*, because such categories (e.g., Islamic precepts) tend to overlook the allegedly mundane experiences that, by framing the historical domain of piety,[38] become religious and therefore transform this very domain. Where shall I start, then?

> [Religious experience] is not solely or primarily what happens in specially designated and consecrated sacred spaces, under the authority of religious elites, but in street and alleys, in the souvenir stalls outside shrines, and in bedrooms and kitchen; [religious experience] does not happen[only] at times determined by sacred calendars or official celestial computations, but by the circumstances and exigencies of people's lives. The [religiosity] is not performed [only] by rote or in accordance with authority; it is [often intuitional] and situational. (Orsi 2012, 150–51)

Here, Robert A. Orsi invites us to consider the in-between normative religiosity. Indeed, do Muslims stop being pious in between the practice of normative precepts? In parallel, I do not perceive religiosity as being framed by a duality between everyday life and normative doctrine. After all, the Muslim prayer, even if practiced inconsistently, is embedded in people's everyday lives.[39] The issue here is rather to understand what makes an experience a pious experience. In this regard, I first put people's lives at the center of the study of religiosity (Schielke and Debevec 2012). While I recognize religion as both alive and normative, existential and prescriptive, I also put forward "the plural, complex, and essentially unsystematic nature of religion as lived practice," because the Muslims I met in Mali were more concerned about how "to navigate [their] course of life" than about "how to maintain the coherence of a religious world-view" (1–3).[40] Although piety is about a morality shaped by religion, this anthropological centering makes clear that Muslims do not necessarily become pious when their conduct follows scripturally based Islamic traditions (see Fadil and Fernando 2015, 63–64). Lara Deeb wrote, "Rather than debate whether or not Muslims are guided by religion, my approach has been to ask how various understandings of morality (including but not only religious ones) come together in relation to everything ranging from fasting to flirting. How does one then define what constitutes the realm of piety in the first place? That in itself should be an ethnographic question, situated and contextual" (2015, 94). Deeb's approach to piety refers more to the study of a local moral sensibility that, as Das stressed, would "allow us to think of the [ethical] as growing within the forms of life that people inhabit . . . [to see] how forms of life grow particular dispositions" (2012, 136). What concrete "forms of life," then, shape the (pious) ethics of Muslim *aventuriers* in Bougouni?

Language is a privileged vehicle for local culture and historic imprint. In a way similar to what Paul Riesman undertook in *Freedom in Fulani Social Life* (1977), I apprehended forms of (social) life from words to values and from these values to people's attitudes. I noticed that in town the terminology of social values converged in debates about what locals called *adama.den.ya* (or *hadamadenya*). This Bambara term is composed of two words: *adama* (Adam) and *den* (child), which together mean "the son of Adam." The suffix *ya* stresses the condition of what is named, so *adamadenya* becomes "the human condition," "humanity," or "humanness" (Gaibazzi 2018, 472). Charles Bailleul (1996) translates *adamadenya* as *état d'homme* (the state of the human being), "humanity," and "savoir-vivre" (manners); he further translates *adamadenya* as "solidarity," "politeness," and "social relations," thereby referring the two sets of meaning to each other. In an insightful monograph on the multiple co-present modes of ethical being that are lived, expressed, and interpreted by music artists in Bamako, Ryan Thomas Skinner translates the notion of ethic-moral personhood with the Bambara idiom *mɔgɔya* (2015). In his study of Massa Makan Diabaté, a Malian writer of *jɛliya* descendant (*griot*, praise singer),[41] Cheick M. Chérif Keïta (1995) similarly translates *mɔgɔya* into *personnalité* (personality). Bailleul mentions that *mɔgɔya* and *adamadenya* are synonyms. In Bougouni's social life, I also heard the term *mɔgɔya* but significantly less than *adamadenya*. I do not have a clear answer for this linguistic inclination. My twofold guess is (1) the etymology of *adama.den.ya*, the son of Adam, refers to the creation myth of Abrahamic religions; its ethnographic recurrence stressed the fact that my interlocutors knew my interest in Muslim life; and (2) unlike artists and *griots*, *aventuriers'* works did not make them public persons; they did not work on stage or around events. As illustrated by Kassim's succession of petty works in Sikasso, Bamako, and Bougouni, most *aventuriers* struggle for a better life; their workplaces were street façades and houses and farming plots of better-off families (see chapters 2 and 5). Thus, Keïta's study of on *mɔgɔya* in relation to the name of someone is telling: while in the traditional Mande society everybody has a *jamu* (family name) that inserts them into a lineage, few only will make a *togo* for themselves, a forename-as-fame that distinguishes these persons from the masses (1995, 42–43). In other words, *mɔgɔya* stresses the heroic dimension of a person. *Aventuriers*, struggling for a better life, could not describe themselves with the lexeme of *mɔgɔ* (person) and its social apex, *mɔgɔba*. Observing the enduring precarity of migrants of Fouta Djallon in Dakar, Susanna Fioratta (2020, 110), too noticed the gap between "real life" (hardships) and "the hero's quest storyline" (goal). *Adamadenya* expresses more the concrete and collective dimension of human life and *mɔgɔya* its imagined and distinct dimension.

The ethnographic recurrence of the term *adamadenya* in Bougouni's social life revealed ethics as a fundamental feature of the human condition in the local culture. Taking this linguistic perspective seriously, this monograph ethnographically explores the fact that *"the human condition is an ethical condition"* (Lambek 2015a, preface, x), insofar as ethics is considered "in the first instance less as a subject of reflection than with respect to action, and then not as a distinct field of action but as a dimension intrinsic to action" (33). In Kenya, the Swahili saying *mtu ni utu* (a human being is humanity) expresses a similar feature of human beings as social (moral) beings (Kresse 2007, 139–75). Besides the possible universal claim of this human condition, I explore its regional hallmarks. In his studies of Mande migrants in Angola, Paolo Gaibazzi speaks about "the human potential for connection" (2018, 471) and how West African ideas of humanity inform us on "how power works" (479). In other words, people's ethical conditions are inherently shaped by, revealed, and discussed through their actions and the connective power of these actions. Coming back to Muslim life, when the ethical and the pious merge, what then?

This ethnographic study of Muslim life refers to an anthropology of religion in which piety is defined as a potential quality of the human condition. This human condition can be lived as a religious experience at any time insofar as it is ethical by nature and becomes intimately recognized as pious in specific moments. By "recognized" (see Lambek 2015b, 5–8), I mean that Muslims "discern" and "elucidate" the pious as "an ethical dimension of living" framed by religion. In this context, the ethical is not objectified as a demarcated field of religion (see Lambek 2018, 138); it is "a kind of sensibility" that grows out of life (Das 2015, 63). I therefore explore Muslim life within ethical life because I put forward the inherent ethical nature of human beings (Lambek 2010a, 2010b, 2012) as the grounds of religiosity. In this monograph, this ethical sensibility is tied to *tunga*.

LIVES IN MOTION ON THE EARTHLY PATH

Analytically, I presuppose that Muslim *aventuriers* strive to live a proper Muslim life for two fundamental religious rewards. They do it motivated by the classic "access to Heaven" betterment of doctrinal orthodoxy, but they also do it to achieve worldly ambitions. Referring to the saying "Tomorrow is in God's hands," my Muslim friends used to say that God already rewards and punishes Muslims on earth. In this way, for these Muslim *aventuriers* moving forward in life (the earthly path) was as important as the gates of Paradise (the afterlife). However, one can argue that concerns about the earthly path and the afterlife are interconnected in Muslim life; therefore, they cannot be apprehended separately. For instance, once during a bus journey between Bougouni and Bamako, I overheard a conversation between two young adult Muslims concerning the recent death of an elder. They were reflecting upon his funeral by linking people's earthly achievements and morality. For them, the fact that his funeral was attended by an immense crowd signified two linked things: the local community, by paying tribute en masse to their elder, acknowledged his prosperous life on earth; therefore, he surely went to Paradise. By contrast, locals said a poorly attended funeral might be a harbinger that Hell was the fate of the deceased. The earthly path and the afterlife can be closely related because people often think that, in such circumstances, the judgment of God does not diverge much from communal appraisal. In Mali the afterlife especially concerns "old men" (*cɛkɔrɔbaw*) and "old women" (*musokɔrɔbaw*)—in other words, those at the twilight of their life. Besides acquiring social status and respectability in the local community, elders' greater devotional practice (e.g., diligent with regular prayers at the mosque), compared to that of younger generations, is motivated by accumulating "divine awards" (*baraji*) in order to prepare for death as the unavoidable gate toward the approaching Day of Judgment (Mann 2003).[42] Although the earthly path and the afterlife cannot be dissociated, I analytically emphasize the former because, among young Muslim *aventuriers*, the earthly path was ethnographically richer and more concrete than the consequences of God's judgment in the afterlife.

The local saying "Tomorrow is in God's hands," moreover, stresses the presence of Almighty God in the lives of Muslims in West Africa. *Aventuriers* perceived God not as an abstract idea but as a living force that is not separate from human existence (Jackson and Piette 2015, 5–8).[43] I thus consider the experiential presence of God in *aventuriers*' lives as relational by nature, hence having neither internal/external dimension nor an added reality.[44] At the same time, the omnipotence of God renders its presence bottomless to the human mind. Unquestioned but bottomless, God's presence was felt as what I refer to as an "obvious mystery" by most *aventuriers*. Exploring religiosity as a kind of ethical sensibility forged in *tunga* (facing the unknown), this monograph investigates the "practical meanings" (Jackson 1996, 34–35) of Almighty God in relation to *aventuriers*' struggle for a better life away from home. The active quality of Almighty God grows out of *aventuriers*' lives in motion.

Inspired by Catherine Bateson's notion of "composing a life" (1989), an edited volume on Japan defines the ethnographic enterprise as "a process of embracing lives in motion" because people and things change over years, including researchers themselves (Long and Clark 1999). In human life, this motion is also felt in the present. In this regard, *lives in motion* can also be explored here and now and amid wider circumstances, what Kalpana Ram and Christopher Houston (2015) call the "horizon" of experience. This monograph explores this existential motion as it grows out of *aventuriers*' struggle for a better life. Walking an earthly path thus becomes a living path within which *one feels in motion*. In addition to concrete achievements that illustrate change over years, prosperity becomes a feeling of creative forward motion or a dynamic of "being on the right track," with "being" meaning moving forward in life. When hardships overwhelm the *aventuriers*, they can also feel motionless on this earthly path, with "being" meaning getting nowhere fast in life. Ghassan Hage would call such inner motion "existential mobility" and motionless "existential stuckedness" (2005, 2009). This exploration of walking an earthly path focuses on how and to what extent God is perceived to set in motion human (Muslim) lives. This focus on lives in motion is also an attempt to "[bring] together the dimensions of past, future, and present" in the ways *aventuriers* live the building of their trajectories on earth (Panella 2012, 25). The past here represents the momentum—the custom of *tunga*—that brought them to Bougouni. The future comprises hopes, expectations, and risks associated with *tunga*. The present consists of their living situations in Bougouni. All of these dimensions shape the backdrop of Muslim *aventu-*

riers' existential perception of prosperity as a custom (momentum), a path (direction), and a walk (motion) at the same time. But what does prosperity concretely entail in neoliberal Mali?

MUSLIM LIFE AND PROSPERITY IN NEOLIBERAL MALI: A MANDE PERSPECTIVE

After the end of the Cold War or the "Second Coming" of capitalism,[45] neo-liberalism understood as processes of political and economic liberalization in a globalizing world (Ferguson 2006; Leblanc and Soares 2008) has accelerated across Muslim societies. Many people perceive this acceleration as being uncontrolled. Following increasing transnational interconnections, neoliberalism also stresses multiplication (of money, goods, and ties). In this specific globalizing context, numerous studies have stressed the linkage between neoliberalism and religion in which the relationship between prosperity and perception of a good Muslim is considerably defined in terms of the market (e.g., Haenni 2005; Rudnyckyj 2010; Sloane-White 2017). The combination of "material success with moral connectedness is coming to be seen as the exemplary contemporary way of being a modern, moral, Muslim" (Osella and Osella 2009, 204). Soares illustrates how in Mali, in the postcolonial era, mercantile logics have progressively supported the development of a "prayer economy" or a "fee-for-service religion." In Nioro-du-Sahel, Sufi leaders deemed saints "trade" their closeness to God (*baraka*[46]) via prayers and blessings to Muslims in exchange for "gifts" (2005).[47] The sainthood of prominent religious leaders has also increasingly been assessed by the public manifestations of their wealth, such as traveling in luxurious 4 x 4 vehicles and living in spacious cement houses with multiple stories. Recent developments in Mali further demonstrate that "entrepreneurialism" has become a "key mode of action" in a religious market characterized by a multiplicity of available options (Soares 2017, 147–48).[48] Social inequalities based on material consumption have therefore increased in this country, and this, it seems, with the blessings of numerous Muslim scholars.

In our globalizing world, however, anthropologists tend to overplay the strength of neoliberalism over the field of religiosity (or vice versa, to a lesser extent). This propensity largely results from two factors: considering both as two separate social-moral domains whereas in reality both "entail processes of subjectification or habituation" (Osella and Osella 2011, 157);

overlooking their long "history of reciprocity" (Osella and Rudnyckyj 2017, 4). It is important to stress that in this part of Africa the relation between practical life and religious motivation as well as the perception of wealth as a sign of blessing long predates neoliberalism. This monograph carefully considers the long-standing relationship between prosperity and Muslim life in contemporary Mali. In this regard, this ethical enmeshment ensues from a dynamic co-penetration of older and newer cultural formations. In other words, older ethical forms of life well up in dynamic co-presence with recent ones, and this occurs in metamorphic ways. In such dynamics of social life, any continuity of tradition is inherently a subjective claim. Inspired by Henri Lefebvre's historical layered-ness of social space (2000 [1974], 103–104), this ethical enmeshment is consequently explored as a "mille-feuille pastry"; it potentially stems from intertwined articulations between ethical forms of life deemed "recent" and "coming from the wider world" within the resurgence and reformulation of ethical forms of life deemed "older" and "local" that, in the case of this monograph, were widely interpreted locally to originate in the historical Mande world.

The term "Mande" (or "Manden," "Manding") refers to a vast historical region of West Africa in which people shared common cultural features and linguistic roots. The historical Mande world now crosses several West African countries,[49] but its heartland was southwest Mali and eastern Guinea, the birthplace of the great Mali Empire established by Sundiata Keïta in the thirteenth century.[50] The golden age of the Mande world is deemed precolonial. What experts called "Mande legacy," however, does more than exist in contemporary Mali: it is still alive. This legacy has, nonetheless, been diffused, interpreted, reappropriated, and regionalized in complex sociohistorical ways. B. Marie Perinbam, in her study of the political unit of Bamako between 1800 and 1900, describes the Mande social field as "prismatic" because, for centuries, it articulates "regional particularisms" within "Mande universalism" (1998, 8–16), such as demonstrated with what is today called the "[Mande] caste system."[51] The historical Mande world, although mostly composed of small communities, also offered "relatively cosmopolitan environments" because it was crossed by "travelers" (e.g., merchants, itinerant scholars) (18–23). This malleability observed within wider Mande frameworks, she adds, "may explain why even today seemingly different people in the Mande-hinterland still insist that they are the same" (54), a remark still on the table in 2021. The daily working of this elasticity within macro configurations exemplifies what Raymond Williams calls a "structure of feeling"

(2011, 69). In this regard, the image of the "mille-feuille pastry" (rather than the idea of continuity associated with legacy) illustrates the layering of the Mande world in contemporary Mali. Thus, instead of associating the Mande world with a static past, I explore it as an intertwined set of sociohistorical "spaces of exchange" (Amselle 1985, 24–26) that is lived through creative, fluid, and dynamic traditions (e.g., Ferrarini 2014).[52] Forms of ethical life deemed "ancient" are still entangled, via "mille-feuille" formations, in local conceptions of prosperous Muslim life.

By exploring mille-feuille formations, however, I do not undertake a historical study of the relation between practical life and religious motivation. My exploration of street life in Bougouni (see chapter 2) revealed to me a recurring yet metamorphic layering of "local origin" that shapes the ethnographic present of this relation: the Mande conception of power (see next section). Studies based on early twentieth-century West African oral traditions disclose that an all-powerful presence of occult nature inhabited people's lives already during the epoch of the historical Mande world. In parallel, inspired by the local saying "Tomorrow is in God's hands," as argued before, Muslim *aventuriers* in Bougouni lived their religiosity as a kind of relatedness with the Architect of the Unknown—in other words, the One Opening to their life ahead: Almighty God. In fact, these seemingly different conceptions of power share the same materiality of the occult.

PROSPERITY: A TWOFOLD MOMENTUM OF POWER

The leader of the Bambara kingdom of Segu (18th century–1861) was named *faama* (or *fama*), a term that derives from *fanga.ma*, which means the strong man, the powerful one (Bazin 1988a, 715). The suffix -*ma* expresses possession; hence *fanga.ma* originally means "to possess" (*ma*) "physical strength" (*fanga*) and by extension to have power. The *faama* of Segu was also a *mansa* (or *masa*), which signifies the suzerain (e.g., the king). However, a *mansa*, such as the Tarawure women-kings who survived the collapse of the ancient empire of Mali by becoming arbiters and peacemakers under the kingdom of Segu (Bazin 1988b), was not necessarily *faama*.[53] The latter term stresses the martial, coercive, and contingent power of a ruler, whereas the former indicates the moral, mystic, and hereditary power linked to people of higher status. In other words, in historical Mande times, people feared the army of *faama* while they also feared the sacred character of *mansa* (Bazin 1998b).

For Agnieszka Kedzierska-Manzon, the Mande suzerain had a privileged link with "the invisible and ritual sphere" (2014, 111). In the same era, leaders of the Bamanan cult called Manyan in neighboring Minyanka areas were also named *faama*. Their strength was based on the *nyama* (occult power) accumulated in the sacrificial altar of the Manyan they worshipped and directed (Jonckers 1993). In reality, these two genres of power were closely related; they coexisted, intermingled, and shaped individuals. Whereas one was rather quantitative and visible, the other was more qualitative and inward or hidden, at least in terms of its source. It was said that the *faama* of Segu had "a particularly loud [hence] disquieting breath," a sign that would announce the power of his *nyama* to his interlocutors (Bazin 1979, 461). Significantly, the oral literature of Mande heroes contains few references to warfare and physical prowess; rather, it focuses on the search for the right *nyama* needed to defeat the opponent (Bird and Kendall 1980, 19–20). Sundiata Keïta, for instance, knew that he could defeat King Sumaoro as soon as his sister Nana Triban, the spouse of King Sumaoro, told him the source of her husband's occult power (Niane 1960, 105–7). Uncovering people's source of occult power meant knowing their weak point. This source must therefore be kept secret. This pattern significantly stresses that *nyama* gives rises to *fanga*, as if the intangible, invisible dimension of power enables its tangible, visible dimension.

The close connection between physical (material) and occult power was a feature of people's potentiality in the historical Mande world. In terms of tangible power, precisely, the genuine source of what was observable is beneath it; what is observable provides clues of what is beneath. This physical (material) power of occult origin provided a prelude to the perception of material wealth as a manifestation of blessedness. In other words, the material accumulation stemming from this power prepared the ground for the development of the early capitalistic economy in West Africa via Islam that later supported the rise of prosperity in its modern sense.

Islam and the Development of Early Capitalistic Economy in West Africa

In historical Mande times, the region was overwhelmingly inhabited by non-Muslims. The presence of Islam, nonetheless, was accepted for centuries. Muslim actors even became part of the Mande balance of power. The first contacts between Mande people and Muslims came in the seventh and eighth centuries with Arab travelers who explored the Sahara Desert from southern Morocco. Muslim traders, commonly called "Dyula" or "Marka," and Islamic scholars, later named *marabouts* (Ar. *murabit*) by the French co-

lonial administration, progressively spread southward down to the heart of
the Mande world, the forest zones, and, to a lesser extent, the coastal countries of West Africa. The *kafo* (*canton*, region) of Bougouni was a vassal of
the powerful Bamanan kingdom of Ségou.[54] *Kafo* designates a political unit
of the historical Mande world. Territories and heads of these units were partially conserved during the colonial period for administrative purposes; they
took the name of *canton* (Zucarelli 1973). As a verb, *kafo* means "to gather,
to assemble and, by extension, a region subjected to one authority" (Turco
2007, endnote 15). During the time of the kingdom of Ségou, the minority of
Muslim traders and *marabouts* coexisted peacefully with the overwhelming
majority of the population (farmers and craftsmen), notables, and the royal family, who practiced what social scientists call "the *bamanaya* religion"
(Bravmann 2001, 35–43).[55] These cohabitations illustrated the centuries-old
processes of accommodation between Islam and local religious practices that
preceded the mass Islamization of the entire Mande world in the nineteenth
and twentieth centuries.

With the progressive southward penetration of Islam, the accumulation of products and goods increasingly shaped the elaboration of prosperity. Muslims' investment in transregional commercial activities gave rise to
a more capitalistic, hence material, economic type of power. According to
local history, for instance, Bamako grew considerably after the settlement of
Suruka families, sub-Saharan Muslim traders and scholars who claimed to be
of Moorish descent.[56] Their commercial activities made Bamako an important market where cola nuts from the Worodugu (south), gold from the Bouré
(west) and salt from the Taoudenit (north) were exchanged (among other
products). The material wealth and occult influence of these families grew
to represent a powerful counterweight to the authority of the family of the
faama (Meillassoux 1963, 207–12; 218–19). The Muslim Touré families, for
instance, were "richer and more consumer-conscious" than the ruling Niare
families (Perinbam 1998, 97). These Muslim families understood their wealth
as a sign of God's blessing. However, it was strategic for non-Muslim rulers to
host and protect a minority of Muslim traders against warfare so as to have
access to prestigious products (e.g., cola nuts, salt, horses, and slaves) brought
by long-distance trade (Launay 1988, 55). The trans-Saharan trade developed along a network of Muslim traders, established in roadside localities
and regional centers, who consequently enriched themselves and stimulated
the material dimension (accumulation and distinction) of prosperity into its
local enactments (e.g., Amselle 1977). In late precolonial times, for instance,

the (current) small town of Garalo in southwest Mali grew as a wealthy Dyula locality thanks to its strategic position along the cola nut trade road to the Worodugu (Peterson 2011, 61, 77). Muslim actors played a central role in the development of an early capitalistic economy in West Africa.

The French conquest of a large part of West Africa during the nineteenth century, however, undermined the balance of power and the complementarity of skills between non-Muslim warriors and Muslim traders that had been present in precolonial times. With the "pacification" of AOF, the development of a road network within AOF (Launay and Soares 1999, 504–6), the spread of Islam in colonial posts and roadside towns, and the imposition of monetary taxation (Peterson 2011, chapter 2), the linkages between Muslim identity, urban life, and economic resources strengthened.[57] With the colonial dominance in the physical (or coercive) power, trade (along with scholarship) became the main avenue to prosperity for locals, to the detriment of warfare (Launay 1988). In parallel, non-Muslim traditions in occult sciences were being increasingly segregated in urban areas and pushed back to the bush (Fr. *brousse*). The independences of 1960 in West Africa deviated from this transformation only partially insofar as physical power remained in the hands of an elite. What certainly changed was that the political and economic powers of Black Africans intermingled more closely because they were not segregated according to skin color. Similar to Adeline Masquelier's findings about Niger (2001, 2009),[58] Islam became equated with status, power, and wealth in most urban parts of postcolonial Muslim West Africa, whereas non-Muslim traditions in occult sciences were being pushed away in the bush.

THE MANDE PROSPERITY IN CONTEMPORARY MALI

In Bougouni, when young Muslims noticed that I did not want to buy a trendy "Jakarta" motorbike but preferred to circulate with a Chinese-made bicycle, they jokingly shouted "*tubabu faantan*" while I was cycling. Jakarta was an affordable Chinese-made motorbike that became the new sign of prosperity in urban Mali (Chappatte 2014a, 29). The term *faantan* is the opposite of the term *faama*. When *fanga* is followed by the privative suffix *-ntan*, it becomes a composite, *faa.ntan*, which means "devoid of power." Whereas the *faama* of Segu was the one who possessed political power supported by an army, young Muslims depicted me as the economically poor white. Indeed, they expected me to buy an in-vogue motorbike instead of a cheap bicycle. They had difficulty understanding why I, the (wealthy) white (*tubabu*), preferred to perspire under the sun rather than to move swiftly and honorably in town. This linguistic shift between a martial power (the *faama* of Segu) and an economic power (the *tubabu*) illustrates how in contemporary Mali, prosperity, the visible side of power, has increasingly relied on material wealth. One of the earliest impetuses that fostered this transformation was the spread of Islam in West Africa, as mentioned earlier.

While recognizing the recent impact of transnational neoliberal forces upon Muslim life in contemporary Mali, this monograph contributes to understanding the importance of being a both prosperous and good Muslim in urban Mali as a subjective experience that layers over the *longue durée*.[59] What can we learn in terms of mille-feuille formations from the old mercantile influence of the trans-Saharan trade in West Africa, which developed along a network of Muslim traders, through a progressive establishment of material distinction in Mali? What can we learn, again, from the ancient Mande connection between spiritual and physical (material) power that still, according to southwest Mali's Muslims, arises and grows, to paraphrase Mariane C. Ferme (2001), out of the "underneath of things"?

Linkages between prosperity and religiosity stem from complex sociocultural mille-feuille formations in which forces of the market and local ethics have been enmeshed for centuries in ways that make it difficult (even impossible) to distinguish them. During his research on the oral epics of Mande blacksmiths, Patrick McNaughton found many references to Islam in Mande traditions. He wrote, "This sort of eclectic interaction with Near Eastern religions occurs often in Mande traditions of all kinds, partly because Islam has been present for so long in the Western Sudan" (1995, 47). In a similar vein, Perinbam noticed that "by the eighteenth and nineteenth centuries . . . Islam and Mande belief systems had been so ethnographically parsed that regional ambiguities and manipulations were commonplace" (1998, 124). Considering Islam "as an integral and authentic part of the African historical experience," the historian Rudolph T. Ware rightly invites us to take Islam as a local religion when we study Muslim lives in Africa (2014, introduction, 35). Similarly, for Jean-Paul Colleyn, it is simply impossible now to study "pre-Islamic" practices in Muslim West Africa. On the contrary, Islam has been "a constitutive factor of traditional African religions" since its arrival in the continent in the eleventh century (2009, 735–36). Islam has indeed been present for so long in the Mande world that it would be implausible to try to isolate its presence in the region. For Charles Stephen Bird, the epic figure of Sundiata Keïta already "represents this union of Saharan mercantilism, deeply marked by Islam, with Mande warrior chivalry strongly rooted in African spirituality" (1999, 290). During the mass Islamization of the entire Mande world in the nineteenth and twentieth centuries, the ethics that underpinned traditional African religions endured but as a constitutive factor of Muslim practices (e.g., for Senegal, see Dilley 2004). In a way, history has turned over this union. In 1884 the *faama* Samory Touré significantly became Almaami (Amselle 1988, 475),[60] the Commander of the Believers, a title that openly specifies the sole root of his power as a chief and believer: God. But the genuine source (God) of what was observable remained part of the occult. Islam has become the dominant religion. The twofold nature of power that characterized the aforementioned union, although protean and innovative, has remained firm in local life;[61] it still shapes the ways people perceive the path to prosperity and its underlying reality. In 2010 in Bougouni, the term *barika* (Ar. *baraka*) expressed the close connection between this physical and spiritual power. To say of a man that *barika bɛ a la* meant "he is a hefty guy"; to tell him *Ala ka barika di ɛ ma* meant "May God give you blessings." Following McNaughton, this monograph demonstrates that "the entangled issues of means and power" (1995, 51) is at the heart of the becoming of human life in Mande societies. Focusing on young male Muslim *aventuriers* of rural origin who move to the provincial town of Bougouni in search of *tunga*, this monograph therefore explores their struggles to be both prosperous and good Muslims through their engagement with this twofold Mande conception of power.

In autumn 2008, I told a Malian scholar, Kadari Traoré, about my wish to live in Bougouni *from within*—in other words, to be hosted by a local family. Kadari then called his "father," a retired professor of mathematics and physics who lived in Bougouni and had hosted him when Kadari was in high school. Without knowing me, this man kindly agreed to accommodate me over the phone. I was given a room in a standard cement wing covered with a sheet metal roof, located next to the main building. I was warmly welcomed and took part in the family life from the first day. This monograph contains only a few vignettes of life in this family due to my focus on *aventuriers*. However, all precious moments shared with this family gave me the confidence to write about the local social life in general.

OUTLINE

The book is divided into two parts: 1, "Navigating Street Life and Public Islam," and, 2, "Motions and Ethics on the Earthly Path." By exploring Muslim life against the backdrop of Islamic revival in contemporary Mali, part 1 (chapters 2, 3, 4) demonstrates that the issue of intentionality among *aventuriers* in Bougouni was framed by an ethics of urban street life deemed of Mande origin. Part 2 (chapters 5, 6, 7) explores the linkages between existential motions and social mobility in *tunga* in relation to a twofold Mande conception of power.

Based on an informed bike tour of the old town, including both colonial and postcolonial districts, chapter 2 explores how Bougouni was increasingly perceived as a "civilized" (modern) locality while still being associated with backwardness when occult accusations and memories of a recent history of underdevelopment and Bamanaya practices arose in public. *Aventuriers* experienced this ambivalence through the three main spaces of sociality (*carré*, *rue*, and *grin*) that characterize traditional urban street (Mande) life in Mali; their open access nurtures an ancient visual ethics that is crucial to understanding the stakes of Muslim life in public.

Chapter 3 examines public Islam on the street. Besides the practice of Islamic precepts, *aventuriers* understood Muslim life as moved by an inner force that informs someone's maturity and blessedness (*barika*). Exploring the debate between public signs of piety and their intentions within a post-1991 context of a growing public Islam, it demonstrates that for those who claimed to be "simply Muslims," the practice of an outward generic Islam does not necessarily subject human beings to a religious path. The older visual and ostentatious character of street life ironically fosters the interpretation of public Islam as a mundane success that attracts charges of hypocrisy. The ambiguity of public Islam reminds Muslims of the need to cultivate an inner force whose values are widely interpreted to be of Mande origins.

Chapter 4 explores how *aventuriers* handle their participation in forbidden activities from *within* a local Muslim community. Analyzing the social significance of the darkness of the night in relation to a public Islam based on sight, it illustrates how forbidden activities were handled through strategies of diurnal conformity and nocturnal discretion in urban Mali. By exploring how Muslims consider the field of *haram* (forbidden) as an integral part of a Muslim life, it offers an ethically wide understanding of Islam's relationship to contemporary Muslim societies.

Based on an ethnography of livelihood hunting in Bougouni, chapter 5 investigates *aventuriers*' negotiation of hardships and their active uncovering of *dakan* (destiny). With feelings of going nowhere fast, *aventuriers* could find themselves being blocked by witches. But Almighty God could set their lives in motion again through a demanding work ethic. This chapter illustrates how *aventuriers* understand the building of their Islamic faith as a complex, concealed, and moral path toward prosperity that lies in the hands of their tumultuous relation with God.

Chapter 6 analyzes locals' understandings of being a genuine male and a good Muslim as they were informed by a set of virtues widely interpreted to be of Mande origin. Echoing the inner force mentioned in chapter 3, it documents the metamorphic resilience of Mande ethical codes in the making of the contemporary figures of "the noble Muslim" and "the blessed child" in Bougouni, figures that considerably framed the ethics of male *aventuriers* in town.

Thanks to the affordability of the so-called Chinese products, chapter 7 explores how *aventuriers* could construct an up-to-date urban way of life since the 2000s. Due to their low quality, however, these products were denigrated as cheap and short-lasting imitations of Western products. Reflecting upon this ambivalence, chapter 8 explores the transience of *aventuriers*' residence in Bougouni in light of the changing political geography of the savanna within West Africa. In doing so, it invites social scientists to value the scholarly under-considered historical connections between the southern shores of the Sahara (Sahel) and lands south of these shores.

PART 1

Navigating Street Life and Public Islam

An Informed Bike Tour of Bougouni

Bougouni was relatively small (60,000 inhabitants) but extended far into the *brousse* (bush). Except for Bamako, the housing scheme in Mali is land-consuming due to its typical single-floor architecture, spacious courtyards, and land availability.[1] Crossing Bougouni by foot from one corner to the other could therefore take more than forty-five minutes. This walk was exhausting under the heat. Since the early 2000s, the motorbike made in Asia has become a popular means of transport in urban Mali thanks to its afford-ability and mechanized motion, which allows people to move swiftly in town (Chappatte 2014a). Such a light motorbike is an especially suitable vehicle for provincial towns due to its mobility on sandy roads and its practicality and comfort for short journeys (Alimia et al. 2018, 13–17). I nonetheless opted for the bicycle for a sporty reason, although local urbanites associated this formerly trendy vehicle with an outdated *broussard* (bushmen) way of life.[2] *Broussard* was a mocking term that defined the inhabitants of the *brousse* as backward and uncivilized by nature.

I bought a Chinese-made bicycle within the week following my arrival in Bougouni.[3] Instead of visiting administrative offices and urban land-marks, working at home, or attending official events in the town center, I explored the town's eight districts by riding daily on this bicycle across its tarred streets, sandy streets, stony streets, narrow streets, junctions, corners, and open fields. Ultimately, this choice of vehicle opened me to a detailed ethnographic discovery of social life in a Malian provincial town. The way you move within a town shapes the way you inhabit the locality, observe its social life, and interact with its actors. As Luis Antonio Vivanco wrote, "Dif-ferent mobilities carry the potential for knowing, sensing, and interacting with [the urban] in specific ways, and are closely related with certain prac-tices of life" (2013, 10). In this manner, cycling offers a specific engagement

Fig. 3. The author with one of his closest informants at the exit of Bougouni toward Sikasso. They had to stop due to a flat tire.

with the urban, a particular "pace and scale of everyday life" (Cox, Horton, and Rosen 2007, 10) adapted to the exploration of most provincial towns of West Africa. Here "most" means towns with less than 100,000 inhabitants.[4] By bicycle I crossed Bougouni from one corner to another in twenty minutes. This speed allowed me to carefully circulate between different urban locations within the same day. Because the bicycle was neither too fast nor too slow, I became a sort of "urban archaeologist" who, in the course of these daily rides, developed an in-depth mapping of Bougouni through a meticulous anthropology of street life.[5]

A BIKING SENSE OF PLACE

Easy to mount, to turn, and to stop, the "bicycle as field vehicle" is a suitable means of transport to cover considerable distance while responding to curiosities and encounters crossing your path (Salter 1969). Riding this thin all-land vehicle in Bougouni allowed me to *perform* this town in the sense of building "an intimacy with the [urban] surrounding" (P. Jones 2005, 826) compared to a motorized vehicle. Adonia E. Lugo (2012), in her study of the practice of bicycling in Los Angeles, speaks about "ethnographic *flânerie*" as a privileged way to undertake urban phenomenology. In his autoethnography of cycling in London and Copenhagen, Jonas Larsen stresses the importance of "movement" in "place-making activity" (2014, 60). Moreover, provincial towns in Mali, by contrast to most Western urban areas, where people bicycle in conditions dominated by fast, motorized modes of traffic (e.g., D. Horton 2013), were still characterized in 2010 with rather light and slow traffic conducive to *social bicycling*. Many times I was stopped by people who greeted, called, or hailed at me from the street façade while I was passing in a "jogging speed" that allowed me to be attentive and respond to social life all around. Although the motorbike made in Asia has recently become a popular means of transport in urban Mali, it is important to stress that most of the movements within Bougouni were still undertaken by foot. Given that walking and bicycling at a jogging speed fall within what constitutes a slow motion, both relate to a similar perception of local social life. Biking also included "go-along as ethnographic research tool." I sometimes joined a friend for a bike ride across the town, or we both walked with me pushing the bike; go-alongs allow you to explore the relational dimensions of places (Kusenbach 2003). In his ethnography of the provincial town of Koudougou (Burkina Faso), Mathieu Hilgers rightly reminds us that urbanites still live in "places" (2009, 2012). A focus on the concept of place goes beyond the physical dimension of space to put forward "a space that is lived in" (see Feld and Basso 1996; Tuan 1977). While biking across the provincial town of Bougouni, I therefore asked myself, What does living in such an urban place mean?

After a month of riding, only the frame of the bicycle remained original because of the bicycle's cheap quality, a fact that made me well known among a few bicycle repair shops overlooking the streets. Many of the people I encountered along the streets spoke only rudimentary French. Besides a pen and a notebook for direct note taking,[6] I always carried a Bambara-French dictionary (Bailleul 1996) that I bought in Le Grand Marché of Bamako in September 2008. In this way I learned the Bambara language by taking linguistic as well as ethnographic notes while talking with these mostly Bambara speakers. This fieldwork on a bicycle in the vernacular did not make me acquainted with those who are commonly perceived as privileged informants of anthropologists, such as teachers, journalists, and nurses. Wishing to go beyond the limits of the French language imposed by its elitist status in Mali,[7] the former settlement of French Sudan, I also did not seek to meet members of the intellectual elite (e.g., civil servants, workers for nongovernmental organizations [NGOs], politicians). Instead I made contacts with those who circulate along the streets and work on the pavements, such as passers-by, people in *grins*, shopkeepers, craftsmen, and street peddlers. My daily commitment to the study of Bambara as well as the prospection of Bougouni by bicycle thus determined the contacts whom I cultivated in the field: young male (Muslim) migrants of rural origin.

This chapter depicts Bougouni's sense of place through *an informed bike tour* of the town. Over time my daily rides across the town connected me to a local history that put the present in the shade. This chapter first introduces the locality's notoriety that "haunts" the social life of its inhabitants. The verb "to haunt" was not locally used to express this notoriety, but I employ it as a metaphorical device to point to a notoriety made of recollections that still loom in people's comments of local intrigues despite the locality's recent urban growth, which is transforming its reputation. This haunting dimension of life is not a mere "byproduct of social reality" (Mitchell 2005, 47); rather, it is constitutive of "the lived world" for people in Bougouni (Hatfield 2011, 73). In other words, it does not point to an "unstable ontology" (Banerjee 2015, 251) but stresses a specific mille-feuille formation of the present that lurks in people's experience of Bougouni. In the course of these bike rides, I also realized the centrality of street life to people's lives. This chapter then offers a bike ride across the districts (old town, colonial, and postcolonial districts) and its spaces of sociality (*carré*, street, and *grin*) to flesh out this centrality that is typical to provincial towns of southern Mali. It finally relates the open character of this centrality to the ways Islam as a public force participates in the moralization of street life through sight.

FROM BOUGOU.*NI* . . .

Bougouni is located in the savanna of southwest Mali, an area of 40,000 kilometers (the administrative *cercles* of Kolondiéba, Yanfolila, and Bougouni). This area of the savanna never played a prominent political role in West African history. This peripheral region "was something of a zone of refuge that had absorbed waves of [non-Muslim] population over the centuries," who fled "state control and enslavement" during the precolonial period (Peterson 2011, 37–38). At that time the region, relatively low in population density, was divided into multiple chiefdoms called *kafo,* each composed of a grouping of villages dominated by a powerful lineage. Villager livelihoods depended on an extensive mode of agricultural production (hoe farming) practiced in abundant but relatively poor soils. Such small kin-based organizations did not control long-trade exchange (in the hands of Muslim traders) and would probably be termed "acephalous" or "chiefless societies" by Jack Goody (1971). Exploring a Mande geography of the region,[8] Perinbam develops the "northern paradigm," "a northern and Islamized [elite] construct" that perceived the north (starting from Djenné) as "urban" and "mercantile," and the south, where Bougouni was located, as the Other "animist," hence "a reservoir for slave[s]" (1998, 96–113). As a "buffer zone" or borderland between the precolonial empire of Wassoulou and the kingdom of Kenedougou,[9] southwest Mali suffered unevenly from the widespread predations that occurred during the wars of Samory in the late nineteenth century. Samory Touré, the founder of the empire of Wassoulou, enslaved numerous inhabitants of this buffer zone to finance his resistance to colonization.[10] The French conquest stabilized the region in the 1880s, but it continued to be a marginal zone. Southwest Mali was on the fringe of colonial policy in terms of investments compared to forested and coastal West Africa (Méker 1980) and therefore during the colonial period remained an area characterized by remoteness, poverty, and lack of economic opportunities. Ever since the implementation of a colonial "head tax" (*nisɔngɔ,* literally "soul price") in 1895, southwest Mali has also been marked by labor migration.[11] Many of its inhabitants moved to coastal countries as seasonal workers in the cash crop economy of plantation. A minority among them settled in Senegal and Côte d'Ivoire (mostly). Southwest Mali is also part of the Bamanan cultural area (primarily southern Mali, eastern Guinea, and northwest Côte d'Ivoire). Historically, Islam achieved relatively slow progress among Bamanan people compared to other Mandinka people (Conrad 2001, 27). As a consequence, the term "Bamanan" has covered somewhat heterogeneous signifiers, but one of them has been "pagans of the south" (Bazin 1885, 101–13). Bamanan as a populous ethnic group who had lately been Islamized tended to stand for what was not Muslim in the past. In contemporary Mali the word "Bamanaya" is still associated with un-Islamic religious practices of Mande origin whether Bamanan or not. The backward identity of southwest Mali has been further reinforced by the fact that this region was one of the last zones of Bamanan country to become predominantly Muslim.

A Late Islamization

In this part of rural West Africa, Islamization was a long-term, gradual, and "drifting" process that took place from below (Peterson 2011). The wars of Samory, with their conversion "at the point of the sword," achieved very little success (49). Instead, Islamization has been the progressive outcome of mobile social groups (freed slaves from 1910, colonial soldiers, migrant workers from 1920) who returned to their homeland and introduced prayer into their villages. A local elder who migrated to Côte d'Ivoire during his youth told me, "It is *yaala* that brought Islam [here]." *Yaala* (or promenade) alone means a stroll. In this context, *yaala* refers to *tunga*. The remoteness of southwest Mali also promoted "ideologies of mobility" that "reveal the centrality of mobility in shaping what it is to be modern" (Blunt 2007, 685). Islam, like new items of consumption (e.g., bicycles, hats, sunglasses), became a marker of the civilized elsewhere between the two world wars. Mass Islamization reached Bougouni's hinterland during the early postcolonial period when conversion spread from within villages. As for Bougouni, Islam also came from above. Bougouni was the only colonial post in southwest Mali from 1894 until 1951.[12] Muslim foreigners settled in this post because of colonial opportunities. Some worked in the colonial administration as civil servants (e.g., translators, clerks, guards). The new colonial post of Bougouni also benefited from two colonial policies: the repopulation of villages along regional trade roads after the wars of Samory (Peterson 2011, 62) and the decrees prohibiting the slave trade in 1894 throughout the colony that caused runaway slaves to congregate in the so-called "liberty villages" (colonial posts) (64). Until the late colonial period, Bougouni and a few old Muslim trade settlements (e.g., Garalo) shaped a sort of "Muslim islands" (35) in southwest Mali where newly converted Muslims sheltered against the segregation that they might undergo in their villages. Other Muslim strangers set up businesses in this locality, which, boosted by colonial investments and policy, turned into a roadside trade town.

The earlier presence of Islam in southwest Mali is articulated to the long-standing influence in this part of West Africa of the two Sufi orders that represented much institutional Islam during the colonial period in Mali: Qadiriyya and Tijaniyya.[13] In 2010, elders of Bougouni remembered the Sufi origins of their Islamic traditions, but the majority were not affiliated to any Sufi leaders (*muqaddam*). By contrast to Senegal (see Cruise O'Brien 2003; Villalón 1995), formal membership in a Sufi order was rather limited in southern

Mali (Soares 1997, 78–79). The first Muslim families of Bougouni had little knowledge of Islam; its practice was often disparate and mixed with local religious traditions (Bamanaya). "Shifting" or "dual" practices were common among newly converted Muslims as well as among practitioners of Bamanaya. According to local elders,[14] in the 1950 and 1960s people who defined themselves as "Muslims" could perform a Muslim prayer, participate in a Bamanan rain-making ceremony, and attend a performance of a *kɔmɔ* initiation society all in the same day.[15] Following Brian J. Peterson, "Even as people began praying and embracing Muslim forms of religious life, the generative cultural grammar, as it were, remained rooted in *[B]amanaya*" (Soares 1997, 13). Islam was not a major force of public life until late in the colonial period. At that time Bougouni hosted a place called *korokoji* (water of peddlers) where locals mingled around small taprooms and drank local millet beer (*dɔlɔ*) in public.[16]

Within the emerging context of an "Islamic sphere" promoted by colonial peace and the development of a road network (Launay and Soares 1999), however, Muslim identity progressively came to be associated with a body of standardized Islamic practices. In Bougouni, "those who pray" (*mɔgɔ min bɛ sɛli*) became distinct from "those who possess fetish" (*jɔtigi*).[17] From the second half of the colonial period, Muslim identity also sharpened with the arrival of foreign scholars (*karamɔgɔw*),[18] who preached in public (*wajuli*) and instructed in traditional Islamic schools (*duguma kalan*).[19] In parallel, these Muslim scholars started to criticize Bamanan religious practices as backward and evil. The worshipping of local djinns (*génies, djinɛw*) became increasingly considered as un-Islamic. With these religious changes, "*Bamanaya*, or indigenous religious practices, became something shameful" (Peterson 2011, 3).[20] Other Muslim scholars even dedicated their life to the annihilation of Bamanaya practices. El-Hajj Ladji Blen (about 1900–1989), who with his acolytes built the second Friday mosque of Bougouni, epitomizes such harsh proselytism. Local recollection of his life recounts the victory of the worshippers of God over the Bamanaya forces of "Satan" (*sitanɛ*). According to his biographer (Sissoko 2007),[21] Ladji Blen was born in a village near Bougouni within an "animist" family. He converted to Islam in 1942 during a journey in Senegal and made the annual pilgrimage to Mecca, known as the Hajj, in 1948. He came back to Bougouni in 1952 and started his fight against Bamanan religious practices, a devotional commitment to Islam achieved through the destruction of numerous fetishes, idols, and power objects, which he pursued until his death. His fight brought him to southwest Mali, the *région* of Kaye, Senegal, and back to Bougouni, where he is buried. Mamadou Sissoko explains the life of El-Hajj Ladji Blen as "*croisades aux pays des idoles*" (crusades in idol countries), a sort of holy war against evil. The public burning of fetishes that happened in southwest Mali echoed other African forms of iconoclasm that, in the name of a monotheistic creed, symbolically aimed at creating new social, religious, and political orders (Sarró 2009, 2–6). In parallel, Islam became progressively associated with wealth, power, and status in town.

While northern Mali has been Muslim since the eleventh century, Bougouni became predominantly Muslim during the early postcolonial period. The first *médersa* (Ar. *madrasah*) in Bougouni was opened in 1961.[22] Besides undermining traditional Islamic school (Brenner 2001), the establishment of such modern Muslim schools brought wider Islamic influences in town because these schools were primarily developed by local Muslim scholars trained in the Middle East. Mosques mushroomed during the last two decades. By 2010 more than thirty mosques had been erected in Bougouni. Muslims prayed in five different mosques on Friday.[23] This recent multiplication of mosques and Friday mosques also stresses the contemporary widening of competing Islamic influences in town.

"A Land of Fragile Faith"

In contemporary Mali, the backward identity of southwest Mali is rooted in the late Islamization of this region compared to the rest of the country. In Bamako, Malians did not understand why I wanted to study Muslim life in Bougouni. For them, Islam was still not fully established in this town; hence, local Muslims were not exemplary Muslims. A religious scholar who had recently settled in Bougouni told me in a private conversation that this part of Mali is "a land of fragile faith." Southwest Mali was still stigmatized as backward by Malians outside this region. With the postcolonial advent of Muslim society in Bougouni, however, Islam became an important moral force of public life. In 2010 most locals defined themselves as Muslim. But Bamanaya, as a set of religious practices, did not disappear; it went underground.[24] Many first generations of Muslims did not abandon totally their "old ways" (*ko kɔrɔ*) because as "legacy" (*facɛ*) they were part of their origin, their identity, and their heirs. An old imam of Bougouni used to tell me that "all the mouths are Muslim" with a point of irony.[25] For him, being Muslim in Bougouni was primarily a public identity. Another elder added that "although you washed your mouth very well, the smell of what you ate is still here."[26] These Muslim elders warned me that appearances can be deceptive. In 2010 Islamization as a process of avowed conversion was nearly completed in southwest Mali. But out of public sight many people were still involved in Bamanan practices, such as during a nightly visit to a *soma* (Bamanan sorcerer) and in a power object concealed underneath someone's clothes.

The backward identity of Bougouni also endured because of its relative underdevelopment in the early postcolonial period compared to other Malian towns with similar colonial pasts. Although electricity arrived in town during the Second World War and a tarred road was constructed in 1962, Bougouni remained a big village of mud housings. The town grew considerably in the 1970s due to the construction of a cotton factory that employed hundreds of locals and developed a cash crop economy in the hinterland. A second cotton factory was built in the 1980s. During this decade, however, cement houses and motor vehicles (indexes of prosperity) were still rare and streets all unsurfaced. Not a single house had more than one floor. Hearsay was that better-off families did not dare to build *maisons à étages* (houses with multiple stories) because they feared falling victim to *mɔgɔw juguman* or *mauvaises personnes*, which literally means "bad persons," an occult dynamic explored in chapter 5. "L'examen de Bougouni" (Bougouni's examination), a tale stressing the animosity of "the people of Bougouni," was widely spread in 2010 Mali. I first heard this tale in Bamako after having told my interlocutor that I was going to live in Bougouni. "L'examen de Bougouni," allegedly based on a true event that happened in the 1960s, tells the tale of a boy from a family of local origin who failed in an exam. His father, who was a witch, used his occult power to cause all children to fail in this exam because he did not want his son to fail alone. This interlocutor wanted to warn me about the nastiness of locals in Bougouni. In 2010 Mali, Bougouni was considered to be "a town of witches."[27] Malians also pointed to the backward character of Bougouni by mentioning a famous reprimand voiced by former president Moussa Traoré following the murder in 1987 of the *secrétaire général* for the Cercle de Bougouni of the single-party Union Démocratique Populaire du Mali (UDPM). His corpse was found a couple of kilometers south of Bougouni on the side of the national road RN9.[28] This tragic event hit the national news headlines and prompted the president to come to Bougouni. Moussa Traoré assembled the town's population in the main soccer stadium. Angry, he shouted at the population the following words, which became a famous saying: *"Bougouni tɛ kɛ Bougouba yé!"* (the small hut [Bougou*ni*] is not a big hut [Bougou*ba*]).[29] This play on words, by stressing the contrast between suffixes "*ni*" (small) and "*ba*" (big), says that Bougouni is and will be a small locality. In the context of the *secrétaire général*'s murder, Traoré's words conveyed the idea that Bougouni cannot develop into a proper urban locality because of the savagery of its inhabitants. According to a former mayor of Bougouni, in the 1980s, "When we told a civil servant that he was posted to Bougouni, this latter became very scared."[30] When a transfer to Kidal (northeast Mali) was interpreted as a sort of punishment due to its extreme geographical remoteness, a transfer to Bougouni was also understood as a kind of career regression because of the threat caused by the occult (hence backward) notoriety of the town's inhabitants. Although elevated to the status of eighteenth Commune Urbaine of Mali in 1982, Bougouni had fewer than 20,000 inhabitants in 1991.

This notoriety still haunted 2010 Bougouni. "Strangers" (those whose family did not originate from the town) feared to fall under the "jealousy" (*kɛlɛya*), "egoism" (*ɲɛgoya*), and "greed" (*nata*) of the "people of Bougouni" (those whose family originated from the town). They thought that an abnormally high number of local people who considered themselves Muslims were in fact witches who did not want others to move forward in life, a dynamic explored in chapter 5. As a cultural backdrop, Bamanaya still shapes local ethics in subtle ways (e.g., Chappatte 2018c). Here, Bamana.ya does not only mean the Bamanan religion. The suffix "*ya*" evokes also a broad Bamanan "condition" or "way of life," a point initiated in the introductory section "Adamadenya: Islam within Ethical Life" and further explored in chapters 3 and 6. With the national construction of Mali as a Muslim country, the Bamanan way of life is increasingly being perceived by some scholars as a past reality that ought to be preserved in museum collections. But, for instance, "the resurgence of *bɔgɔlan* and the continued vitality of such institutions as Ciwara and Sogow attest [to] the resilience and dynamism of Bamana social and aesthetic traditions" (Frank 2001, 51). In Bougouni I daily observed the Bamanan way of life on the street, especially its (mille-feuille) forms of ethical life. Its ubiquity is difficult to recognize because human beings do not mention the obvious. The Bamanan way of life is there, full stop. As a mille-feuille formation, its presence is also diffuse, hence easily contested. Its forms of ethical life are increasingly being Islamized in their labelings also because "Bamanaya" is associated with the un-Islamism in contemporary Mali. In Bougouni local conceptions of Muslim life were being shaped by the Bamanan way of life in different domains of social life whether its influence was mentioned, denied, or confirmed.

. . . TO BOUGOU.*BA*

Nahawa Doumbia is a popular Malian singer who comes from southwest Mali. She was born in 1959 in the village of Mafele, next to the small border town of Manankoro. According to local recollection, her mother, who died shortly after Nahawa's birth, predicted that Nahawa, although the daughter of a blacksmith (*numu*), would perform songs, an activity that is traditionally the realm of *griots*. Defying her father, she started to perform locally in the 1970s. Spotted by agents of the Ministère de la Culture, she took part in and in 1980 won La Biénnale de la Jeunesse in Bamako.[31] Her career then took on a national and even international dimension; however, she has mostly performed in Mali, where she is often called the "Queen of Didadi," a rhythm of the Wassoulou on which young people challenge each other during festive ceremonies.[32] Nahawa is also nicknamed "child of djinns" (*djinɛw den*) because she often refers to djinns in her repertoire. This connection with occult forces makes her an awe-inspiring artist in Mali. Part of Nahawa's popularity is also due to her empathic lyrics, which are related to the difficulties of everyday life. She has remained close to ordinary Malians by living in Bougouni, where she worked for twelve years as a nurse in the local hospital. She wrote a praise song called "Bougouni" (released in 2009), in which she interpreted local traditions as inherent to the recent development of the town. Refuting the notoriety of Bougouni, this song invites the listener to appreciate this provincial town for what it has recently become: a "crossroads" (*kunbenyɛrɛ*) between Mali, Côte d'Ivoire, and Guinea.

The Crossroads of Southwest Mali

I first reached Bougouni by bus. After a three-hour trip on the newly repaired 170-kilometer tarred road from Bamako to Bougouni (financed by the EU) I arrived in the town's bus station around 10:30 p.m. The place was still full of street peddlers, travelers, *coxers* (local brokers), and *gargotes*—small restaurants composed of a table, a bench, and cooking pots. I had to make my way through the crowd, buses, and worn-out taxis. My host waved at me. We then drove on his old Yamaha 100 through tarred streets lit by street lighting and along which various kiosks were still open. We next took a sandy street to arrive at my host's courtyard. The ride lasted seven minutes. After customary greetings, I then took a walk in the vicinity. Malik, a fostered teenager who also lived in this courtyard,[33] accompanied me. We heard a loud *coupé-décalé* music coming from the neighborhood.[34] A civil wedding party was still going on in a vacant lot. The place was lit by a strip lamp fixed at the top of a post next to a DJ. Electronic equipment was connected to two car batteries. Children were raising dust by dancing energetically. A group of youths wearing jeans, colorful shirts, elegant jackets, and hats were chatting and smoking cigarettes. In darker spots, others were flirting. Midnight passed and I decided to go to bed. In the morning, I did my first tour of the town on the back of a trendy Jakarta. My driver, Alou, a student of the Institut de Formation des Maîtres (IFM),[35] brought me to what he thought would be the best locations to show a newcomer in town. We crossed the center without stopping, passing by the Siraba Togola Auditorium, the Conseil de Cercle, and the big market. On the way he pointed out the new three-floor cement building of the local police. Passing by some opulent houses, we took the exit toward the town of Yanfolila. Riding on a smooth asphalt road, I learned that the section of road between Bougouni and Yanfolila (82 km) had recently been tarred by a Chinese company. After one kilometer, Alou stopped in front of a massive football stadium that included athletic lanes and VIP boxes. He proudly informed me that "this stadium, which can host international games, was inaugurated in December 2008 by the Malian president and the ambassador of China in Mali." Next Alou took the exit toward Bamako to show me an Indian-owned cottonseed oil factory and told me that "two hundred locals worked there." My first twenty-four hours in Bougouni gave me a guided glimpse of an urbanizing locality shaped by wider connections. This Bougouni was rather far from the allegedly big village of mud houses that Moussa Traoré visited in 1987. More than twenty years have since elapsed, however.

In the last two decades, Bougouni had expanded considerably. Its growth was due to macro and regional factors. I will first introduce the infrastructural and institutional factors that supported this urban growth. Both put forward the provincial town as the first recipient of African urbanization. I then explain its regional factors. They point to the geo-economic resentments that assisted the 2012 coup d'état in Mali.

Bougouni has followed macro tendencies of African urbanization. The intra-African mobility has increased because of the development of modern transport and road networks in much of the continent (Bruijn, Dijk, and Foeken 2001; Gugler 2002). This development has particularly preoccupied states of landlocked countries. In Mali the post-1991 governments promoted a policy of *désenclavement* (opening up) through inaugurating new international tarred roads and maintaining older ones. Amadou Toumani Touré, the president of Mali between 2002 and 2012, used to say that "tarred roads are the harbours of Mali." Bougouni is strategically located along the international tarred road between Bamako and Abidjan, the only tarred road crossing the border between Mali and Côte d'Ivoire. The Malian section of this international road has benefited from works of maintenance. As a roadside town along the trading axis of Bamako–Abidjan, Bougouni has therefore drawn international traders. As a crossing town between Mali and Guinea, it has also attracted smugglers of cigarettes and motorbikes (among other products) due to the weakness of the Guinean franc compared to the CFA franc.

The post–Cold War era opened up to the decade of "second independence" in many West African countries (Clark 2000). These democratic and liberal shifts have often been followed by institutional reforms of decentralization. From the Jacobin and paternalistic Malian states of Modibo Keita and Moussa Traoré,[36] the Third Republic of Mali triggered in 1993 a complex bottom-up participatory process called *la Décentralisation* (Kassibo et al. 1997).[37] This reform led to the creation in 1999 of three new levels of territorial collectivities mentioned in ascending order: 701 *communes*, 46 *cercles*, and 8 *régions*.[38] In 2010 the Malian decentralization was being achieved through the second mandate of locally elected representatives.[39] Bougouni, already a Commune Urbaine since 1982,[40] was elevated to the administrative center (*chef-lieu*) of Le Cercle de Bougouni, a vast area of 20,082 kilometers that is composed of 26 *communes* spread over 482 localities. In 2010 approximately 450,000 people lived in this populous *cercle* of Mali. By elevating small towns such as Bougouni to administrative centers of *cercles*, *la Décentralisation* brought numerous state services that have in turn boosted the development of modern services and retail outlets in town.

For instance, three Centres de Santé Communautaire (CSCOMs) one Centre de Référence,[41] three private clinics, one state high school, two private high schools, five professional schools, NGOs and bilateral governmental projects (thirteen in 2010), a bank with a cash machine,[42] three modern gas stations,[43] three internet cafés, six hotels, four radios,[44] two modern bakeries, and few big shops (clothing and food) have since been erected in Bougouni. Canal+ Group, a mass media company, and Orange Mali, a telecommunications company, also set up in town with the opening of official outlets. By bringing civil servants, qualified workers, and businessmen into town, new economic opportunities have supported the emergence of a local economic elite and provided work for a series of lower-level urban employees, such as schoolteachers, policemen, and secretaries. An important migration of country dwellers who, motivated by these new urban opportunities, have consequently moved to Bougouni in search of money and more (*tunga*), like the *aventuriers*. Many among them start offering their services as seasonal workers at the end of harvest and thereafter decide to settle in town. Besides working in peri-urban agriculture, or as housemaids and houseboys for better-off families, an increasing number of migrants also make a livelihood as small traders of Chinese goods in town, a new trading opportunity explored in chapter 7. Other countryside people seek to hide in town to avoid taxes back in their villages. They became what Malians name *populations flottantes* (fleeting populations).[45] Small towns have also grown more quickly than big towns due to a combination of factors (see Dubresson and Bertrand 1997; Tacoli 2001), including profitable trade competition. Provincial towns, such as Bougouni, benefited from a "gradual migration"; that is, migrants who first settle in small towns before continuing to big towns (Foeken, van Dijk, and van Til 2001), such as Bamako, where opportunities are supposed to be more profitable but risks bigger.[46] This monograph illustrates the same point but in reverse.

I met Boubacar, a small trader of frippery, in 2009. He was an established stallholder who had a fixed trading spot in the central market of Bougouni. With his little bit of savings, he built a small sheet metal hut where he sold *yuguyuguw* previously bought in Bamako. Boubacar grew up in a village near the town of Mopti (central Mali). When Boubacar was a young boy, his father sent him to a traditional Qur'anic school on the outskirts of the town of Ségou, where he divided his time between learning the Qur'an and helping his master in farming activities. He eventually left the traditional Qur'anic school during his late teenage years to work as a hawker in Mopti. He decided to turn away from his parents' traditional occupation of *sɛnɛkɛla* (farmer) mostly because of its limited access to a cash economy. For him, "money" (*wari*) was more than a mundane necessity; it was the unavoidable door to a prosperous life. He thereafter moved to Ségou and then to Bamako. As he told me, "Money is where the crowd is. . . . I wanted to go to the capital, to earn money, to get married." Bamako, the political and economic center of Mali, is by far the biggest town of the country, where most Malians wish to live. The Malian capital is "the destination of desire and promise, especially for Mali's young people" (Arnoldi 2007, 19). After a couple of years in Bamako, Boubacar managed to start a family. As a head of family, however, he faced additional difficulties making ends meet. Hearing about new trade opportunities related to the contemporary growth of Bougouni, he then settled there with his family because, he argued, the markets of the big towns were already overcrowded with hawkers. When I first met Boubacar, his monthly income was less than 50,000 FCFA (US$100). In Bamako his family would just barely survive with such an income; in Bougouni they would live better. Besides the deterioration of infrastructure that characterizes the urban growth of big towns of sub-Saharan Africa (Tacoli 2001), the life trajectory of Boubacar illustrates a recent intra-urban migration to small towns because big towns are increasingly associated with greater risks due to their growing rental costs and trade competition.

Coming to the Fore of the Savanna

Regional factors also explained the recent urban growth of Bougouni. The emergence of the Ivorian crisis in late 1990s, with its ethnic tension, caused a partial return of migrants to their home savanna. The decade of Ivorian crisis (2002–2011) particularly hit southern Mali, where all families had members working in the former Ivorian El Dorado (Gary-Tounkara 2008). Malik, for instance, comes from southern Mali but grew up in the town of Divo (Côte d'Ivoire). His biological parents sent him to Bougouni due to the Ivorian crisis. Others, such as Kassim, lost their assets and fled to southern Mali to pursue *tunga*.

The recent urban growth of Bougouni also stresses the geo-economic resentments that assisted the 2012 coup d'état in Mali. The savanna of southwest Mali, a transitional zone between the Sahel of northern Mali and the coastal and forest regions of Côte d'Ivoire, has increasingly become an important zone of migration. The 1980s droughts initiated a gradual environmental degradation (e.g., desiccation) of the Sahel.[47] The high birth rate of its population has since led to wild oscillations in food production. This ecological pressure has consequently fostered a general "southbound migration" in West Africa (de Bruijn and van Dijk 2003). In Mali this southbound migration has further been supported by the failure of the state to also give an economic response to the long-standing instability of northern Mali; the recurrence of its cycle of conflict has accelerated since the 1990s (1962–64; 1990–95; 2007–9; 2012+). The resulting demographic pressure has progressively transformed the Malian savanna into a regional hub where northern people migrate to avoid the troubled Sahel by carving out work opportunities there, such as Boubacar the small trader and Fousseini the carter.

In parallel, traders and smugglers have increased their operations in the borderland of southern Mali in adaptation to changing economic flows. By contrast to the north and central areas, land resources are still available in southern Mali, considered as *le grenier du Mali* (the granary of Mali). For instance, southwest Mali has witnessed significant rural-rural migration since the late 1980s, as illustrated by the arrival of Dogon farmers in the region of Wassoulou (Konaté 2003). The West African savanna is low in fertility and sensitive to erosion compared to forest and coastal regions, but it still benefits from a longer and heavier rainy season than the Sahel. Migrants from northern Mali stressed that "the issue of water" (*ji.ko*) is much less pressing than in their native Sahel. As a relatively small town, Bougouni still offers complementary farming opportunities. As Tacoli wrote, "In these less densely populated centres, urban and peri-urban agriculture could more easily be combined with other urban occupations as a livelihood strategy" (2001, 145). Most families in Bougouni indeed complemented their urban activities with small breeding, gardening in the courtyard, and farming in the vicinity of the town.

Bougouni had tripled its population since the 1990s to become by far the biggest locality of southwest Mali. In 2010 its weekly market attracted merchants from as far as Bamako, Sikasso, and Guinea. Its *forains* (stallholders) supplied a regional network of weekly rural markets down to Manankoro. What was formerly a large village had been transformed in two decades into a provincial town of more than 60,000 inhabitants, the third biggest town of the Région de Sikasso. This monograph, by documenting the recent acceleration of the urban growth of Bougouni, illustrates the migratory impact of the geo-economic resentments that have hit northern Mali in an accelerating cyclic way. These resentments, which recently also hit the center of the country, fueled the 2012 coup d'état in Mali. This enduring and expanding instability has turned the formerly marginal savanna of southwest Mali into a crossing point and destination of southbound intra–West African migration. Beyond the specific case of Mali, the study of this migratory mutation and its articulations to forest and coastal areas will contribute to a rethinking of the political geography of the savanna within West Africa.

The Old Districts

Bougouni was composed of eight districts in 2010. Dougounina, Niébala, and Faraba constituted the old town. Its inhabitants were mostly descendants of the founders of Bougouni who settled there during ancient times. With the growth of the town, these three small districts became enclosed in the center of Bougouni (see fig. 4).

According to local history, Bougouni was initially a lazaretto for small-

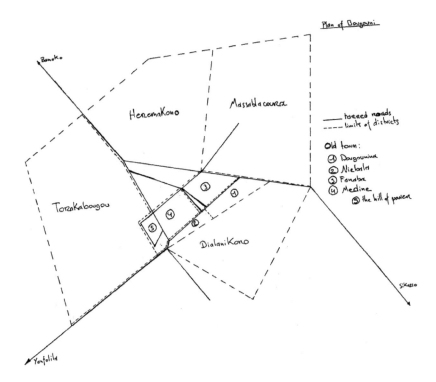

Fig. 4. Plan of Bougouni's districts

pox.[48] The Diakité family's local chieftainship narrates that in precolonial times, a Fula Diakité of Kita (Kaye region) moved to southwest Mali and became the shepherd of the Bamanan Coulibaly of the village of Kola. The Coulibaly hosted (*jatigiya*) the Diakité and gave him one of their daughters in marriage.[49] Later the Diakité built a lazaretto composed of a small hut (*bugu* [hut]; *ni* [small]) within the lands of Coulibaly but away from the village of Kola, because members of his family were infected by smallpox. When they recovered, the Diakité decided to stay in the small hut where the current district of Dougounina stands.

The couple gave birth to children. When they grew up, two sons settled next to their parents and founded the district of Nièbala. A third son then established what became the district of Faraba. The hamlet also grew by attracting hunters. At some point, however, the Diakité took over the chieftainship of Bougouni. How precisely their locality became the center of an independent chieftainship is not explained. The Diakité's narration is sig-

Fig. 5. The monument (small hut) marking the foundation of Bougouni

nificantly restricted to a unique plot: they are the genuine founders of Bougouni. The shift to colonial power most likely led the Diakité to sever their links of submission to their hosts, the first traditional landlords of the area. Encouraged by the growth of what became the colonial post of Bougouni, the Diakité imposed their own chieftainship by taking control of surrounding lands. Over time, the village of Kola stood inconspicuously in the vicinity of an expanding Bougouni.

The small hut that marked the foundation of Bougouni has inspired the only monument of contemporary Bougouni: a small hut made of stones, cement, and thatched roof fenced with wire netting (fig. 5). This monument stands at the center of the town in front of the Conseil de Cercle of Bougouni. The anthropologist Rosa De Jorio wrote in her book on cultural heritage in contemporary Mali, "The emergence of a diversified public culture is one of the most significant changes in Mali's democratic and neoliberal era" (2016, 9). It implies, in this case, the traditional chieftainship among the numerous actors of local heritage politics. In 2010 the Diakité families still occupied most of the old town of Bougouni. Its three districts were composed of large residential plots where Diakité *gwaw* (Bamanan traditional families[50]) lived in a mix of old mud houses and new cement buildings. The head of family, his wife (or wives), their children, the wives of their sons, and their grandchildren all shared the same courtyard. Compared to the other districts, the old town was marked by uneven sandy and narrow streets that rendered slow, difficult, and winding travel by car. The house of the Diakité's patriarch (*dugutigi*, chief of village) was strategically located in the oldest district, Dougounina, next to the oldest Friday mosque of the town and its big market. At a short distance lay the well-maintained tomb of Diakassan Moussa Diakité, a great warrior who, according to the Diakité's oral tradition, converted to Islam and fought for the king of Ségou during the precolonial period. Locals praised the Mande ethics of their illustrious ancestor and venerated the *barika* of this tomb through a sort of hero cult (explored in chapter 6). The Diakité in turn associated their ancestry with the prestige of being an early actor of Islam in southwest Mali.

The rivalry between the Coulibaly of Kola and the Diakité of Bougouni still shapes contemporary politics. Although the two localities are separated by only a ten-minute motorbike ride, they do not belong to the same municipality. The grassroot consultations of *la Décentralistion* often resulted in the formation of *communes* according to ancient affinities and old rivalries (Toé 1997; Coulibaly and Hilhorst 2004). The village of Kola did not want to join the Commune Urbaine of Bougouni. Its chieftainship opted for the creation of the Commune Rurale of Kola, a municipality that includes eight other villages, but tensions remained. A land dispute between the two chieftainships ended in dramatic events in 2009. Early in the morning of June 7, a group of Diakité destroyed several houses constructed at the border between the two municipalities. They chased off their occupants, arguing that they did not ask permission of the Diakité to settle there. According to the sole local newspaper, *Le Relais*,[51] this ransacking was led by Diakaridja Diakité, son of the traditional district chief of Dougounina and a former political candidate of the Rassemblement Pour le Mali (RPM) for the National Assembly of Mali. The *préfet* of the Cercle de Bougouni, the highest representative of the central Malian state in town, and the police did not intervene. The Malian law on *Décentralisation* promoted "the re-enchantment of tradition" and "the rehabilitation of origins and of belonging" (Mbembe 2000, 37) by giving traditional chieftainships the right of consultation and the task of tax collecting,[52] but not the right of coercion. Strangers who lived in Bougouni interpreted this ransacking as an "abuse of authority" from the local chieftainship that again revealed the backward identity of the "people of Bougouni."

The Fula arrived in southwest Mali through ancient waves of migration from mostly the current *région* of Mopti (Amselle 1987). They progressively settled in southwest Mali and took political power due to their military strength. However, they gradually abandoned their language to adopt the language of their first hosts: the Bambara. In 2010 Bambara locals joked about these "fake Fula" who settled in their villages and married their sisters. They teased them, saying that their "Bamanan sisters," in turn, taught "Bamanankan" to their Fula children instead of the Fula language. Progressively, these Fula became farmers and adopted the local lifestyle. Only their patronym remained of Fula origin. Their former hosts used to say, "They have been 'Bamanised,'" some of them with a revengeful spirit. This teasing expressed a sort of "joking relationship" that certifies the matrimonial alliance established over time between when the Fula and the Bambara settled in southwest Mali.[53] At the same time, it reminded the Fula that, although they hold many chieftainships in this region, their Fula ethos no longer exists due to the cultural domination of Bamanan society in this region.

The Colonial Town

The fourth oldest district of Bougouni is Medine. This enlargement of the town was planned in the colonial period. Its division into plots was ordered by Maurice Méker, the French *commandant* of the *cercle* of Bougouni (1947–1952), who wrote a memoir containing references to Bougouni (1980). Méker also drew up the first "modern" urban plan of Bougouni that provided the framework for the postcolonial extension of the town. During the colonial period, Medine was called Mékerbougou. Upon the independence of Mali in 1960, the district changed its name and became Medine. With the expansion of the town, this district, like the old town, became enclosed by new districts. In 2010 the eastward part of this district was integrated into the current center of the town. It hosted the hospital of Bougouni and the first football stadium of Bougouni, which bears the name of Sakoro Mery Diakité, a *chef de canton* of Banimonotié during the colonial period.[54] In terms of architecture, Medine differed from the other districts because of its colonial buildings. These old sturdy cement houses, standing in large courtyards, were deteriorated due to lack of maintenance yet ventilated by open terraces and empty squared-pattern walls. Their residents also differed from other districts due to their employer. In Mali "most colonial buildings [. . .] became the residence or the workplaces of the Malian bureaucracy, thus providing continuity in the geography of power after independence" (De Jorio 2006, 85). In 2010 these colonial buildings were still used as residences of civil servants transferred to Bougouni. This typical colonial planning and, thereafter, the Malian state's requisition of colonial buildings transformed part of Medine into the civil servants' section of the town.

The district ends westward at the bottom of a hill that locals often compared with *la colline de Koulouba* (the hill of *kuluba*) in Bamako.[55] The hill of *kuluba*, nicknamed *la colline du pouvoir* (the hill of power) by inhabitants of the capital, is the site of the Palais de Koulouba, the former residence of the governor of French Sudan. Erected in 1907, this residence became the Presidential Palace of Mali. The French *commandant* of Bougouni also lived in a big Sudanese-style house built at the top of a hill nicknamed "the hill of power" by locals. In 2010 this colonial residence overlooking Bougouni was, not surprisingly, the house of the *préfet* of the Cercle de Bougouni. Other, smaller colonial houses stood on the hill. They were the homes of families of important state officers such as the *sous-préfet*, the judge, and the chief of police. At the eastward foot of the hill, the state jail stood in the very place of the colonial jail. Next to the jail, traces of the abandoned *cimetière français* (French cemetery) were still visible. Other, more recent state buildings extended this overlooking concentration of power. At the entrance of the hill's plateau, stood the state Radio Kafokan, the voice of the people. This radio station broadcast appointments to state agents and official information across the Cercle de Bougouni. More recently, the powerful Orange Mali company erected an antenna at the top of the hill. Bougouni's hill of power illustrated the continuity of the colonial state's geography of power in contemporary Mali.[56] Fifty years after the country's independence, locals still referred to the *préfet* of Bougouni in informal discourses as *le Commandant*.

The New Districts

My host family was an example of educated Malians who moved to Bougouni because of the recent development of its services sector. The head of the family, a retired professor of mathematics and physics, comes from Kita. He first arrived in Bougouni in the late 1970s to work as a teacher in the public high school. He then settled in town, where he achieved a distinguished career in teaching. His wife, also from Kita, found a job in the Bougouni post office. Over time, they built a cement house in Bougouni, where they raised a family. Their children represented the second generation of migrants in town. In 2010, however, most of Bougouni's inhabitants were first-generation migrants—in other words, migrants who had settled in town en masse since the 1990s. In less than three decades, the demographic structure and size of Bougouni changed radically. In the late 1980s, Bougouni looked like a big village whose inhabitants mostly originated from the town itself; however, in 2010 most of Bougouni's inhabitants did not originate from the town. Most first and second generations of migrants lived in the four districts that developed after the independence of Mali: Massablacoura, Heremakono, Torakabougou, and Dialanikoro.

These mostly residential districts were large and growing even larger. The acceleration of urban growth created inflation in land prices of districts of the town's center. First and second generations of migrants, the new majority of the town's inhabitants, were thus buying building plots in the new districts. Torakabougou possessed its own food market due to its distance from the town's center. Massablacoura hosted a chicken market. As the town's demographic growth had been accompanied by inflation in land prices in its enclosed districts, inhabitants were thus buying building plots in the new districts. Their edges bordered the *brousse* and were more than a thirty-minute walk from the center. In 2010 these new districts depicted the struggle of Malian households to build their first cement houses, the marker par excellence of a prosperous life in West Africa (see Choplin 2020, 160–70). The purchase of a building plot was shortly followed by the construction of a basic infrastructure, such as a well. An informal rule stipulates that a building plot that remains empty over a certain period of time is still considered as ownerless, hence saleable by the state. The buyer of the plot then started to build a cement house. First, the groundwork was laid. The walls were thereafter erected and eventually the roof. A cement roof with iron rods indicated the owner's plan to erect a second floor. This building process took years, a genuine lifetime project for Malian households with limited income. The new districts also illustrated the emergence of an economic elite who invested their wealth in the building of opulent private houses and houses to rent. The rapid expansion of the town was also accompanied by corruption and illegal housing schemes. For instance, it was not unusual to hear stories of building plots sold to more than one owner. Land disputes between the traditional chieftainship and communal authorities had also punctuated the urbanization of Bougouni. In 2010 entrepreneurs in construction were among the richest inhabitants of Bougouni.

SPACES OF STREET SOCIALITY: *CARRÉ, RUE, GRIN*

People in Bougouni did not spend their days indoors. While few urbanites had the privilege of working in offices, the daily life of most of them was based on outdoor activities in courtyards, neighborhoods, and on the streets. People spent most of their time in three spaces of sociality (*carré, rue*, and *grin*), which are still common to all Malian towns. Taken together, these three spaces of sociality shape a sort of "outdoor living room" and, at the same time, a working place.[57]

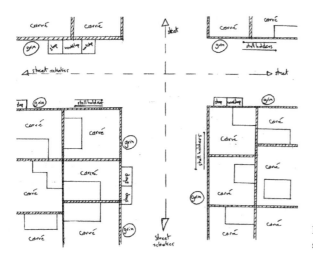

Fig. 6. Plan of urban street life

Le carré (Family Compound)

An urban district is divided into households (*du*) that vary between the traditional extended family (*gwa*) and smaller units such as the nuclear family. Each household inhabits a space enclosed by a wall (of mud or brick) that gives a sense of intimacy to its members. This space, commonly named after its shape (*le carré*[58]), is composed of buildings and an open-air courtyard. People do not spend much time indoors. With the heat of the sun, the air inside the houses tends to be stifling during the day, and houses are therefore mostly used as dormitories and shelter for the night. Malians are also abandoning their traditional thatched roofs for roofs made of sheet metal. This material shift bakes the inside of the house even more. Social life happens within the courtyard, where people spend most of their time when they are at home. In his study of modes of ethical being of music artists in Bamako, Skinner describes the courtyard as "a locus of urban African civility" (2015, 29). The courtyard is usually split into open zones (kitchen, laundry, corral, and playground), and the washroom stands in one of its corners. Daily life in *le carré* unfolds around meals, chats, naps, comings and goings, and prayer. It is also structured by gender. Women usually stay home, where they do all household chores and take care of children, going outside only to do shopping in the market, to attend a wedding or a baptism, or to greet someone or visit a sick person. With men's increasing difficulties to make ends meet, however, more and more women are getting involved in the local economy.

Wives of *aventuriers* considerably help their husbands to cope with family expenses, a point illustrated in chapter 7. Men eat at home and take naps but otherwise spend their time on various activities in town. Family members often gather together in the shade of a big tree after lunch for chats and to watch TV after dinner.[59]

Although *le carré* represents what is the Malian "private" (or domestic) space, it is still framed by shared activities and subjected to collective sight.[60] The main entrance, moreover, is open to comings and goings of many kinds. People come to greet the family, to ask for someone in particular. These meetings occur without invitation. As is customary, the foreigner is always welcomed with a seat and a glass of water. What was planned as a short visit often extends to the next meal for the person who does not know how to say no. Although enclosed by a wall, *le carré* is an open space during the day because people move in and out freely. As such, *le carré* is a porous space where the private and the public merge. At the end of the day, when the head of family and his wife (or wives) go to bed, lights are switched off and doors are shut. But cunning teenagers, students, and young unmarried adults still find a way to enjoy a nightlife and to be involved in forbidden practices out of the public gaze of the day.

La rue (The Street)

Each cluster of *carré* is separated by a grid of streets. Except for main streets, most of them are unsurfaced and do not have street lighting. The urban street is the place where the three spaces of socialities connect. The outer walls of familial compounds, the street façades, are punctuated by commercial units in which locals set out small retail stores and workshops. At the sides of the street, some run shops *par terre* (stallholders), while others come together in informal spots called *grins* (see next section), where men sit, drink tea, play cards, chat, and scrutinize and comment on street activities. Some hail street peddlers to come closer. Others wink at young women on their way to school. A shopkeeper respectfully greets an elder on his way home. Some pedestrians also observe and envy the new cement and multistory buildings of rich families. Vehicles, such as donkey carts, motorbikes, and 4 × 4s, slowly circulate on the uneven sandy streets. The street is also a space of celebration where families welcome parents, friends, and the neighborhood under a big tent with music and food during baptisms and weddings. Apart from shaping an economy of the pavement where social life and business intermingle, these street activities constitute the foreground of public morality in town because of their visibility.

All of these activities animate social life between families in the neighborhood. They also nurture gossip among its inhabitants. Malians say that what happens outside the familial compound mirrors what happens inside it. Consequently, people's manner and clothing on the streets engage their honor (*danbe*) through moral evaluation based on sight. In parallel, public life is also rooted in respect (*bonya*), which implies self-restraint and concealment of shameful practices, a point explored in chapter 3. The surveillance of movement and the body in these open spaces, however, cannot be reduced to strategies of social control. Chapter 3 demonstrates how people also use certain tactics (Low and Lawrence-Zúñiga 2003, 32) so as to take advantage of life's visuality through ostentatious practices. Chapter 4 examines how some people bypass its constraints through nighttime activities.

Le grin

In contemporary Mali (as well as in Burkina Faso and northern Côte d'Ivoire) the *grin* (or rarely *thé-club*) is an important element of urban social life.[61] In Bamako, Skinner introduces the "neighbouhood grin" as a kind of "conversational club" (2015, 18). The origin of the *grin* is confused and seems to come from a distant past.[62] Often associated with a broad Bambara-Dyula culture, the *grin* is to a certain extent comparable to the *fada* in Niger (Masquelier 2019) and the *ataya* in Senegal (Moulard 2008, 88–93). Similar to the *fada*, the *grin* has a "capacity to simultaneously become part of public space and constitute[s] private spaces" (Masquelier 2019, 62). According to Schulz, the *grin* is an informal male group based on friendship and neighborhood connections that "cuts across divides of socio-economic background, age, occupation and educational background" (2002, 811).[63] The men meet on a daily basis at home or at the workplace of the *grin's* leader, usually the one who can afford to provide sugar and tea for the group. The *grin* is therefore the place where men can address concerns to people outside the control of their parents and their household while drinking tea. Women can spend some time in the *grin* on their way to the market, but they usually do not linger there. Men wave to women, who sometimes then sit for a couple of minutes. Then they move on to pursue their activities in town. The *grin* is, above all, a space where people talk (*baro*). For Schultz, the dimension of *baro*—"talk-as-action"—is the cornerstone of the *grin* that brings men together and forges their sociality (2002, 812).[64]

In Bougouni, however, men also tend to meet in *grins* according to their age, their activities, their marital status, and their economic power. During my early period in Bougouni, I spent time with a *grin* of youths who were especially active after dusk. A group of teachers had their *grin* next door. A group of apprentices and students used to sit together in front, on the other side of the street. Around the corner from where I lived, neighbors of all social backgrounds set up a kind of *grin* by regularly sitting in front of the TV of a local shopkeeper. Membership in a *grin* can vary greatly, from a group bound by a common criterion to a loose group that shares time in front of the same TV. The increasing formation of an urban elite and variety of lifestyles and educations can sometimes undermine the social mix of the *grin*. Moreover, *grins* are not stable spaces of sociality. They come together and disperse during the same day because people move from one *grin* to another. They also come together and dispserse over time because people move or their relations change. One can also be a member of several *grins*. Some are daylight *grins*; others are nocturnal. Among the three spaces of street sociality, the *grin* is the one that is the most protean by nature.

Talking in *grins* is punctuated by the making and drinking of tea, a daily ritual for many Malians. The tea maker puts twenty-five grams of green tea in a teapot and boils it for a long time (10–40 minutes). He then adds lots of sugar, cools the tea down by slowly pouring it from the teapot to small cups, and finally serves it. The ritual is started again with the same tea leaves a second time and a third time. In this way, the first tea service is strong and bitter. It is the tea of men and guests that wakes them up and gives them strength. The second infusion is mild and slightly bitter. The third one is light and sweet; it is the ladies' tea. The first served are usually leaders of the *grin* along with guests and elders. If you sit and wait here until the third tea is served, more than one hour will have gone by. Between tea services, people kill the time by talking, playing cards, and listening to music.[65] They not only socialize but also watch and comment on movements of pedestrians and vehicles on the street. Given that most people struggle to find full-time livelihoods, they spend time in *grins* where life flows *dɔɔni-dɔɔni* (slowly). Meeting, joking, and gossiping are dimensions of *grins* that are stressed in a popular Malian TV series called *Le Grin*, which shows life in a *grin*: ordinary Malians sit by the side of a street, drink tea, exchange, and chitchat in Bambara about daily life matters and interact with passers-by in humorous manner.[66] Social activities in *grins* nurture comments and moral evaluations of street life in Bougouni. In this regard, *grins* are the eyes and ears of Radio Trottoir that convey street happenings to households. Following a similar vein of social life, they are also the eyes and ears of public Islam, an increasing form of ethical life that is explored in the next chapter.

CHAPTER 3

Public Islam on the Street

One evening in May 2009, I was sitting in a *grin* by the side of the tarred road that runs between the Medine and Dialanikoro districts. This main road had street lighting. Passers-by frequented several shops that stayed open late into the evening. As usual, I was spending my evening drinking tea, chatting with friends, and observing the nightlife around me. As the time approached 10:30 p.m., we noticed a well-groomed man wearing a clean white robe and sunglasses, with Islamic prayer beads around his neck, walking along the street. He was coming toward us while chanting in Bambara, "God is protection. God is help. God is cover."[1] Arriving at the *grin*, he stopped, looked around, and then stared at a group of young (unmarried) women (*sunguruw*) sitting in the shadow of a big mango tree on the other side of the road. He brusquely shouted, "Women put newborns in toilets.[2] At night, mothers sleep when their daughters are outside. Women whiten their skin. I do not understand!" Reactions within the *grin* were mixed. Some shrugged. Some smiled and responded, "This is true."[3] Others just listened carefully. Afterward, this odd person started to dance to hip-hop and reggae music coming from someone's mobile phone. A couple of youths gathered around him. They encouraged his performance by clapping their hands. Suddenly he stopped, pointed skyward, and said, "Obama and the White House fear me because I can trigger the Third World War by planting something in the soil." Everybody around started to laugh out loud. One person thanked him and bought him an ice cream from the neighboring shop, after which he continued his evening walk along the streets of Bougouni, repeating, "God is protection. God is help. God is cover."

This strange character was well known in Bougouni. According to local recollection, he was a promising and even gifted student of Islamic studies who had attained a good level of competence in the Arabic language and knew about some esoteric aspects of Islam. When asking God for a favor during a long, lonely, and demanding session of prayer, running the prayer beads between his fingers (*ka wurudi kɛ*), he lost control of himself and fell into madness (*fatɔya*), from which he had never recovered fully. Many interpreted his madness to be the result of occult forces that unsettled his mind during his prayers to God so that he lost his way. In other words, he asked God for powerful forces that only pious men, such as elders, can handle. Haste and immoderate ambition led him onto the path of madness, but his insanity gave him the ability to catch glimpses of an invisible occult world that most Muslims do not see. Therefore, locals also feared and listened to him because, as a member of the *grin* said that very evening, "even if he is mad, he can sometimes tell the truth."[4]

Muslims conceive Islam as a multidimensional phenomenon. Certainly it involves a set of rituals, signs, and moral discourses that shape public life. In Mali, Islam also involves an inner force that informs someone's personality, maturity, and *barika*. And these two dimensions do not necessarily connect. In Bougouni the self-described "simply Muslims" understood piety as both the practice of Islamic precepts and self-discipline (virtuous ethos), the interplay of which was not imperatively spontaneous and straightforward. As a thread running through local Muslim life, this twofold nature of piety reminded *aventuriers* of public Islam's potentiality of moral ambiguity. Public expressions of Muslim piety, supported by Muslim leaders and their followers, shape someone's reputation of being a good Muslim but do not necessarily index pious intentions.

THE ISSUE OF INTENTIONALITY IN PUBLIC PIETY

The *seere* is "the dark, sometimes circular, spot or mark on some Muslims' foreheads. . . . The mark indexes regular prayer beyond the obligatory five ritual daily prayers and presumably appears on the forehead from touching the ground during prayer" (Soares 2004, 206). Thus, the *seere* should index piety. Nonetheless, it is frequent that Muslims question the "moral character" of its bearers when they are accused of "charges of corruption, embezzlement, or illicit sexual activities" (222). Others accuse some bearers of *seere* to have intentionally created it in order to make people think that they are pious.[5] What can we learn from the debate over the validity of the *seere* as a genuine index of piety in Mali? Soares states, "It is perhaps unwise for the anthropologist to speculate about the intentionality of actors" (222), and concludes by asserting the existence of publicly recognized signs of piety. Soares is right in stating that public signs of piety exist in Mali, but I also think that inserting the dimension of intention (or motivation) into the analysis can illuminate the ambiguity that is intrinsic to the twofold nature of piety. The *seere* means "proof" in Bambara. As proof, the *seere* is notwithstanding one that can be "falsified" for mundane (non-pious) purposes. Whereas the outward signs of Islam indicate the presence of a Muslim identity, they do not automatically certify piety, because they can be duplicated by selfish intentions. The source of intention is by nature inward and, as Muslims say, known only by God. The presence of intention in someone's mind still gives outward hints about its "underneath" source. So the source of intention has a phenomenal imprint. This relatedness, however, remains subject to moral evaluation because sight can be deceptive. The inward source–outward imprint of an intention resonates with the ancient Mande feature of the twofold nature of power (see introductory chapter): the genuine root of what is observable lies beneath it, or the spiritual (occult) power; and what is observable may provide an ethical glimpse of what is beneath, or the physical (material) power.

A focus on intention allows the analyst to explore the relation between outward signs of piety (appearance) and inward states of mind (intention). Instead of analyzing how religion subordinates subjects to its precepts, a focus on intention also explores "the formation of subjectivities" in order to "understand how people (try to) act on the world as they are acted upon" (Ortner 2005, 41). In Mali the debate around the problem of intentionality in outward signs of piety involves an anthropology of ethics and freedom for two main reasons: to widen the range of motivations that support the display of outward signs of piety; and to explore how the formation of subjectivities can give rise to the intentional display of outward signs of piety for mundane purposes. I do not say that Muslims can stand "outside Islam," but the fact that people's attitudes toward outward signs of piety can be ambiguous shows how Muslims engage with rituals, public signs, and moral discourses in complex and tactical manners that deserve to be explored. The debate around the issue of intentionality in public piety links the study of piety with the intricacies of daily life. When we investigate the making of pious life, the challenge is to take into consideration "the complex and often contradictory nature of . . . experience" (Schielke 2009, 26). The analyst should not fall into the "illusion of wholeness," which tends to overemphasize the coherence and perfection of religious experience (26).[6] As Magnus Marsden observed in Pakistan's former North-West Frontier Province, the Qazi (Islamic judge), a pretended example of piety, also express "inconsistencies" by making sexy jokes during public sermons in the mosque and by showing off a "playful" appearance (smart clothes, slick haircuts, and expensive perfumes) in public (2005, 5–6). How, then, do Muslims in Bougouni consider the possibility of discrepancies between the twofold nature of piety in their assessment of proper Muslim life?

Bambara language does not have a word for "good Muslim" or an adjective for "pious." When I asked my fieldwork assistant to translate *vrai musulman* (true Muslim) into the vernacular, he replied by saying "*silamɛ yɛrɛ yɛrɛ.*" The term *yɛrɛ* is a particle of insistence that expresses the idea of absolute and legitimate (Bailleul 1996). It can stress any word. For instance, "true friend" becomes *terikɛ yɛrɛ yɛrɛ.* Most people simply say of a bad Muslim that "he is not Muslim" (*silamɛ tɛ*) and of a good Muslim, "he is Muslim" (*silamɛ don*).[7] The intonation of the voice completes the intensity, depth, and contour of a moral evaluation. However, when piety is assessed beyond a specific moment—in other words, as an Islamic path—Muslims recognize human weakness and earthly challenge as inherent to the making of a proper Muslim life. Being Muslim was synonymous with virtue, but this did not mean that the Muslim is perfect. Most Muslims in Mali considered Islam as pure; however, like Indonesian Muslims, they differentiated "the perfection of Islam" from "the messiness of the human world" (Simon 2009, 258). As my friend Alou the teacher explained, "The Muslim is the one who sins and asks for forgiveness. The true Muslim is the one who never sins. According to the Qur'an, the true Muslim is called *mu'min.*[8] This latter is extremely rare among Muslims." The figure of *mu'min* depicts more an ideal type than what Muslims in Bougouni observed around them. Abdramane the street peddler significantly said, "We are like a scale. On one side we collect *barajiw* [divine awards]. On the other side we amass *jurumuw* [sins]." Some approach the Islamic path more through precepts; others put more emphasis on virtues. But all Muslims assert that only few of them live their life in full accordance with the Islamic path. In Bougouni it was in this human, hence elusive, path that someone's religious experience was assessed. How, then, do local Muslims relate the Islamic path to the twofold nature of piety? We first need to consider how the main Islamic currents that are present in Bougouni impact on the Islamic path. Secondly, we will explore how local Muslims responded to these influences.

BOUGOUNI: THE RELIGIOUS CROSSROADS OF SOUTHWEST MALI

In Mali historic centers of Islamic studies are often characterized by the presence of prominent religious leaders and their network of followers who manage to keep other Islamic currents at bay. The two Sufi orders (Hamawiyya and Tijaniyya) of Nioro-du-Sahel, for instance, still dominate the Islamic debate in town and therefore prevent other (more recent) Islamic influences to take root locally (Soares 2005). Bougouni, a town marked by a late Islamization, was not characterized by any religious dominance or monopoly over the local Islamic debate. Following the new civic liberties brought by the events of 1991 in Mali, Bougouni, like many Malian towns, had undergone a rather competitive process of Islamic renewal. The town became the religious crossroads of southwest Mali, where numerous Islamic currents work toward making their influence in town tangible.

At the beginning of my stay in Bougouni, my host father recounted the following anecdote when I asked him about the Islamic currents present in town.

> The other day the *pieds-nus* [barefoot] visited the mosque. They are a grouping of fundamentalists who wear traditional cotton clothes. They proclaimed that there are seventy-three Islamic religious paths, but only one, theirs, leads to God. I disagree because Islam cannot be reduced to one path.

This anecdote about the Islamic path points to dogmatic discrepancies between Islamic currents found in Bougouni. It also illustrates that the style of dress can name the identity of a distinct Islamic current, such as the barefoot. In Bougouni, Muslims tended to divide the identity of Muslims into five different categories. Louis Brenner rightly defines identity building as "a process of naming: naming of self, naming of others, naming *by* others" that happens in local as well as wider political contexts (1993b, 59). Categories of identity thus do not exist for themselves. They are articulated to other categories of identity in ways that reflect dynamic religious orientations, markers of Muslimness, and expressions of piety instead of fixed criteria. In line with Brenner's approach to identity building, the following section examines the main categories of Muslim identity employed in Bougouni as they were shaped by the Islamic renewal enabled by the Third Republic of Mali. These processes of naming thus involved fluid, situational, and incomplete categories.

THE BAREFOOT

The so-called barefoot is a Muslim current founded in Mali by Cheick Ibrahim Kalil Kanouté in the 1980s. According to its founder, the true Muslim should live as the Prophet Muhammad. His followers must therefore refuse any technology subsequent to the epoch of the Prophet. Thus, the barefoot did not drive any motorized vehicles and did not wear modern shoes. It is why they were nicknamed "barefoot." They were also called *sirawo* (the path of hole) because it was commonly said that Cheick Kanouté developed this peculiar Islamic path during the years when he lived in the hole of a big tree. His followers were also known to wear traditional hand-woven cotton clothes and to refuse modern medicines. Women were confined to the house (chores and child rearing) and men mostly farmed. Their strict discipline of life prompted clashes with civil servants who consider them to be rebellious citizens because of their rejection of modern services (e.g., vaccinations). A few conflicts even ended in tragedy. The barefoot mustered only a thousand adherents in the entire country.

In Bougouni barefoot were composed of a few families settled at the edge of the Heremakono district. They built their own mosque, the only mosque that was not registered in the AMUPI's record of mosques. The barefoot were not part of the AMUPI because of religious views rooted in a refusal of contemporary modernity. Local Muslims considered them to be "mad people" and "extremists" because they denied living in the epoch when they were born. The barefoot, however, attracted public scrutiny. Their outfits "from another [past] epoch" were easily recognizable. Barefoot encountered on streets often provoked mocking remarks from passers-by. In town, their small but visible presence aroused more laughter than suspicion.

THE WAHHABIS

Bougouni was also home to the so-called Wahhabis.[9] These Muslims, who named themselves "Sunnis," had been labeled with the pejorative colonial-era term Wahhabites by those not affiliated with their doctrines.[10] The self-label Sunni indicates their claim to be the genuine followers of Sunni Islam, whereas the label Wahhabite stresses their imported Islam beliefs (Chappatte 2018b, 234). Although such Muslims covered heterogeneous groups, they were all inspired by reformist currents of Arabic influences for two main reasons: many members of their religious elite studied Islam in the Middle East; and they vehemently criticized the superimposition of local social structures of power on religious offices, the *maraboutage* practices, and the cult of saints adopted by most local Muslims.[11] The Wahhabis took hold first in the big towns of Bamako, Bouaké, and Sikasso.[12] In 2010 the provincial town of Bougouni, located halfway between Bamako and Sikasso, hosted an important minority of Wahhabis.[13] In charge of four mosques (one Friday mosque) and two *médersas*, the presence of this minority was highly noticeable due to their "Arabic dress code."

Women were mostly confined at home; when they went outside, they wore black veils over ordinary clothes. Men wore white robes and trousers. Their pants were shorter than ordinary pants. They were cut in the calf region to avoid picking up dirt from the soil, which can invalidate the prayer. Men let their beards grow. Wahhabis prayed with their arms crossed, as opposed to their arms hanging by sides as adopted by all other Muslim currents. The Wahhabis promoted rational (modern) Islamic school (*médersa*) because they disagreed with both the esoteric education of the traditional Islamic school and the modern but secular Western-style public school.[14]

Wahhabis were perceived with mixed feelings in Mali, mostly due to their dogmatic strictness and its social consequences. I met numerous Muslims who shared the opinion of Sidy the builder: "Wahhabis are knowledgeable about Islam, but they exaggerate." He told me that one of his *promotionnaires* (schoolmates) became a Wahhabi. Despite their religious divergences, they stayed friends over the years. Sidy respected his friend's knowledge of the Islamic sacred texts, but he thought that by struggling to find an Islamic explanation for everything, and by restricting his conduct to religious guidelines only, his friend went too far: "The Wahhabis are walking on a thin red line. They think life is within religion. For me, however, it is the opposite. Religion is within life. It is tough for them. They sometimes drop it." Sidy's comment about "walking on a thin red line" depicts local perceptions of the Wahhabi path as like a tightrope walk because its religious rigor makes life complicated.[15] Many educated Muslims who read Islamic sacred texts by themselves also criticized the Wahhabis for their *islam littéraliste* (Holder 2009a, 241),[16] which seeks to consistently encapsulate Muslim life into a set of written norms. These educated Muslims thought that the world-as-it-is (the real) cannot be fully grasped by textual knowledge, so Wahhabi analytical process was often blamed for its speculative tendency. For Bakary the engineer, when the nature of Islamic authority is systematically enclosed in literal interpretation of textual material, one risks reducing the conception of proper Muslim life to "all that is not written is condemned" to the detriment of "all that is not condemned is allowed." Put differently, Bakary compares the Islamic sacred texts to a finger that points at God: the Qur'an and Hadiths indicate the direction of the religious path. However, the Wahhabis study the finger instead of the direction it reveals, because their textual approach to Islam keeps them from seeing the wider world into which religious life is inserted.

More significantly, local Muslims of all educations criticized Wahhabis for undermining *adamadenya*. They had contempt for the fact that Wahhabis tended to socialize only among themselves and therefore did not attend the life-cycle rituals of other Muslims. Wahhabis were commonly depicted as those who weaken traditional community life because they do things differently: their public codes, their way of praying, and the praying times in their mosques differed from the rest of Muslims. Wahhabis were also the only Muslims in town who did not join the celebration of the Maouloud (Mawlid, the celebration of the birth of the Prophet) (Holder 2009a). It was not anodyne that in 2010 Malians kept naming them "Wahhabites." Whereas colonial administrators perceived Salafiyya ideas as subversive to colonial order, numerous Muslims of contemporary Mali blamed the Wahhabis for confounding Islam with Arabic culture, thereby neglecting (even betraying) their own cultural legacy. Malians still considered them as a "threat" but to *adamadenya*. They argued that the long tradition of Islam found in central and northern Mali certifies local Islam as being as legitimate as Islamic currents coming from the Arabic world.

THE SUFIS

The category "Sufi" covered the "phenomenon of new Sufis" found in Bougouni (Soares 2007). These recent currents were articulated around "new Muslim public figures" that emerged due to the post-1991 process of liberalization, freedom of association, and new media of communication (80). Among these currents, the Sufi branch of Cheick Soufi Bilal was present in Bougouni. This new Sufi movement attracted public attention because of

the media coverage of its spiritual leader. In 2010 Bilal was a prolific writer and a preacher with a growing saintly reputation in Mali. His media-
mediated charisma, along with his bricolage of various Sufi orders (85) and
dreadlocks indexing "youth urban culture" (83), supported his reputation of
open-mindedness among younger generations of Muslims in Bougouni. The
followers of Cheick Soufi Bilal opened a *zawiya* (place of religious activities
associated with Sufism) in the Dialanikoro district in the late 1990s. Despite
Bilal's small number of followers in town, the public sermons that they organized during the evening often drew a crowd of young Muslims.[17] Malian
youth also appreciated the new Sufis because of their acceptance of dance and
music in their conception of a proper Muslim life. By contrast, elders were
more suspicious toward such movements, which they depicted as immature,
defiant, and lacking good manners.

THE ANSARS

The market of religious media and paraphernalia in Bougouni was full of
imprints of Chérif Ousmane Madani Haïdara and Ansar Dine,[18] the Muslim
association founded by Haïdara in 1983. Initially, this Muslim organization
based in Bamako operated clandestinely under the totalitarian regime of
Moussa Traoré. The advent of the Third Republic of Mali thereafter boosted
the growth of Ansar Dine thanks to the new freedoms of the press and association. In addition to his oratorical skills and outspokenness (Schulz 2003,
2006, 2007; Soares 2005, 234–35, 252–55), Haïdara has become "a veritable
media star" in Mali (Soares 2007, 80) due to the promotion of his Islamic
teachings in Mali's lingua franca through the media on a large scale, such as is
illustrated with the numerous audio recordings of his sermons found in local
markets. In less than thirty years, Ansar Dine had turned into one of the most
powerful Muslim associations in contemporary Mali.[19]

In 2010 the branch of Ansar Dine in Bougouni was growing. Its committee was also supervising the opening of new sub-branches in the big villages
of the town's hinterland. The association's members, the so-called Ansars,
were especially active. They organized public sermons on a weekly basis.
These events often ended with two public oaths of allegiance. According to
Haïdara, the profession of the Islamic creed (Shahada) does not completely
certify adherence to Muslim faith.[20] An individual adheres fully to Islam only

through making the six promises in front of witnesses who already did so, such as at the end of a public sermon.[21] I was told that through this public act, Haïdara aims to foster an Islamic religiosity based on human conscience rather than a mere religious identity by birth or a classic Shahada-based conversion to Islam. After the first six promises, one was invited to make a second public oath, which consists of a pledge of allegiance to Ansar Dine and its "spiritual guide," Haïdara. This second *baya* (sermon) evokes the meaning of this concept in Arabic: an oath of loyalty, often to a ruler. By doing so, a certified Muslim becomes a member of the organization—that is, an Ansar, a genuine guardian of Islam. What was sociologically at stake with these two public oaths of allegiance was faithfulness to Islam through Haïdara.

Ansars did not pray in specific mosques. Men did not wear recognizable symbols of allegiance. As for Ansar women, they wore partial hijab-style veils. This Islamic accessory made them easily recognizable within a crowd. Although members of Ansar Dine were on the rise in Bougouni, they represented only an active religious minority of the local Muslim community. On the other hand, Haïdara was an unmissable figure in the field of media in town.

The figure of Haïdara was noticed through the circulation of his sermons on local radios, DVDs shown in *grins* and courtyards, and through the presence of his image on trucks, cars, and shops. The four radio stations of Bougouni broadcast eleven and a half hours of Islamic programming every week, among which Haïdara- and Ansar Dine–related programming accounted for 56.5 percent of all Islamic radio programs. Such wide media coverage promoted the evocation of Haïdara in informal discussions between Muslims in town. Many among them quoted his teachings when debating religious issues, while others argued about them. At the very least, nobody felt indifferent to Haïdara. In this media success, what struck me the most was Haïdara's popularity among the youth of the town in a country where they are in the majority. But many of these young people were not Ansars. How, then, can we qualify their bond to Haïdara? The numerous but loose bond between Haïdara and these young sympathizers—neither close disciples, nor members of Ansar Dine, nor certified Muslims—was mostly based on the media practices through which his name and teachings were regularly heard in daily social life in town (Chappatte 2018b). Among these media practices, the youths listening to the numerous *zikiri* cassettes found in local markets played a considerable role in establishing this bond.

THE SIMPLY MUSLIMS

> There are many paths within Islam; the Ansar, Sufi, Wahhabi, Barefoots, and those who walk on Muhammad's path. I am among those who follow Muhammad only. We do not have a chief except God himself. (Boubacar the small trader)

The category *silamɛ dɔron* (simply Muslim), the way *aventuriers* identified themselves as Muslims among affiliated Muslims, accounted for most Muslims found in Bougouni.[22] These Muslims agreed with some teachings of definite Islamic currents, but they were affiliated with none of them. Being not affiliated with an Islamic current means being neither a member nor a follower of an Islamic current and its religious leaders. Boubacar, for instance, was a sympathizer of Haïdara because he appreciated the flexible teaching of the latter's moral guidance (Chappatte 2018b, 19). For instance, Haïdara's emphasis on "correct intention" resolved the long-standing dispute over the proper position of the arms during the prayer (19). He sometimes attended public sermons organized in town by the local branch of Ansar Dine. He also listened to Haïdara's preaching on local radio programs when at work. On occasion, Boubacar also attended public sermons organized by followers of Cheick Bilal because he appreciated the openness of Bilal's Islamic teachings. Although he did not support the rigidity of Wahhabi doctrines, he agreed with their criticism of the custom of ostentatious weddings that burden families with debts. Boubacar cared about Islam because, among other goals, he wanted to live a proper Muslim life. However, he did not feel the need to be affiliated with a specific Islamic current, because his religiosity, as an object of individual scrutiny, did not require a firm affiliation.

Filippo Osella and Caroline Osella (2008) mention the existence of "just Muslims" in Kerala. In private these Muslims declare not to be aligned with a particular religious group. In public, however, they take a clearer religious affiliation due to an overdetermination of identity by political events. Such a situation of political pressure over the choice of a specific Muslim affiliation did not exist in Bougouni. How, then, did simply Muslims position themselves within Bougouni's competitive process of Islamic renewal? Although these Muslims did not follow a specific body of doctrines, they related their Muslim identity to a sort of presumed universal Islam.

THE FORMATION OF A GENERIC ISLAM

The history of Islamic debate in Mali is related to what Louis Brenner (2001) terms "doctrinal politics." Muslim scholars have mostly enunciated Islamic disputes around discourses of "truth and ignorance": "Consequently, doctrinal political debate inevitably includes claims and counter-claims about what is 'true,' and about which scholars are truly knowledgeable and possess a full command of Islamic texts, and which are ignorant" (135). Doctrinal politics between Muslim scholars have therefore been characterized by the following equation: "Whoever knows tells the truth; the others are ignorant." In this way, "the expansion of each movement was accompanied by one, or several, doctrinal initiatives which simultaneously challenged a pre-existing doctrinal position and sought to demonstrate the superior Islamic knowledge of the leader in question" (137). The dynamics of doctrinal politics resonates with Roman Loimeier's theory of religious reform, which defines any reform as a change with a program (Loimeier 2016, chapter 2). How do self-described "simply Muslims" live their religiosity in relation to doctrinal politics? How do they perceive the unity of Islam when divergent conceptions of proper Muslim life coexist and compete where they live? In Bougouni, Muslims still base their unity on Islamic consensus (*ijma*); however, it is a "generic" one that is reduced to the assumed universals of Islam.

Dale F. Eickelman defines "generic Islam" as the outcome of modern mass education and religious policy of the Oman state whose aim was to develop Islamic studies as a "scrupulously non-sectarian subject" (1989, 5). In this context, state authorities promoted a generic Islam as the means to foster a shared Islamic curriculum and to avoid sectarian divisions between Ibadis, Sunnis, and Shi'ahs. In Bougouni, generic Islam was also a sort of shared Islamic curriculum, but its development differs from what is found in Oman because it was not the result of a particular religious policy.

Muslims in Bougouni used to tell me that "Mali is a *laïc* [secular] country" to stress that the Malian state is not ruled by Muslim scholars.[23] They also told me that "Mali is a Muslim country" because more than 90 percent of Malians identify themselves as Muslims. Are these two statements contradictory? For local Muslims, Mali was part of the "the global Islamic community" (*umma*). As such, they perceived Islam as an important cultural referent of Mali. In contemporary history, Islam as a cultural system is imagined (Anderson 1983) as one of the "world religions" (Cook, Laidlaw, and Mair 2009).[24] Both these ideas—of *umma* and world religion—reinforce the perception of Islam as an

authentic, coherent, and encompassing system to Muslims. However, following the arguments of Joanna Cook, James Laidlaw and Jonathan Mair, this
system does not exist out there as if it had an existence separate from Muslims: "The widespread assumption by adherents of self-consciously world
religions that there *must be* a coherent whole of which they are part is itself a
religious commitment" (54). This system thus needs to be continuously produced and explained by Muslims in order to exist and to endure. In Bougouni
the practice of a generic Islam systematized Islam as the common religious
culture for "simply Muslims" who were facing the competitive Islamic teachings set by Islamic currents. Following John R. Bowen's (1998) line of inquiry
between "universal" and "local" Islamic traits, how, then, has generic Islam
as a putative element of universal Islam been appropriated in southern Mali?

As a reminder, the first Muslim families of Bougouni had little knowledge of Islam; its practice was often disparate and mixed with local religious
traditions. Within the emerging context of an "Islamic sphere" promoted by
colonial "peace" and the development of a road network (Launay and Soares
1999), Muslim identity progressively came to be associated with a body of
standardized Islamic practices. The Muslim prayer, for instance, became an
idiom that brought together people of different origins during economic
migration across AOF. This process of standardization accelerated after the
independence of Mali with the implications of small media, civic reforms,
and modern technologies. How has this process been shaped by competition
between Islamic currents? What unites Muslims when such religious competition creates dogmatic discrepancies among Muslims? Muslims assemble around a generic Islam, a sort of lowest common Islamic denominator
accepted by all Muslims.

> Muslims throughout Mali agree on the five Islamic pillars.
> The rest is only disagreement. (Imam, Bougouni)

When asked what unites Muslims in Bougouni, Boubacar the small trader
of *yuguyuguw* and Kassim the handyman and mill worker pronounced the
first pillar of Islam—that is, the Islamic creed (Shahada): the Muslim declaration of belief in the oneness of God and acceptance of Muhammad as his
Prophet. Salif the tailor uttered the *sura Al-Fatiha*,[25] which is intoned in each
prayer and during every life-ritual ceremony. The above quotation, collected
during an informal chat with a couple of elders in the courtyard of a mosque,
illustrates in a nutshell the Islamic consensus found in town: the five Islamic

pillars, which are the Islamic creed, the regular daily prayer, the ritual fasting, the almsgiving, and the pilgrimage of the Hajj.[26] The unity of Islam stopped at the five Muslim pillars. This sounds rather simplistic, but local Muslims took *ijma* as a straightforward statement that did not need the backing of any religious authority to be verified. Muslims in Bougouni could achieve consensus over other points, but such consensus was never immediate; it stemmed from debate, the outcome of which was partial, changing, and situational.

STREET LIFE AND PUBLIC ISLAM

The post-1991 democratic and liberal processes in Mali granted civil liberties (e.g., freedom of association) that have in turn supported a peculiar process of Islamic renewal. Contemporary Mali is characterized by the formation of an *"espace publique religieux"* (public religious sphere) within which a mushrooming of new Islamic associations and their followers advocate public expressions of piety (Soares 2004), while politicians seek to seduce a Muslim electorate (Holder 2009a).[27] By contrast to a logic of rupture with its claim of an Islamic state, the contemporary articulations between Islam, politics, and public life in Mali follow a *"logique d'accommodement"* (logic of accommodation) (Holder 2009b) in which these articulations are potential resources of power. How have Muslims responded to the moralization of public life supported by Muslim scholars, Islamic associations, and their followers? How has this increasing visibility of Muslim activism acted on the daily life of Muslims in general? The practice of generic Islam has become marked by an acute display of outward signs of piety.

In Bougouni daily life was about a street life that mostly unfolded around three spaces of sociality: the *carré*, the *rue*, and the *grin*. As these spaces were open, hence visible, street life in urban Mali tended to bind the quotidian to a public performance. Similar to a Mozambique suburb, when "daily life is spent outdoors under the gaze of neighbours or passers-by," one "lives in a quasi-constant state of surveillance, comparable, in some respects with Bentham's panopticon" (Archambault 2010, 123). The open character of Bougouni's urban street life also stemmed from an urban architecture of local (Mande) origin. The dry and hot climate of the savanna coupled with the availability of land "naturally" obliged people to live outside. In roadside towns, with the development of an economy of the pavement where social life and business intermingle, street activities of all kinds became the foreground of daily life. In this centrality of street life to people's daily lives, practices of ostentation potentially went hand in hand with practices of dissimulation insofar as "to dress" implied "to cover" as well. The "logic of ostentation and dissimulation" ensuing from such outdoor living rooms resonated with the close connection between physical (visible) and spiritual (occult) power found in the historical Mande world.[28] Therefore, the dynamic between the open and the concealed has been a key tension of urban street life and its public morality in southwest Mali.

Following the coup d'état of 1991, the emergence of Islam as a public force, which accompanied its massive spread into southwest Mali in the 1950s through the 1970s, has gained new momentum. The Islamic renewal observed in contemporary Mali has strengthened the authority of Islam in public through moral evaluation based on sight. And Muslims responded to this Islamic renewal by the practice of a generic Islam marked by the display of outward signs of piety. These signs advertise the shaping of moral subjects in public: "To be" is also informed by "to appear/look." Observers are also attentive to what people do in public because it shapes their "reputation [honour]" (*danbe*). Social order in Mali is rooted in respect (*bonya*), which implies, above all, self-restraint in public; it is also rooted in honor, which insists on correct behavior, good manners, and ostentatious display. In Bougouni the significance of values, respect, and honor were encapsulated in the following local French expression: *Il/elle est quelqu'un de considéré(e)* (he/she is someone respected). This expression carries two constitutive sets of meaning: (1) someone who is not just anyone because he/she is known among the community to be distinguishable from the masses; and (2) someone regarded with esteem; a person of standing.

Muslims of Bougouni (especially the economic elite, family heads, and elders[29]) displayed outward signs of piety, such as the white robe of Arabic style, the rounded small white cap called *silamɛ fugulan* (Muslim hat), and white Moroccan-style slippers, among other items and clothes of the Muslim dress code. In 2009 the first imam of a mosque in Torakabougou was criticized because he wore a *veston* (blazer) over his white *boubou* (long, flowing garment) during communal prayer. His detractors did not appreciate his blazer, because they thought it was not a proper Islamic cloth. They added that the imam should be an exemplary Muslim. In order to stay in office, the imam had to remove his blazer. During a bus trip to Bamako, I heard someone calling his unknown neighbor *karamɔgɔ* (teacher in Islamic studies). This person was a well-groomed young man with a sharp-cut beard; he wore

a white robe of Arabic style, small rounded cap covered with golden embroidery, and white Moroccan slippers (*silamɛ sabara*). He also had Islamic rings
of luck on his fingers. He spent most of the time picking up his ostentatious
mobile phone and conversing with his interlocutors in a calm voice. He also
occasionally listened to a reading of the Qur'an through his white earphones.
His neighbor did not call him *karamɔgɔ* by accident. Owing to his Muslim
look, he was respectfully referred to as a teacher in Islamic studies. Furthermore, his clean appearance and his extravagant mobile phone were indicators
of wealth. One should respect an apparently pious and rich stranger. In *Muslims and New Media in West Africa: Pathways to God* (2012, 159–67), Schulz
focuses on the female face of the post-1991 Islamic renewal in the urban localities of San and Bamako. Through her discussion of the decision of "taking the
veil" as an act of public self-expression, she illustrates how in southern Mali
the public practice of piety became an important element of religious identity
among female participants in the Islamic renewal. In Bougouni the minority
of Muslim women who traditionally covered their hair did not act in a solely
religious fashion. They also wore colorfully aesthetic foulards in *bazin* called
musɔr (in French, *mouchoir*) that partially covered their hair, whereas older
women loosely draped over their head and shoulders a scarf called *kunna.biri*
(literally, to cover the head). Often used as a prayer shawl, this accessory highlights the respectable status associated with old age in contemporary Mali. In
Bougouni an increasing minority of women wore partial hijab-style veils. On
the streets they would often be pointed at as "Ansar women," although not all
women wearing such veils were affiliated with Ansar Dine, a designation that
illustrated the influence of Ansar Dine in town.

During the day, prayer times in town unfolded as religious duties within
carrés, around the shops, and along the street façades.[30] Men and women
looked for the colorful plastic pots (*selidaga*) that they commonly use to
perform their ritual ablution (*ka seliji ta*). They took or borrowed someone's
prayer mat. If there was not a mat, they used a plastic or jute bag instead. They
then prayed. Except for elders, Muslims did not necessarily seek to pray in the
mosque. They prayed wherever they happened to be during the coming of a
prayer time (e.g., within *carrés*, in workshops, in shops, on the waysides) with
little concern for the noise and bustle crossing their prayer space. Kassim
the handyman confided to me that as a single man he often prayed outdoors
(rather than indoors) to let the neighborhood know and spread the word that
he is an observant Muslim. He added that it is important to build a reputation
of being an observant Muslim in the eyes of local parents who are looking to
marry their daughters to "respectable Muslims."

The communal Friday prayer constitutes the collective core of the weekly holy day of Islam. It therefore illustrates well the visual, social, and ostentatious character of public piety found in urban Mali. Every Friday just before 1 p.m., the streets of Bougouni became packed with Muslims walking toward the five Friday mosques for the communal prayer. At that time, one could observe processions of finery and "Friday best." Men carried prayer mats and prayer beads and wore immaculate traditional white clothes (*grands boubous*) or robes of Arabic style and elegant Muslim caps and turbans. Old women wore loose-fitting traditional clothes and partial veils decorated with colorful and golden embroidery. Amid a typical environment of reddish dust along the streets and in the air, a sharp-eyed observer could notice numerous polished shoes among the crowd as well. Locals said that those who arrive first at the Friday communal prayer and manage to find a place in the front row receive more *baraji* than the others. The Friday mosques were so packed that latecomers had to pray in rows outside the mosque. At the precise moment of the prayer, the streets of the towns were half empty and silent. Those who missed the communal Friday prayer remained quiet while the Muslim community was praying together. When the prayer was over, the processions of finery started again and scattered as Muslims went back home, eating and relaxing with family and, later, visiting relatives and friends in town.

The relationships between street life, power, and Islam have transformed Muslim identity as a mundane resource that is active in the broader politics of prosperity in contemporary urban Mali. A good Muslim was *quelqu'un de considéré(e)* in Bougouni, a form of respect that entails a public identity. Although the public expression of piety shaped social status, Muslims knew, however, that Friday parades of Muslims were not necessarily aligned with their intentions. The twofold nature of piety, both public and personal, which I explained through my opening anecdote of the madman, reminded them of the problem of intentionality linked to the practice of public piety.

THE ISLAMIC PRAYER: A PRACTICE BETWEEN FAITH AND MUNDANE STATUS

I met my friend Yaya, a sympathizer of Haïdara, during a public sermon organized by Ansar Dine. At that time, he was a newly married man who worked as a carpenter in a workshop in the district of Dialanikoro. Yaya and his wife shared the same courtyard with his parents and younger brothers and sisters. His parents had moved to Bougouni a decade earlier from the hinterland of

Segou. He used to invite me for lunch when women of his courtyard were not cooking *to* with *gan* sauce because of my dislike for glutinous meals.[31] One day we ate my favorite Malian dish: rice with peanut sauce (*tigadεgε.na*). Then we relaxed a bit. His younger brother was preparing tea. Yaya suddenly waved at me to look at his uncle, who was visiting that day. He was praying a few meters away. A mobile phone was laid on the right-hand corner of his prayer mat. Holding a red hair comb in his hand, his uncle was intoning *sura*. Yaya smiled at me and whispered, "You see, my uncle is always ready for business and seduction, and this even when he is praying!" I saw many Muslims placing their mobile phones on their prayer mats during prayer as if this mat also became a sort of external pocket or a handbag during a moment when the body must be free and available to the prayer. Yaya's remark was more a joke than a critique. Holding the comb in his hand while praying nonetheless indicated that a prayer can be animated by numerous intentions, mind-sets, and focus, either pious or more mixed ones.

The prayer (*sεli*) is an important vehicle for the Muslim faith (*limaniya*).[32] It is the second pillar of Islam that is constituted by five daily prayers performed at precise moments during the day. My friend Boubacar, the small trader of *yuguyuguw*, used to say, "Praying is about bringing God within you."[33] The Muslim prayer therefore concerns the relationship between the worshipper and God. Boubacar added that Muslims "communicate" with God through the five daily prayers. The Muslim prayer is about an intimate set of moments that should ideally be neither distracted nor interrupted.[34] In other words, it is a ritualistic performance that demands pious intentions to be valid. True intentions of the worshippers are known only by God; however, small signs (e.g., the red comb) hint that worshippers can be distracted during their prayer.

Many times I entered shops and found a person praying behind the counter. I went outside and waited until the shopkeeper completed his prayer. Comings and goings and street activities can also affect someone's space of prayer.[35] In Bougouni such interferences were coped with differently. Some people remained focused on their prayer no matter what happened around them. Others seemed to lose focus; their bodies were in a prayer posture while, for instance, their eyes were looking at movements around them. Once I went to a workshop because my bag had a big hole that needed to be fixed. There I came across a man praying on a mat between two doors. He looked at me while intoning *sura*. I stopped for a couple of seconds. He kept looking at me while intoning and used a body language (with his eyes and hands) that I interpreted as "what do you want?" I did not respond and waited until the end of his prayer. Others were affected by more subtle breaches of focus, such as worries (e.g., a debt) arising in the shape of negative thoughts during prayer. All of these breaches indicate that the mind of the worshipper is dissociated from the focus of the prayer: God. This lack of concentration evoked more laughter than mockery among Muslims in town because to remain all the time focused during prayer is challenging. Moussa the *bogolan* maker,[36] a local individual whose life personified an ethical nobleness that was present in a diffuse way in Bougouni and its hinterland, once commented, "Muslims even forget God during the prayer. For instance, during their prayer they think, 'Heee, I did not close the door of the shop; shit! What if the robber comes?' What kind of Muslim is that? [laughs]." Muslims who remain firm and unshakable in their prayers demonstrate a link with God that is deemed direct and deep. Their alertness and attentiveness during prayer connote devotional concentration, hence pious intentions. Their prayers thus express a genuine piety. Most Muslims, however, struggle to stay on the Islamic path due to their somewhat shallow faith. Their breaches of concentration during their prayer remind them that the Islamic path is demanding. In Bougouni, Muslims faced perturbations during prayer because, according to local discourses, God puts their faith to the test. A period of recurrent lack of concentration could sometimes be interpreted as a harbinger of misfortune. However, when lapses were interpreted as the presence of insincere intentions and duplicity of the Muslim prayer, they could give rise to criticism that goes beyond the symptoms of a weak faith.

Public buses between Bougouni and Bamako stopped at each prayer time. Although Islamic orthodoxy allows a traveler not to pray, most people got off the bus to pray. A young traveler confided to me that "we do not let people think that we do not pray, because this is ill-regarded." In the 1980s only elders respected Muslim prayers. In 2010 young adults increasingly prayed in such public situations because declaring one's Muslim identity did not necessarily make a person Muslim anymore. Regular daily prayer also informed someone's reputation. A Muslim who prayed regularly was also deemed more respectable than a Muslim who did not pray. As already stressed by Kassim the handy man, many times I heard people saying that local Muslim families no longer let their daughters marry men who did not pray. Social representations of the Muslim prayer and its regular practice also inclined young Muslims in Bougouni to pray in public not only for the mundane status it brought them but also to avoid being stigmatized as bad Muslims. These vignettes of

Muslim prayer illustrate the tension between the relational world (social life) and the reflexive domain (personal intention) when the fulfilment of religious duty increasingly shapes social status among Muslims.

In Bougouni public Islam inclined Muslims to pray in public for its social merits. The Muslim prayer has also become a mundane ritual, sort of social tactic that does not require a genuine faith to be activated. Similarly to the Minangkabau people of Indonesia, however, many local Muslims "complained that so much of public religious life was hypocritical, a mere show" (Simon 2009, 270).[37] Public Islam therefore generated the issue of hypocrisy.

"ZIGZAG MUSLIMS"

Many Muslims in Bougouni questioned the profession of public Islam as an avowal of piety because it did not necessarily index pious intentions. The social merits associated with the practice of a generic Islam marked by outward religious signs put the sincerity of public piety in question and reminded Muslims of the twofold nature of piety, both public and inward. When moral failings were involved, Muslims responded to the discourses of "truth and ignorance" of Muslim scholars and the moralization of the public life supported by Muslim scholars and their followers through discourses of "sincerity-hypocrisy." Such discourses especially concerned prosperous Muslims who did not follow the twofold nature of piety in their public Islam.

The nature of hypocrisy can be manifold because, as deception, it can appear in many different situations. As Judith Shklar explains, hypocrisy, whether conceived by a naïve or wicked mind, is a socially learned behavior that aims at profit (e.g., being considered a good Muslim) through the art of pretense: the fact of "assuming a false appearance" with "dissimulation of real character or inclination [genuine intention]" as a means to an end (1979, 3). An accusation of hypocrisy can uncover a wide variety of moral issues, from a mere moral insecurity to the unmasking of evil schemes. In Bougouni a Muslim who did not pray was seen as a bad Muslim. The sincere attitude imputed to his mind toward non-practicing Islam, however, could work as a partial protection against odious accusations, an evaluation that decreased with aging. At first his faith was just deemed weak, unless proven otherwise through, for instance, involvement in harmful activities. People were nonetheless more fearful of the so-called zigzag Muslims because the fact of praying without faith could betray the presence of a malicious mind.

During my fieldwork, discourses of "sincerity-hypocrisy" were particularly directed against Muslims of the economic elite (e.g., big traders, heads of wealthy families, civil servants, politicians), Muslim scholars, and followers of Islamic movements who emphasized outward signs of piety but revealed a lack of sincerity in their religious practice through moral failings they failed to dissimulate in life. Such Muslims were accused of just wanting to look pious in public while acting in an un-Islamic manner when out of sight. Muslims viewed these pious-looking Muslims as not walking straight on the Islamic path; their practice of Islam was despised because it was bound to selfish aims, such as building a reputation of being a prosperous (good) Muslim, rather than manifesting a genuine faith.

Sekou grew up near Bandiagara (central Mali). Two years ago, a relative in Bougouni suggested Sekou look for a job in this fast-growing provincial town. Sekou agreed to the idea because he wished to move away from the weight of customs. Back in Bandiagara, indeed, the little money he made was spent for the needs of his extended family. When I met him, he worked as the night watchman for a hotel in town. In our exchanges on Muslim life, he used to say, "Those married men who bear Muslim names, pray in public and say, 'God is the greatest,'[38] but bring prostitutes to the hotel during the night are not Muslims; they are zigzag Muslims."

I used to stop at the bus station, where I chatted with people I met in restaurants and shops of this busy area. In this way I became acquainted with Adama, a single man in his mid-twenties. Adama grew up near Bla (central Mali) and then moved to Bougouni to pursue his studies because his sister married in town. He had completed high school three years earlier and now got by with doing small activities in town. I once encountered him around 11 p.m. wandering alone in the bus station. He looked sad and angry at the same time. I invited him for a *sucrerie* (soft drink) to cheer him up. We sat at a table of a nearby restaurant. He told me what was disturbing him that evening. Adama often had comical stories to tell about flirting in Bougouni, but this time he was hurt by such a story. A couple of months ago, he said, he fell in love with a young unmarried lady. He had since tried to seduce her. He felt that the affair was not a usual flirt due to his sentiments. He also thought that she was a serious match because of her good morals. For instance, she did not go out at night. One evening, while hanging around the bus station, he encountered two people standing in the dark on a side street of Bougouni. They then swiftly moved to a car parked under a tree and left as if they did not want to be seen. But the dim light of a nearby lamp betrayed their identity: it was the woman Adama had fallen in love with and an elder of a neighboring family. Such a late furtive meeting between an old man and a young woman could only be traces of an affair of illicit sexual activities. He was choked. The woman turned out to be loose and the elder not who he pretended to be. This elder was a wealthy trader and the head of a respectable family, known to be a good Muslim who never missed common Islamic duties. Moreover, he used to criticize youths who spend their time in *grins* instead of farming for their parents as lazy and useless. He openly accused them of being more interested in women than in their family. This very evening, however, Adama discovered that this elder also belonged to those seniors who took Islam as mere appearance: "It makes me laugh when I see them in the big mosque. They pray with the so-called Islamic clothes and moralize the youth there. Then during the night they go visiting their [young] mistresses in secrecy. This is just *maquillage* [makeup]!" Adama also lamented being in a powerless situation. As a young unmarried man without a proper job, he felt that he could not compete with the older man: "He is a wealthy trader and a head of a respectable family of Bougouni. He is our elder. What can I do? Nothing!" His account would at the very least circulate among friends in town, hence fueling the discourses of "sincerity-hypocrisy" toward the acute public Islam of local big men.

During the evening, Salif the tailor and I used to visit Amidou and his wife, Rokia, at their home in the district of Torakabougou. Amidou was a local youth leader involved in many projects. Rokia worked as a midwife in town. I met them through Salif, who had recently become involved in a gardening project thanks to Amidou. This newly married couple hosted an evening *grin*, where friends came to chat, watch TV, and drink tea in the living room and on the terrace. Their home was located at the dead end of a quiet and small sandy street. They rented half of a cement house. The other half was occupied by another young married couple who had recently moved there with their baby. The two families shared the same courtyard. One evening Salif, Rokia, and I were sitting quietly at the threshold of the living room. It was shortly after midnight. Amidou was already in bed and Salif and I were about to leave. However, low voices and movements coming from the other half of the house drew our attention. We saw a male figure leaving the house, walking out to the gate, and disappearing into the darkness of the night. Rokia was stunned. She told us that the husband of the female neighbor was not at home. He traveled to Segou for work. For her, such a late visit by a man to a married woman was scandalous! Nobody recognized this late evening male visitor. His specific look, however, partially unmasked his identity. We discerned a man with a long beard wearing a white robe and white trousers cut in the calf region. Salif chuckled. He then commented, "These Wahhabis foul the name of God! They hide themselves behind their Islamic dress, but this is just a façade!" Who was this late evening male visitor? A lover? A *marabout*? A *soma*? A doctor? Whatever the truth, a late evening visit by a man to a married woman in the absence of her husband would unavoidably nurture gossip about adultery.[39] By revealing tensions between appearance and intention in Muslim practice, such stories of zigzag Muslims question the nature of the real person.

> Many Muslims pretend to be Muslim. When they go to the communal Friday prayer, they show their Islamic *masque (mask)*. However, when they go back to their activities, they are capable of un-Islamic acts to obtain what they want. (Boubacar, the small trader of yuguyuguw)

Metaphors of sight abounded in such accusations of hypocrisy. Terms like "zigzag," *maquillage*, façade, and *masque* indicated the presence of a mask-like identity, hence a concern about "the underneath of thing." For Kassim the handyman, a good Muslim is sincere with his heart: "If what you say is what is in your heart, then you are a good Muslim. If you say something that your heart disagrees with, this is bad." For *aventuriers* in town, people's intentionality lies in their conscience or their *dusu* (heart), an innermost being that "cannot escape from God." Sekou the hotel guard often said, "Here people hide themselves to drink alcohol, but your conscience cannot escape from God." Kassim added, "Islam dwells at the bottom of heart. It is not a makeup." *Aventuriers* often explained to me that Islam is between themselves and God by putting their right hand on their chest and looking at the sky. Here "the underneath of thing" points to issues of trust (*danaya*) and shifting allegiance. In terms of the politics of prosperity, it transforms public Islam into an ambiguous resource.

AN AMBIGUOUS RESOURCE

Public expressions of Muslim piety can be ambiguous because human beings engage with rituals, signs, and moral discourses in complex, reflexive, and strategic manners that deserve to be explored not only in their personal dimensions but also in their social consequences. Public life in urban Mali unfolds against a peculiar backdrop: the open character of traditional street life. Logics of ostentation and dissimulation are thus inherent to urban street life in this country. By grafting to this backdrop, its recent liberal-oriented civic context has certainly reinforced the reading of public expressions of piety as mundane resources that are active in the broader politics of prosperity. But this acute focus on ostentation has also reinforced the social concern of practices of dissimulation. Not surprisingly, the debate between public expressions of Muslim piety and their intentions demonstrates that outward signs of piety do not necessarily indicate human beings with a virtuous path. In most societies the truth is not always welcome in public. Human beings, for instance, can opt for deceptive politeness or silence to preserve social harmony. But hypocrisy was especially despised among Muslims in Bougouni because, apart from insulting Islam, it potentially connoted the presence of malicious intentions. Zigzag Muslims were deemed a threat to social harmony because such mask-like Muslims were accused of conspiring through treachery (*janfa*) and lie (*nkalon*). In other words, a person able to display a mask-like Muslim identity in public could ally with occult forces when out of sight. Accusations of hypocrisy could go so far as to signify that the devil (*sitanɛ*) had been unmasked. Muslims often felt powerless when this unmasking concerned a powerful person, a point that is further explored in the next chapter.

CHAPTER 4

Islam under Street Lighting

An Ambiguous "Civilization"

In 2010 I was surprised to notice a big *ronier* palm tree standing in the middle of one of the main streets of the old town of Bougouni. I asked why it was there. According to local recollections, when Bougouni was composed of three separate districts, locals feared this *ronier* because it hosted powerful djinns; nobody settled next to it or dared to cut it down, because they did not want to provoke the wrath of its occult inhabitants. Over time Bougouni expanded, becoming a locality of seven contiguous districts. The *ronier* remained but it stood right in the middle of a street, and the locals gradually changed their mind about it. By 2010 they were no longer afraid of the *ronier*, which had lost its occult character. An elder who lived near the *ronier* told me, "The djinns left the *ronier* owing to the growth of the town. Djinns do not like industries, urban products, and their smell. Neither do they like electric light. Therefore, they moved away." In Bougouni, with the arrival of street lighting in 1952, the "backward" forces of Bamanaya progressively moved to the bush country. In parallel, Islam "civilized" the town. The Muslim identity became equated with status, power, and wealth. The once notorious tree was eventually cut down shortly after the end of my stay. As a friend told me over the phone, "It disturbed the traffic too much." In Mali, Islam and electricity are "civilizing" forces that urbanize a locality.

In contrast to the darkness that invades villages during the night, in Bougouni one could find numerous shops and activities open until midnight under street lighting. In southwest Mali, villages did have a nightlife;[1] however, not to the extent that it could be called an "everynight life." In this regard, locals' sense of nocturnal urbanity stemmed from the presence of a regular nightlife under street lighting. This expensive infrastructural investment, moreover, stressed the presence of a powerful actor: the state (Alimia et al. 2018). Locals praised such nocturnal opportunities brought about by electricity by saying, "Bougouni is a town because of its night activities."[2] The encounter between the two "civilizing" forces generally associated with urbanization and modernity in Mali, Islam and electricity, did not, however, result necessarily in a homogeneous moral order.[3]

The night has historically been defined and judged in negative terms such as "chaos," "fear," and "occult." In Mali the night (*su*) is associated with witch (*subaga*). The etymology of *su.baga* is composed of two words: *su* (night) and *baga* (poison). *Subaga* is thus the poison that devours people from within during the night, the time of darkness, fear, and treachery in Mali. Societies have tried to master, to colonize, and to domesticate the night in many ways. A decisive breakthrough in the pacification of the night was the discovery of electricity in the nineteenth century. However, electrical light is not as efficient as daylight. Electricity cannot enlighten all the darkness of the night. Popular wisdom advises people not to wander at night into an unlighted narrow street, for instance. We never know what malevolent intentions lurk in the dark street corners. In Bougouni, as in most of urban Mali, the domestication of the night by electric light was peculiarly partial. Only the main streets in the center and a few of the bigger streets in residential areas benefited from limited, patchy, and dim street lighting. Power cuts occurred with such regularity that locals nicknamed the power company Energie du Mali as "*Energie du Mal*" (power of evil); the capacity of its two big, aging generators was insufficient to support a galloping urban growth. Other than the sporadic light from shops and TV screens, the inner streets were shrouded in darkness.

The night is often depicted as the prime time of secrecy because of the concealing nature of its darkness. Many anthropologists working on Muslim West Africa have examined the notion of secrecy in relation to Islamic esoteric sciences. In this context, esoteric secrets (Ar. *sirr*) are specific knowledge crucial to building up religious authority (e.g., Dilley 2004). My approach here, however, is the realm of secrecy as a specific field of experience. The night in Bougouni, beyond visual proximity, was lived as the time of "shadow play" because the dim penumbra of the West African urban night "'reveals the silhouettes' of activities but hardly their 'faces'" (Alimia et al. 2018, 13–17). The "shame" (*maloya*) provoked through the public gaze therefore becomes seriously reduced.[4] Anthropologists, however, have tended to ignore the night, taking ethnography as a daytime activity only, thereby considering the night as simply the continuity of the day.[5] Promoting the nascent anthropology of the night related to nightlife (Galinier et al. 2010; Schnepel and Ben-Ari 2005; Steger and Brunt 2003) in West Africa (Fouquet 2016, 2017), this chapter investigates the night as a chronotope (space-time) when "certain practices of secrecy provide their performers with the means to engage with the wider world" (De Jong 2007, 11).[6] Inspired by Georg Simmel's pioneering essay on the social significance of secrecy, "the secret produces an immense enlargement of life" (1950, 330) because daylight observance no longer frames nocturnal activities. Put differently, the darkness of the night creates a specific marginality in which forbidden activities can hide away. People in Bougouni were involved in chores and obligations during the daylight; the day was primarily devoted to work (*baara*). However, after dinner, urbanites enjoyed a period of free time (*lafyia*) before sleeping time.[7] The notion of *lafyia* here refers to leisure, pleasure, and hedonism. While some people fear the unseen, uncontrollable, and malevolent character of the night, others welcome the night as a darkness that hides. The wife of Boubacar the small trader of *yugu-yuguw* worried about occult forces, which lurked in the darkness of the night, because these forces were known to harm sleeping people. She therefore used to wash her two young boys with protective inky liquid. As he had learned during his years of Qur'anic studies near Mopti, Boubacar would write names of God with ink on a wooden slate (*walaha*), wash this work of writing with water, and then keep the inky liquid in bottles. Infused with names of God, this blessed water allegedly prevented *subaga* from harming their children at night. By contrast, Salif the tailor appreciated how he could visit his girlfriend under cover of the night. As visual perception became limited, the street ambiance altered; activities seemed wrapped with mystery. In corporeal terms, the "nightscape" blends people in with their surroundings by altering their sight; in other words, as the "thereness" of the day disappears into the darkness, social contact has to be done within "hereness" (Handelman 2005, 253–54). In this way, nightlife is simply less bound to control by sight than day life. People who want to "obtain relief from the structures and strictures of the day" (Schnepel and Ben-Ari 2005, 154) thus use darkness to bypass daytime morality. Moreover, the withdrawal of sight places other senses at the fore, such as tactility and hearing. This specific sensorium, caused by the absence of daylight, is conducive to close contact, privacy, and sensuality. In Bougouni, Muslims experienced the night as a sort of counter-hegemonic time when alternative lives were sought away from the scrutiny of public Islam.[8]

This emphasis on sight does not indicate the presence of a "modern occularcentric epistemology" of Western origins (Hirschkind 2006, 18). It reveals the centrality of the street as an arena of morality in urban Mali, a point already stressed in chapter 3. Arguing that the senses are also "bearers of culture" (Howes 1991, 17) and that sensory orders can vary based on "cultural traditions" (Geurts 2002, introduction), the traditional (Mande) built form of Bougouni's urban street life nurtured a pervasive public gaze during daylight, hence a public Islam based on sight. In parallel, some activities were nocturnal due to the alteration of public morality within the twenty-four-hour quotidian cycle between day and night (Chappatte 2017). This chapter attempts to bring the intelligible and the sensible together by demonstrating how the interplay between secrecy and display *and* the interplay between daylight life and nightlife were both important dynamics of morality in urban Mali.

BOUGOUNI AT DUSK

Schools and civil administration closed around 5 p.m. Activities in the center of Bougouni significantly decreased when approaching the time for the fourth prayer of the day (Maghrib), a quarter of an hour before sunset. After dealing with the last clients of the day, most traders tidied their shops. Then they performed their ablutions, prayed, and closed their shops. After the fourth prayer, the big market and its vicinity emptied out quickly. Artisans, laborers, merchants, and street peddlers headed home accompanied by the setting sun, which refracted through the reddish dust suspended in the air. As the sky darkened and the horizon disappeared, the traffic became indistinct, not least the many vehicles without lights. Southwest Mali is close to the equator; therefore, there is little difference in the length of daylight between seasons. Sunset in Bamako varies between 6 p.m. (in November) and 7 p.m. (in July): the day-night transition is almost unchanging through the year in Bougouni. Moreover, the closer you come to the equator, the quicker darkness falls.

At the same time in residential areas, children were playing around *carrés* and adjacent streets. Wives and housemaids finished preparing dinner. A little later, families came together in their respective *carrés* for dinner. Those who spent their day in town asked after those who stayed in the neighborhood. Dinner was usually eaten quietly, but at 8:15 p.m. everyone gathered in front of the TV to watch a popular soap opera (the *Marina* telenovela) on ORTM, which ended at 8:45 p.m.[9] By then the street lighting was on and darkness otherwise wrapped the town. Babies and small children showed signs of tiredness. Sleeping time was coming for the youngest. The other members of the family surrounded their elders and the head of family, who were watching the national news (9:00–9:45 p.m.). The end of the national news coincided with sleeping time for older children and their elders among them; after a long day, some were nodding off. Not without difficulty, the rest of the children were sent to bed. If they had not already done so, Muslims completed their fifth and last regular prayer of the day. The town was then ready to sleep. However, a minority of urbanites decided to stay awake a bit longer to get involved in "everynight life."

WOMAN AT NIGHT: AN ECONOMIC OPENING

Southwest Mali is traditionally characterized by a gendered division of work. According to local customs, a man's duty is to provide food (*nasɔngɔ* or *les prix de condiments*), shelter, clothing, and medicine for his wife (or wives) and his children. In complementary fashion, a woman is associated with the home— that is, cooking, household chores, and child rearing. In practice, due to growing difficulties in making ends meet, men have increasingly welcomed women's involvement in the local economy.[10] Married *aventuriers* especially appreciated when their wives could help them in difficult days by earning some coins, as illustrated with Boubacar's wife, via small-scale catering and street peddling. Women have taken this opportunity to support their husbands with family expenses and to meet their female needs; they save money to purchase perfumes, clothing, jewelry, and other goods and services that shape *musoya* (womanhood). In Bougouni many women sold vegetables, clothing, and jewelry in the big market. Others sold cakes, water, soft drinks, and fruits to travelers making a stopover at the bus station. In the morning and late in the afternoon, women also sat outside their *carrés* in residential areas to sell passers-by dishes and finger food, such as salty pea fritters (*shɔ furufuru*) and sweet-potato chips (*woso jiranen*) with chili (*foronto*).[11] Although linked to home, women enjoyed a degree of mobility during the daytime (e.g., shopping, courtesy visits) and were important actors of the local economy. When darkness fell, however, women were bound to traditional norms of nocturnal female confinement. Unless they were going to *halal* (licit) events (e.g., attending a nocturnal public sermon, visiting a sick person), women, especially those who were married, remained within the confines of their house after dusk.

These norms should not be understood as strict rules acting like insurmountable obstacles. Rather, in Bougouni they shaped a disposition of female ethos toward good manners,[12] so a woman seen on the street after dinnertime did not necessarily raise suspicion. It was indeed not rare to see a woman who, wearing decent dress (traditional wrapper, *boubou*, plain jumper), was heading toward a local shop.[13] Men in nocturnal *grins* would simply think that this woman was commissioned by an elder because her presence was visible, her look decent, and her activity discernible.[14] In other words, at night women should not stroll (*yaala*) without good reasons. When darkness falls, however, a stroll possibly connotes secret activities. In this context, the verb *yaala* can also signify flirting. A woman could therefore go out at night without raising suspicion only for a known and accepted reason. A woman with such a reason therefore sought to make her presence obvious at night in order to preserve her reputation. The silhouette of a woman who was determined to be taking a nocturnal but unrecognized stroll would comparably raise suspicion. Her attitude of indiscretion would hint at loose morals (in contrast to an unrecognized male in the same situation). Men in nocturnal *grins* would think that such evasive, furtive, and unfathomable behavior could cover only shameful activities. In case her identity was discovered, her reputation would be undermined through gossip. Such woman would be labelled a *sunguruba* (prostitute), *bandite* (bandit), or *vagabonde* (hell-raiser). For men in nocturnal *grins*, only women who were deceiving their husbands and unmarried women involved in casual sex sought to go out at night under the cover of the darkness. Although *sunguru.ba* and *kamalen.ba* have similar etymological logic, *kamalenba* did not necessarily have a negative connotation; it simply meant a seducer (and not a male prostitute).[15] When a woman was *regularly* observed out at night, her habit would also raise suspicion, even if her nocturnal presence was discernible and associated with *halal* activities.

After experiencing increasing difficulties in making ends meet, however, men have recently allowed more and more women to set up small trading activities at night.[16] Men accepted their wives' economic activities as long as they were not carried on to the detriment of household chores.[17] Others hired housemaids and delegated to them their household chores. Some women gave a hand to their husbands at their nightly livelihood activity. Others, helped by their daughters, set up small trades on the threshold of their *carré*. But nightlife, as a daily chronotope of outdoor free time, was still interpreted as the domain of men.[18]

"EVERYNIGHT LIFE"

The courtyard of my host family was lit by a nearby streetlight. Its entrance opportunely overlooked one of the new districts' sandy streets that benefited from street lighting. On its right, the next-door *carré* occupied a busy junction that attracted most of the daily nightlife of the neighborhood. Adjoining the wall of the street façade, two cement-built commercial units housed a grocery and a clothing workshop. Both remained open every evening until midnight. The shopkeeper used to bring a TV set, a bench, and a couple of chairs to the grocery's threshold. Men from the vicinity and passing customers came together, drank tea, and chatted while watching night TV programs on ORTM (sport, folklore, Indian movies, and religious programs).[19] Such circles of men constituted one of the numerous nocturnal *grins* scattered alongside the streets of Bougouni. After dinnertime women quickly popped into the tailor's shop so as to check on their most recent order. The mother of the family living at the street corner, helped by her two eldest daughters, installed a sort of small restaurant (*gargote*), which was open on an evening basis between 7:00 and 10:30 p.m. Latecomers who found empty pots at home and passers-by who felt hungry could order soft drinks, salad, peas, rice and sauce, and other foods there. In front of the grocery on the other side of the street, motorbikes stopped to buy gasoline in an *essencitigi* stallholder run by an *aventurier* from the northern région of Kaye.[20] In another corner of this busy junction, young men spent their coins at a video game spot. Lonely students studied for exams under streetlights located farther down the street. A couple of children defied sleeping time by playing a worn table football game standing to the right of the small gas station. The kind of nightlife described in this busy street corner of a residential area went on daily until midnight. I hence call it "everynight life."

COVERING ONE'S TRACKS AT NIGHT

Young women slightly delayed their bedtime to enjoy a short romantic meeting with their boyfriends. In dark corners of street façades, female silhouettes were often spotted just outside the threshold of *carré*s in the company, presumably, of their lovers, male silhouettes next to motorbikes. They stayed in range of their *carré* in case their elders or parents called them from within the house. Hearing their name, they could quickly respond and move back into their *carré*. *Bonya* (respect) is central to the social order in town. At night respect works through practices of concealment.[21] During the daytime I often met Salif the tailor at his workshop. I once encountered him reprimanding his girlfriend. He was warning her not to dare meeting young men in his sight again. He then told me:

> I know and she knows we will not get married. We just do it for pleasure.
> I know she is with other young men as well, but I do not want to see that
> in front of me. The other day, I observed her speaking suspiciously with a
> young man on a Jakarta motorbike. She should not do that in front of me. She
> should respect me instead. Here respect is like that.[22]

Malik, the fostered teenager who lived in the same courtyard as I did, waited until the rest of the household fell asleep to go out in town. Malik occupied the only room within the main house that had its own proper door, a different entrance from the main door of the house where the head of family, the housemaids, and the children slept. Because of this extra exit, his comings and goings could easily go unnoticed at night. I guessed that the head of the family had offered Malik this room on purpose. He knew that young men need to go out at night as part of their educational transition to adulthood. I also enjoyed a room located in the annex of the house. I used to go out by bicycle shortly after dinner when the rest of the household was closing the main entrance of the house. Both Malik and I went out to join our respective nocturnal *grins* in town. When I came back after midnight, I found the gate of the *carré* closed. No worries. I parked my bicycle in front of the gate and walked along the wall to a pile of wood, which I used as a ladder. After climbing over the wall and landing softly within the courtyard and away from the goats and chickens, I opened the latch of the gate, put my bicycle in my room, and went to bed. Malik and I circulated discreetly during the night so as to avoid public attention, especially within our neighborhood. We had to preserve the reputation of our host family. We were aware of each other's nocturnal life, but we never talked about it. We knew that night activities were unspoken matters. Our complicity resided in our respective silence about the other's nighttime activities.

Most nocturnal *grins* were characterized by the subtle comings and goings of men.[23] Members of the *grin* sat, chatted, drank tea, and took shorter (or longer) trips in towns. They took their own motorbike or borrowed someone else's, disappeared into the town, and came back after a while. These short tours were announced by expressions such as "I go and I come" and "I go on an errand."[24] What struck me the most is that people did not ask for further details about these tours. Nightlife in *grins* unfolded through the arrivals and departures of people. These unquestioned apparitions and disappearances of people into the darkness of the night continued until the *grins* emptied. When I dared to question why, people just told me, "Each of us has his *affaires* [intimate business, in this context])." Of course, some men knew exactly what was going on out there. They just routinely covered the activities of their friends. Social life in nocturnal *grins* illustrated that the secrecy of the night was more about discreet trails that led to the mute darkness of the urban night. In many cases, such "empty" idioms meant that night is primarily understood as a time for private and unspoken matters. Others lied by saying "I go home" or "I go to sleep,"[25] but they just moved away and unobtrusively looked after their own business in town. This kind of lie (*nkalon*) is not motivated by malice and does not aim to harm someone. The lie here is more a "mode of deception" (Barnes 1994, 1–19) that points to covering one's tracks in the night. In this way, these empty idioms and white lies were just common techniques of dissimulation highlighting the night as a time of secrecy. Inspired by Ramon Sarró's (2009) analysis of the secret in his study of religious change on the Upper Guinea Coast, the sociological dimension of secrecy here is not only about concealing content but also about "creating remoteness." Members of *grins* knew that "the real ground [of such empty idioms] is elsewhere," yet they did not verbally inquire about this situation (8–9). By not discussing these empty idioms, members of *grins* understood comings and goings of nightlife as private and unspoken matters. They expected the same sort of silence about their own tours in town.

In a wider perspective, this creation of remoteness also demonstrates that "control over secrecy and openness" is about managing privacy that is someone's autonomy and vulnerability (see Bok 1989, 18–25). Members of *grins* rarely spoke about their nighttime activities. They preferred to gossip about other people instead of speaking about themselves. As a friend used to say, "I do not speak about my plans in *grin*. The *grin* is about distraction and pleasure instead." In what I call "nocturnal *grins*," men talked about others but rarely spoke about their nocturnal activities. In this way they were not necessarily linked by trust (*danaya*). Rather, these *grins* functioned as meeting points for preparing serious nocturnal activities, such as romantic meetings, going to nightclubs, and going to local bars called *maquis* (see Chappatte 2014b, 2017).

Men might voice intimate matters in the *grin* but not to all members of the *grin*. The *grin* was about speaking (*kuma*) and chatting (*baro, causer*) in the group, whereas trust was considered more as a dyadic value forged between two individuals.

When my friends and I planned to go to a *maquis*, for instance, we nearly always proceeded in the following manner. As usual, we first met in a *grin*. We sat for a while. We chatted, joked, and drank tea. When my friends felt ready, we left other members of the *grin* and disappeared into the darkness of the night. Like the others, we quietly went about our own intimate business in town. "Feeling ready" here was also a question of discretion. It was rare that my friends were ready before 11 p.m. They preferred to move to a *maquis* late into the evening, when most small restaurants and stalls located under street lighting had closed.

THE *MAQUIS*

The French term *maquis* originates in Corsica. It refers to a type of Mediterranean vegetation comprised of low, scrubby, and thorny ground cover where Corsicans used to hide themselves after a vendetta or acts of banditry. During the Second World War, the terms *maquis* and *maquisards*, respectively, designated groups and members of the French Resistance who secretly fought against the German occupation of France.[26] The expression *prendre le maquis* still signifies the act of taking refuge in the wilderness so as to escape state authority. In the early 1980s, "unauthorized" and therefore discreet and makeshift restaurants, where people of lower urban classes chat while eating national dishes and drinking alcohol, started to appear in Abidjan, Côte d'Ivoire (N'Guessan 1983, 546). Because of their clandestine nature, people named them *maquis*, a term probably brought to Abidjan by the Corsican mafia, which has long been influential in the city (see Ellis 2007, 169).[27] During the 1990s, the *maquis* became legal and spread outdoors; they quickly turned into popular spaces of festivity where Ivorian youth would hang out to *faire le show* in public (see Newell 2012, chap. 3). Pervaded by the cultural influence of Abidjan within West Africa, spaces of entertainment also called *maquis* progressively sprang up in Mali. Although legal under the secular state of Mali, *maquis* in Mali have remained close to their original Ivorian counterparts in relation to concealment, because alcohol consumption is socially stigmatized in this predominantly Muslim society.

In Bougouni three small restaurants selling alcohol were located along the main tarred roads crossing the town. Muslims did not go there, because these spots were too exposed to the public. They attracted essentially the town's Christians, travelers, and truck drivers on their way to Bamako, Sikasso, and Abidjan. Owing to their visibility, many locals referred to them as restaurants or bars, instead of *maquis*. One of the oldest *maquis* of Bougouni, Le Robinet (The Tap), overlooked a busy area of the town: the bus station. As the crowds and activities shaping these important spaces of transit are difficult to monitor, Malians often labeled them "dens of thieves" due to their alleged association with petty crime and banditry. Locals said that people of good manners do not linger there. The visibility of Le Robinet was therefore relatively unobserved because it was consonant with the negative depiction of bus stations made in Mali.

Otherwise, most *maquis* in Bougouni were inconspicuously located just off the tarred roads and on the fringe of residential areas. They were not obvious to those who were not seeking to go to such bars. When I started being interested in the *maquis*, I realized I had passed a *maquis* every day without noticing it for months. This *maquis*, called Chez le Burkinabé (Burkinabé's Place, named after the nationality of its owner, who was from Burkina Faso), occupied one of the first compounds in the residential area found behind the Bamako-Sikasso tarred road. No sign whatsoever indicated the presence of a *maquis*.[28] From the outside, it looked like a typical familial compound fenced by a mud wall, above which big mango trees and iron roofs were visible. Its door, overlooking a sandy inner street, was behind a small restaurant, which usually stayed open late into the night. It was only when a Muslim friend brought me there at night that I realized it was a *maquis*. After passing an open vestibule, we entered a vast courtyard characterized by a subdued atmosphere. Tables and chairs were scattered in the corners. Some seated areas were enclosed by walls made of straw mats and covered with vegetal roofs. I noticed human silhouettes here and there, but they remained unidentifiable. A single lightbulb illuminated the whole place from the interior of a dilapidated house standing in the middle of the courtyard. This building sheltered the most expensive element of the *maquis*: a big refrigerator to keep beer cold. The barman sat next to it and was watching DVD movies on a small TV set. From time to time, a client hailed with a "Barman!" or "*Psssssst!*" He then stood up and came to take an order. The barman used a flashlight if the client wished to check the change he received.

A typical Malian *maquis* does not seek to domesticate the night. On the contrary, darkness constitutes the main feature of its ambience. Besides being hidden from the street, Chez le Burkinabé welcomed clients into a somber atmosphere that blurred their identities as, inside, sight became limited to the tables and the people sitting around them. Indeed, the combination of the darkness of the night and the dim light spreading from the single bulb created an atmosphere of shadows conducive to privacy from within the *maquis*.[29] Some Muslim consumers of alcohol, and men who take women out, seek *maquis* with a dark ambience because they want to appreciate their beer or romantic date without being observed from within the establishment. The *maquis* is also a space for extramarital relations, where unofficial lovers meet in secret. A minority of *maquis* showed porn movies and had rooms called *chambres de passe* in their backyards that were rented on an hourly basis. Other *maquis* were brothels.

Owners of the *maquis* in Bougouni were aware of the importance of the secretive character of their businesses. Muslim neighbors tolerated them as long as their presence remained unnoticed and did not disturb public order. As a consequence, it was difficult to know the exact number of *maquis* in the town. Locals nonetheless told me that the *maquis* were lucrative and that their number had tended to increase over the years. As Salif the tailor jokingly said, "There are more *maquis* than mosques now in Bougouni!"[30] This is obviously difficult to assess, as most *maquis* were unobtrusively inserted at the margins of the local society (Chappatte 2014b). However, sometimes a *maquis* will move from the margins of society to the center of public attention. Muslim activists then tend to denounce these nocturnal encroachments and lobby for the closure of the establishment.

THE RISE AND FALL OF LE VATICAN

Salif and his co-tailors hosted a *grin* at the threshold of their sewing workplace. Workers in the next-door commercial units and friends would pop into this *grin* for a chatty tea break. They often stayed there until late in the evening to complete pressing orders. The *grin* overlooked a main street of the town, the tarred road bordering the district of Heremakono. Across the street stood the ruins of an NGO's office that had operated in the region in the 1980s. After years of decay, a promoter rented this plot and renovated it to make a restaurant. Called Le Vatican, this catering space was turned into an entertainment venue a few months later for economic reasons; it then had a short life due to its disturbing the gaze of passers-by. Members of the *grin* and I witnessed the brief story of Le Vatican from the threshold of the sewing workplace. Our "gossips from afar" about this space illustrated the kind of gaze that nurtures public Islam in Bougouni.[31]

The building under construction attracted the curiosity of passers-by due to its originality. A big house with a thickly thatched roof, a brick wall to its rear, and an open-work wall made of white and blue planks of wood was taking shape facing the street. A large terrace had been added at the front. When I met the promoter, a local Muslim who had lived most of his life in Bouake but came back to Bougouni owing to the Ivorian crisis, I asked him about his project here.

> Here in Bougouni there is no proper restaurant. They've mostly got little restaurants where people eat off poor plastic plates and sit on worn benches and even on the ground! Me, I know how to welcome clients. You need to set a decent table with tablecloth, napkin, and nice cutlery. You need to have comfortable seats with chair backs as well. You know, I just want to do the same as they rightly do in the restaurants of Côte d'Ivoire.

The promoter was as good as his word. When the construction work was completed, passers-by could admire a well-designed half-open house decorated with the words "Le Vatican" in red characters painted on the front wall of the terrace. Inspired by his previous work at a restaurant called Le Vatican in Bouake, the promoter chose the same name so as to associate his business with the "civilized" restaurants of Côte d'Ivoire. He inaugurated his restaurant by organizing a dance party at which he offered food and soft drinks to the population. His party was announced over the radio, so masses of people came.

After the inauguration, however, his restaurant remained empty most of the time. The tables were delicately set, and the food was well cooked, but people still preferred to pay less and continued to eat local dishes at the smaller restaurants. The promoter was also reluctant to sell alcohol to the locals because he did not want his place to become a *maquis*. There was no market for expensive restaurants in Bougouni because most of its inhabitants did not want to waste their already limited budget on what they saw as an unnecessary luxury when they could eat their favorite meals at home. Bougouni is simply not Bamako. The poor business done by Le Vatican forced its promoter to sell it after only two months.

The two new owners had a totally different idea of what Le Vatican should be. The younger brother of one of the owners became the manager of the new Vatican. Within two weeks he started selling alcohol and employed a local woman to cook affordable local snacks. The clients came slowly. A week later, Le Vatican also started to rent five *chambres de passe*. The manager found an empty house connected to the backyard of Le Vatican by a small hidden path that went behind the residential house located on the left. He investigated who the landlord was. The manager called the landlord and they arranged a deal together. Shortly afterward, a big sound system with speakers was installed in the restaurant. Two weeks later five prostitutes arrived and settled into the rooms. Within five weeks Le Vatican had been transformed into a sort of *maquis*/brothel. When they saw the prostitutes, members of the *grin* facing Le Vatican exclaimed, "Oh, this is really a *maquis* now!" From the very moment the prostitutes came, Le Vatican started to be a hit. It became crowded every night, and beer was frequently out of stock. Ironically, Le Vatican turned into a space of forbidden pleasures rather than a "civilized" restaurant worthy of the morality of Vatican City. During the holy month of Ramadan, activities slowed down, but the crowd was still there.

Kassim the handyman and mill worker, in fact, was also a regular of this street section. Before the construction of Le Vatican, he opened next to the future restaurant a small street food shop as a night activity supplementing his day work in the mill (see chapter 5). Besides visiting Salif in the nearby *grin*, I also popped into Kassim's shop, where I ordered an egg sandwich and chatted for a while before heading home. Although located under street lighting, Kassim's small business suffered from a lack of clients. Apart from two nearby *grins* and a few trucks that parked along this street section for the night, the area was quiet after 10 p.m. Later, however, when Le Vatican turned from a restaurant into a *maquis*/brothel, his daily turnover increased considerably. During the evenings of the holy month, I found him busy serving clients at his shop. Kassim fasted during the day yet was happy when night fell because the clients of Le Vatican consumed his food. Business was prospering. He commented, "As an Ivorian song says, 'One man's meat is another man's poison.'" Kassim agreed that alcohol and prostitution are bad; however, these forbidden activities brought him many clients. Because of the changes that had been made to Le Vatican, his daily turnover multiplied fivefold. He concluded, "What can I do? I accept them. I need to survive here."

However, the success of Le Vatican quickly started to spill onto the street. After a couple of weeks, the prostitutes dared to come outside the building;

they sat on the terrace and ordered food next door as well. Within the tranquility of the night, the activity of clients also produced perceptible noise within the neighborhood. One family complained about the nocturnal nuisance of the prostitutes and their clients, who had to pass near the courtyard of their residential house in order to enter the *chambres de passe*. Given that this courtyard had an opening in the wall as a door, families could see prostitutes and clients passing by from within their compound. As Le Vatican was close to the street lighting of the tarred road, it also attracted the gaze of passers-by.

Three weeks after the end of Ramadan, I heard in town that "Le Vatican has fallen!" Apparently, someone called the landlord of the house that had been turned into *chambres de passe* and warned him about what was going on there. The landlord then gave Le Vatican's manager two days' notice to leave his house. Meanwhile, a brick wall was erected across the small path connecting the backyard of Le Vatican to the former rooms. As soon as these rooms were closed and the prostitutes left, the clients abandoned the place. Soon the owners removed valuable material from Le Vatican. Only an empty straw hut then remained. Kassim, discouraged by the lack of clients, left the area as well.

No one knew exactly who had put pressure on the landlord. It may have been the neighbors who had openly complained to the manager. But this family ran a business that benefited from clients brought in by Le Vatican. The so-called Wahhabis were also spotted scrutinizing Le Vatican from the tarred road after the night prayers of Ramadan; the closest mosque to the business was the main mosque where they prayed. Finally, it may have been someone whom no one suspected; many possibilities remain. The gossip from afar uttered by nearby nocturnal *grins* and the gazes of passers-by also activated the regulatory forces of public Islam through word of mouth.

One thing is sure, however: the landlord was approached secretly. Suspicions about where the responsibility lay might be entertained, but the conflict could not become open because the informers' identities remained uncertain. The landlord might have publicly kept quiet the fact that he knew what was really going on there. As long as the rooms did not disturb public order, he could have gained money. His big cement house was indeed costly and had been empty for months since the departure of his last tenant, an NGO project. Any client wanting to rent the house, I imagine, would have been welcome. Once the forbidden activities started disturbing public order, the landlord (living in another town) could have protected himself by denying any knowledge of what was going on. The interplay between discretion and display through secret deals and hypocrisy is also an important part of setting up forbidden businesses.

Le Vatican lasted two months as a restaurant and three months as a *maquis*/brothel. For members of the nearby *grin* who witnessed its rise and fall, it was doomed to failure because its forbidden activities were not sufficiently hidden from public scrutiny. They said we should not forget that Mali is a Muslim country. Besides the absence of a wall and the proximity to the street lighting, when Salif compared Le Vatican to other long-standing *maquis* and brothels in town, he observed that it "did not have a back door" overlooking a dark inner street.

THE DARKNESS OF THE NIGHT AND THE VEIL OF POWER

The head of my host family never asked me anything about what I did at night. Once, when I dared to tell him, "I am going out for a stroll," he smiled and replied, "May God grant you a peaceful evening." As long as Malik and I behaved correctly in our daily life, our nocturnal activities did not matter. But the day we learned that Oumar had failed the Diplôme d'Études Fondamentales (DEF) exam, the head of the family openly scolded him: "Instead of doing your homework, you have been wasting your time the whole year by going out every night!"

I met Souleymane, a married senior civil servant in his forties, in a *maquis*. Noticing my regular presence there, he once struck up a conversation with me, and we became friends. Later I asked him what his wife thought about his nocturnal activities. He replied, "My family do not like the fact that I drink alcohol, but they cannot prevent me from doing so because I give them food, clothes, a roof, and medicines. . . . I am the head of the family." Many of the so-called *maquisards* (regular clients of *maquis*) I met were wealthy married men (Chappatte 2014b, 533–35). Their respective families were often aware of their consumption of alcohol because their frequent absence during the night raised suspicions, and the smell of alcohol definitely betrayed them. Their spouses, however, covered for them so as to preserve their honor. Their larger family kept a low profile with regard to their consumption of alcohol as long as they, as heads of family, were financially able to support them. Souleymane's authority as head of the family allowed him to take his motorbike and go into town after dinner without giving any explanation. But he still had to act toward his family with a respect based on the visual concealment of shameful practices. Besides fasting and praying regularly, his alcohol consumption was also under the cover of a charitable Muslim life. For instance, he paid the travel expenses for the Hajj pilgrimage in 2009 (roughly US$3,500) to his mother, who lived in the same familial compound. Such a generous gesture honors the one who does it by granting him many *baraji*. Because of his privileged job, he "bought" the silence of his kin and the neighborhood regarding his alcohol consumption through various gifts and arrangements.

The fact that Souleymane could be known as a respectable member of the local community who never missed the Friday communal prayer while at the same time being a suspected *maquisard* during the night illustrates that ways of being both Muslim and a consumer of alcohol were handled through strategies of display and discretion. People do not shift their identity during the night. A Muslim remains a Muslim when he is drinking alcohol in the *maquis* insofar as *haram* is part of a Muslim's life. Even while drinking, a Muslim does not forget his Muslim identity. An example is a friend of Souleymane who admonished a waiter because he had dared to play a cassette of Qur'anic recitation in a *maquis*. For him, one should respect God even in a *maquis*. Only true Muslims—those who were called the *mu'min*—live a life unsoiled by *haram*. Forbidden activities were part of daily Muslim life in Bougouni and were handled through strategies of diurnal conformity and nocturnal discretion.

The interplay between display and secrecy as the interplay between day life and nightlife is an important component of morality in urban Mali. Nocturnal activities can therefore be explored as discreetly inserted into the day. In this way "night and day are viewed as a pair of mirrors, out of which grow reflection and truth of the other" (Galinier et al. 2010, 837). When the night covers the sphere of *haram*, its actors are hardly segregated. The Muslim community integrate their forbidden activities as "an absent presence" (Valentine, Holloway, and Jayne 2010, 16) because their occurrence is mostly suspected to be shameful moral gaps that should remain out of public sight.

However, a single and jobless young man would not handle forbidden activities with the same level of secrecy as an established head of family. He would try to keep his forbidden activities secret (unknown) as much as possible because his incomplete adulthood, hence "frail" social status, does not protect him within the local community. He would rather care about his reputation as a male Muslim becoming a responsible adult, especially when searching for a possible local bride. On the other hand, Souleymane was already a wealthy civil servant and a head of family. He consumed alcohol out of his family's sight but did not bother erasing all the traces of his regular nocturnal tours to *maquis*. As a wealthy head of family, his respectable social status put him beyond the reach of some of the moral forces of public Islam in Bougouni. In fact, he was locally considered as a *mɔgɔba*, literally "a big man." Such high social status veiled him against shameful public reprimands about his alcohol consumption in the *maquis*. Therefore his nocturnal activities there were guided more by his personal discretion than by secrecy. Power in the Muslim society of Mali often works as a veil that helps to keep traces of forbidden activities by its holder as no more than an open secret.

PART 2

Motions and Ethics on the Earthly Path

CHAPTER 5

Struggles for Better Lives in the Hands of God

The adventure does not benefit indolent people.[1]

Aventuriers acknowledged the presence of powerful nonhuman actors on their earthly paths toward a better life. By "presence" I mean they did not take God and witches (among other occult actors) as abstract ideas but as living forces that are not separated from human existence (Jackson and Piette 2015, 5–8). Rather than examining the epistemological statuses of these occult actors, this chapter investigates the "practical meanings" of these occult forces (Jackson 1996, 34–35) for *aventuriers* in relation to the building of a prosperous life, a central theme of this book. In this way, prosperity is not only defined by material, familial, and symbolic stages to reach; prosperity also becomes a form of being defined by an existential dynamic through which one feels prosperity *moving forward*. By considering prosperity as made of both concrete achievements and feelings of forward motion, this approach allows us to go beyond the classic (socioeconomic) figure of the prosperous (wealthy) man.[2] This exploration of lives in motion is also an attempt to "[bring] together the dimensions of past, future, and present" in the ways *aventuriers* actively live the unfolding of their trajectories on earth (Panella 2012, 25). The *past* here represents the momentum—the custom of *tunga*— that brought them to Bougouni. The *future* comprises hopes, expectations, and risks associated with *tunga*. The *present* consists of the interpretation of their living conditions in Bougouni. All of these dimensions shape the backdrop of *aventuriers'* perception of prosperity as a path (direction) and a walk (motion) at the same time.

In Mali it is said that whereas witches obstruct the earthly path (motionless), God may clear it when one behaves accordingly (forward motion). This chapter thus analyzes how these *aventuriers* discern the unfolding of their earthly path as an existential dynamic, the motion of which can be influenced by powerful nonhuman and occult actors. The quality of motion is lived through specific emotions. In Bougouni these emotions were socially cultivated and debated against a backdrop of the quasi-unavoidability of money in the making of a better life coupled with money's scarce access and disparity in contemporary Mali. How come *aventuriers* find themselves being blocked by witches? What do young countrymen's feelings of going nowhere fast tell us about social inequalities in contemporary Mali? How do *aventuriers* deal with these feelings? What do their strategies inform us about the nature of their relationship with occult actors? As Muslims, *aventuriers* used to say that God is the Almighty mediator of their destiny (*dakan*) on earth. To what extent could they then ask God to bring forward motion onto their earthly path? What kind of religiosity actuates the search for this forward motion? Although destiny is said to be "in the hands of God," an exploration of its "causes" (*sababuw*) puts forward a "dialectic view of life" (Jackson 1989, 2) that demonstrates the importance of self-responsibility in human destiny's upcoming design. This existential analysis will be illustrated by a detailed ethnography of Kassim's attempt to conduct a small evening trade business through various strategies, among which was the economy of charity. The chapter concludes by offering a few thoughts of these *aventuriers'* metaphysics of Almighty God and its related kaleidoscopic notion of destiny.

RESENTMENTS: WHEN MONEY MATTERS

Jane I. Guyer wrote that "money is probably the single most important 'thing/ good' in ordinary people's ordinary lives" in West Africa (1995, 5). Since the neoliberal turn of the 1990s, the Malian society has been marked by a general polarization of prosperity in life in terms of wealth and consumption. This acceleration of a rampant form of economic liberalization has accentuated the "over-monetarization" of everyday forms of sociability (Olivier de Sardan 1996, 1999) in the country, such as illustrated by the increasing centrality of cash in bride wealth transfers in a context of capitalist expansion (Wooten 2005, 25–26). In Bougouni access to "money" (*wari*) was actually perceived as the main key to build a prosperous life because of its necessary ubiquity in daily life (e.g., to buy potable water). The financial power of *wari* was the "door" to concrete earthly achievements. For instance, how could an *aventu-*

rier marry or build a cement house without money? In parallel, *wariko* (money troubles) kept one's mind busy because money was scarce, so it made access to money an even greater concern. And money turned out to be volatile when in one's possession. Ibrahim, a local civil servant whose life is especially developed in the second half of this chapter, used to say that money was elusive because "it comes as it goes." The elusiveness of money was caused by what Malians called *le social*. Due to his privileged job, for instance, Ibrahim faced a particularly intense flux of requests coming from kin, friends, and the neighborhood. He had to be careful of not being accused of egoism—in other words, of not moving forward in life alone. Locals apprehended issues of wealth and the power it conveys in moral terms (see Ferguson 2006, 74). Money was also understood as shrouded in mystery (Guyer 1995, 26) because of the opacity of its origins.

In most Western countries, people's financial power is basically represented by their wage. In Mali the wage does not have the same significance. Ibrahim used to tell me that "my wage accounts for less than 50 percent of my monthly income. . . . Without *les affaires* [businesses] I would not be able to run the [extended] family."[3] He had to support the whole family because he was among the rare family members who benefited from paid employment.[4] I never knew exactly what Ibrahim meant by *les affaires* because Malians do not reveal the totality of their income and its sources. Ibrahim's authority within the family, as well as his degree of freedom in terms of personal expenses, was mostly based on the fact that his financial power was kept secret. For him, "someone who shows his limits [whether financially or not] reveals his weaknesses." The same logic of secrecy around the amount of and access to money applies in an even more obvious manner to traders given that their sales fluctuate constantly. Except for themselves, people in Bougouni did not know exactly who earns what. Someone's failures and successes on the earthly path were consequently subject to speculations that gave rise to rumors and gossip in town.

The speculative nature of these conversations rendered them conducive to moral debates. Three words recurrently occurred in comments about a person's contingency on the earthly path: "jealousy" (*kɛlɛya*), "egoism" (*ɲɛgoya*), and "greed" (*nata*). During 2009, for instance, the construction of a new Centre de Santé Communautaire (CSCOM) in Heremakono Nord was delayed due to discord between the traditional chieftainship of Bougouni and the communal administration. This logjam animated conversations in *grins* late into the evening for some time in town.

The CSCOM was financed by an American who married a local woman.[5] The communal administration, after having negotiated with the traditional owner of the land (the chieftainship of Bougouni), allocated a piece of land for the realization of this social infrastructure. The chieftainship, however, impeded its construction because it did not receive its share of money in this land tenure process. Whether or not the *commune* attempted to bypass the chieftainship's traditional rights over the land is not important to my analysis. What matters is that many inhabitants of Bougouni thought that the "egoism of people of Bougouni" were behind this blockage. They were disappointed that these families "jeopardized the development of Bougouni" in order to pursue their own greed.

In 2010 Mali was characterized by a blatant unequal distribution of and access to money that, in turn, fostered jealousy between people and made egoism a source of public concern. In Bougouni I met prosperous people who deployed strategies of economic concealment (e.g., modest lifestyles and hidden investments) so as to contain jealousy toward them in town and, consequently, to avoid becoming the target of occult threats.[6] Karim, for instance, wore simple, faded, and plain working clothes. He did not have the look of a wealthy man. He certainly lived in a decent villa, but he only rented it and did not equip it with a refrigerator, air-conditioner, parabolic antenna, "Western-style" shower, and toilets, among other features of most up-to-date houses. Moreover, this villa was inconspicuously located at the edge of the town and away from streetlights, tarred roads, markets, and shops. Karim was, in fact, a rich trader who occupied various economic niches in south, west, and central Mali. He owned a dozen trucks in various regions of Mali and constructed expensive cement houses in Bamako for rental and his coming retirement. He confided to me, "I do not want to attract people's eyes upon my family."[7] As a wealthy *allochtoon* (displaced person), he also feared the bad reputation of Bougouni, a sentiment that also played a role in his will to publicly show a modest lifestyle. Poorer persons, such as *aventuriers*, also attempted to control occult threats to their earthly path.

"THE BAD PERSONS"

I once wanted to greet the *secrétaire général* of a Commune Rurale of southwest Mali before my departure from his village. Arriving at his home early in the morning, I found nobody there. I therefore decided to leave, as a gift, a hat and a shirt on the threshold of his room. I then left and took a bus to Bougouni. I called him in the afternoon because I wished to verify that he noticed what I left for him. He started to laugh and thanked me for the relief of my call. He had indeed gone back home around twelve o'clock and saw the hat and the shirt lying in front of his door. However, he had no clue about what it was. Instead of thinking of a gift, he immediately suspected that he was the victim of an occult threat. He did not touch the clothes and went directly to consult someone knowledgeable in such affairs in order to counteract this potentially malicious act toward his person.

In southwest Mali people feared becoming the target of an evil force that lurks in the shadows of social life. This force, named *mɔgɔw juguman* or *les mauvaises personnes* (the bad persons), has particularly shaped the reputation of Bougouni in postcolonial Mali, a point stressed in chapter 2. The so-called bad persons could either be triggered by people who asked a sorcerer to harm someone or by witches themselves who attempted to devour someone from within. Here I am interested in the fact that these bad persons covered a protean morality that brought "the underneath of things" (Ferme 2001) at the center of the town's social life. Victims of bad persons were deemed hit by a surreptitious and malevolent form of occult power, which could be counteracted through either *maraboutage* (Islamic esoteric sciences[8]) or *somaya* (Bamanan sorcery).[9]

The *marabout* and the *soma* (sorcerer) deal with the occult.[10] Both follow divinatory systems that have been intertwined for so long that none of their respective practices can be qualified as pure or having a single origin (Kassibo 1992, 545–46). A table of sixteen signs used by *soma* as well as *marabout*, for instance, dated back from a famous treatise of divination written before 1230 by an Arab named Mohamed Es Zenati (Colleyn 2009, 735). In southern Mali, a priest of a Bamana cult once told the anthropologist Jean-Paul Colleyn, "Islam is strong, but it has not been able to stop *saragha*." For this priest, sacrifice (*saragha* or *saraka*) referred to pre-Islamic practices. But Colleyn reminds us that this term comes from the Arab term *sadaqa*, which means "prescribed charity" (2010, 13), an etymology that stresses an ancient Islamic influence. At the same time, this linguistic argument does not mean that this Bamana priest was wrong. We need to seriously consider that Islam has been "a constitutive factor of traditional African religions" since its arrival in the continent in the tenth century (2010, 735–36). The relation between Islam and Mande could thus be described as one of correspondence, not of consequence, yet both types of divination invoke different channels of power: *mar-*

abouts invoke God (*Dieu, Ala, Allah*), whereas *somaw* invoke djinns (*génies, djinɛw*). Although the former diviners invoke God, they remain, like *somaw*, ambiguous figures because of their relationship with a power that is occult by nature.

Muslims in Bougouni used to say that because of their Muslim faith, true *marabouts* refuse to harm people; those who harm people are in fact sorcerers disguised as *marabouts*. Sorcery, by contrast, was stigmatized as un-Islamic. In town, sorcerers therefore kept their identity secret and practiced sorcery sheltered from public view, but one was able to locate them by word of mouth and this without much effort. Locals knew who they were. More precisely, they differentiated between the *sorcier* (sorcerer) as healer and diviner (*soma*) and the *sorcier* as witch (*subaga*).[11] Whereas the latter was feared, the former was tolerated. Given that a sorcerer was allegedly not Muslim, people thought that the *soma* was able to harm people through occult means. It was said that someone could pay the *soma* to undertake *baara juguman* (bewitchment, literally "evil work") on someone else by means of different sorts of *dabali* (evil spell) of Bamanaya origins. In Bougouni people especially feared *kɔrɔtɛ*, a deadly evil work that is thrown at people in order to kill them. Locals often related *korotɛ* to sudden death.[12] The *soma* was also known to prepare *pudiri* (Fr. *poudre*; powder) that people mixed with victims' meals so as to charm them.[13] When someone was suspected of being the victim of such occult threats, people say *elle/il a été travaillé*. This French expression is the literal translation of its corresponding Bambara idiom in which the verb *ka baara* (*travailler*, to work) means "to bewitch." The *soma* (or *sorcier*) and the disguised *marabout* were ambiguous figures in terms of morality. People suspected their protean intentions.

In fact, the word *subaga* expresses the very explicit evil character of sorcery. *Subaga* is translated as *sorcier malfaisant* (evil sorcerer) in French spoken in France (Bailleul 1996, 380). I translate it in English by the word "witch." Its rendering in native French indicates that a *sorcier* in West Africa is not necessarily evil, a linguistic observation that reinforces the local distinction mentioned earlier between the *sorcier* (sorcerer) as healer and diviner (*soma*) and the *sorcier* as witch (*subaga*). Witchcraft in Bambara is hence *subagaya* (or *subaaya*). The etymology of *su.baga* is composed of two words: *su* (night) and *baga* (poison). *Subaga* is thus the poison that devours people from within during the late night (3 a.m.+) when all the town is asleep. For many in southern Mali, this deep night is the prime time of darkness, fear, and treachery. In Bougouni witches were depicted

as humans (whether male or female) who were able to change into various evil creatures during the night. Nocturnal animals, such as the owl,
were unsurprisingly among the many shapes that witches could take during
the night to attack their victims. Witches were certainly feared, but they
remained uncovered; at most, they were only suspected. Their obscure
identities reinforced the atmosphere of suspicion and mistrust pertaining
to occult schemes in general and stressed the abhorrent but clever nature of
the evil agent (Parkin 1985, 1). More importantly, Patrick R. McNaughton
(1995) rightly states that the semantic field of *juguya* (malevolence) in the
historic Mande world does not necessarily connote a reality in which evil
and good stand in clear-cut opposition. Most people in Bougouni acknowledged witches' presence in town but were not able to identify them. During
daylight good and bad people rubbed shoulders with each other—in other
words, both types of persons shared the same face in public.

I explore in the next section how "evil refers to various ideas of imper-
fection and excess seen as destructive; but that these are contestable concepts which, when personified, allow mankind to engage them in dialogue
and reflect on the boundaries of humanity" (Parkin 1985, 23). *Aventuriers*, for
instance, were inclined to associate *mɔgɔw juguman* with resentful persons
who did not want others to move forward in life.

KO KA CA! HARDSHIP, MOTION(LESS), AND BEWITCHMENT

In the *grins* of Bougouni I often heard people moaning *ko ka ca!* This idiom can be translated as "difficulties are numerous" or "affairs are many and
manifold" (Jansen 2009, 113). *Ko* is a catchall colloquial word that, depending on the context, can signify "affair," "problem," "difficulty," "need," "envy,"
"custom," "action," or "behavior" (Bailleul 1996, 202–3). Altogether, these signifiers express hardship in life. *Ko* can also be employed as a suffix so as to
specify an issue. One might say *dumini.ko* (food concern), *baara.ko* (work
concern), and *wari.ko* (money troubles), for instance. *Ka ca* means "there are
many." People often accentuated the *ca* (many) so as to stress the sentiment
of powerlessness that inhabits them in the very moments when they think
about ways to overcome hardship in life. *Ko ka ca* thus conveys the manifold
hardships one faces on the earth path.[14] The causes of these hardships were
often associated with human egoism.

In Bougouni I often met people who complained about the egoism of their patron. Madou grew up in the hinterland of the small town of San (central Mali). Already married, he had gone off on *tunga* in Bougouni a few years earlier. He worked as a builder. As Bougouni was a fast-growing town, he did not worry about finding a job. But he was concerned about the low wage he received from his patron. He confided to me that he did not eat a proper lunch while at work because his daily wage was just enough to cover his family's expenses back home. But his patron lived in "a cement villa equipped with parabolic antenna" and drove "a 4 x 4 Toyota." For Madou, his patron was "a selfish man" who did not care about his employees. The tailor Salif had learned his craft by working for three years in the workshop of an established local tailor. He was at first happy when his patron started to give him jobs. However, he noticed over time that these jobs had little earning potential because they remained basic. Consequently, he was not able to accumulate any savings for financing two projects (his trade and his wedding) that would make him move forward in life. He thereafter left this workshop because his master craftsman "did not want to teach him the [lucrative] craft of embroidery." For him, "Ibrahim [his former patron] is not good. He does not want people to move forward in life." Other accusations of egoism were more hidden, complex, and insidious.

Alou, a student in the IFM, was in Bougouni "*malgré lui*" (despite himself). He grew up near the town of Koutiala where he achieved the Diplôme d'Études Fondamentales (DEF). His father compelled him to move to Bougouni, where his older sister married a local merchant. He then started working in the two shops belonging to his sister's husband. But "it did not work out," Alou said, so he started attending the IFM. Although benefiting from a state grant, his studies turned out to be unsuccessful. When I first met him, he had recently failed the year-end exam. He was also engaged in a complex love affair. His girlfriend, already married,[15] had two other suspected lovers in Bougouni. Over a couple of years, Alou had undergone successive failures in the building of his life. He had attempted various initiatives; however, their outcomes were mixed. Salif the tailor also subsumed successive failures with the initiatives he took to move forward in life. He left the workshop of the established local tailor to open his own workshop. He was fed up with being a mere apprentice and thought that this initiative would bring him a genuine clientele; however, he did not manage to have many clients. One of his friends, employed by a local NGO, then recommended him to work on a new gardening project. After a promising start, however, the project collapsed because of mismanagement. Because Salif had a reputation for being a good farmer, he then agreed to farm for a family of civil servants so as to be able to accumulate enough savings to eventually start a trade in the seed business. The head of this family promised him a "substantial sum of money" at the end of the harvest. But the yield, as well as the generosity of his patron, proved to be not as Salif had hoped.

Despite all of their efforts, Salif and Alou felt that their lives had stagnated. Both men started to think that something beyond their will did not want them to move forward in life. It happens that in Bougouni as elsewhere, hardships tend to weigh upon people, especially those with modest incomes. They may become overwhelmed and feel blocked. The impression of going nowhere fast, despite their efforts to be in motion, leads them to think that their inability to move forward in life results from occult obstructions provoked and nurtured by the jealousy and egoism of bad persons toward them.

DIVINATION: THE POWER TO FACILITATE DESTINY

Salif and Alou consequently began to visit a *soma* in order to assess their occult situation. I accompanied Salif to sessions of divination, which happened after dinnertime. I met him at the entrance of the courtyard of his host family, a better-off family for whom he worked as a farmer. Night had fallen, and a dim penumbra invaded this residential area, which did not benefit from street lighting. Salif usually would take his employer's Jakarta motorbike to ride around town. But for these occasions, he always opted for moving by foot following dark back alleys. Instead of taking the lit tarred road, we walked toward the back of a row of commercial units made of cement. We then took an unlit little street parallel to the lit tarred road that we would normally use when going in this direction. Salif confessed to me that he used to walk to the *soma* in darkness (*dibi*) because such visits ought not to be public. The divination concerns an intimacy of the self and a probing of the occult that should be secret. Muslims, moreover, do not want to be seen with a diviner (*soma*) because of his association with Bamanaya, hence un-Islamic practices.[16] After a walk of twenty minutes along unlit back alleys, Salif stopped at the entrance of a courtyard. Its door was open. From the street one could see the door of a room on the right thanks to the faint presence of a lit lightbulb coming from the back of the courtyard. Salif scrutinized the place for a few seconds. It was quiet. With his head close to the door, he softly uttered a male Muslim first name. Someone responded from within. We entered the room without greeting the families living in this courtyard. The avoidance of a greeting (*foli*), a central custom of social life, stressed the secrecy of our visit.

We found a man playing with a young child. A woman swiftly came in from a back room and took the child away. This room, lit by a yellow light-bulb, was full of objects made with natural materials (e.g., bone, cotton[17]) and waste bottles. Some were empty and others filled with leaves, roots, and powders. Leather bags decorated with cowry shells hung on walls. In Mali this vegetal type of paraphernalia is commonly associated with Bamanaya. The man moved to sit behind an oval ground space covered by a few centimeters of brown sand. A dozen cowry shells were scattered on the sand. Salif, who had been in touch with sorcery since his previous periods of village life, introduced me to the *soma*. We then both asked him for a consultation of sand divination. The *soma* asked us for 200 FCFA each (less than thirty cents) to make our respective "occult diagnoses." Rather than focusing on the practice of sand divination itself,[18] I explore how this divinatory consultation is related to the issue of lives in motion on the earthly path.

Salif asked the *soma* to probe the possibilities for fulfilling his longing for improved trade and a wedding. The *soma* then let the djinns speak about Salif's request through the sand divination. At the end, the *soma* told Salif that he "had been bewitched by persons close to him." In other words, his stasis in life was the result of "bad persons" whose evil forces were obstructing his earthly path. He also learned that an old relative did not want him to move forward in life. A young woman whom he saw frequently also wanted to harm him. *Somaw* never name bad persons. At the utmost, their precision stops at gender and an approximate age. Suspicions were heightened. Salif immediately thought about the young woman who sold mobile phone credits next to his *grin*. She seemed not to like him. Doubts remained. The *soma* continued. Alou then learned that he had also been bewitched by an old man who lived in the neighborhood: "[This man] does not want him to succeed in life." After the occult diagnosis came "the treatment." The *soma* suggested performing a sacrifice (*saraka*) on behalf of Salif so as to contain the occult threat. Depending on the gravity of the occult diagnosis, the *soma* could ask a client to bring him kola nuts[19] and hens for minor threats and cocks, goats, and even money for major threats.

How concretely, then, is divination related to lives in motion? Salif told me that "*somaw* can remove difficulties only; they ease your path." He illustrated this point by stressing that the *soma* did not tell him to invest in trading or to seek a wedding. In other consultations, I also observed the client asking the *soma* to probe the path of a given project. A *soma* facilitates a destiny but does not change it radically by telling his clients the projects they should invest in. For Muslims, only God can change your destiny. The *soma* could only "remove difficulties out of [his] path" (*ka gelɛya bɔ ne ka sira la*) by means of sacrifice. In Salif's quotation, *gelɛya* (difficulties) mean bad persons stemming from *subagaya* or *sababu juguman*.

The cycle of occult diagnosis and sacrifice can continue until the occult threat is completely contained. The client can also decide to stop this cycle or to visit another expert in esoteric sciences. In 2010 a hen cost 1,500 FCFA (US$3) and a cock 3,000 FCFA (US$6) in Bougouni. People with modest incomes could afford to buy one or two hens, for instance. Such purchases, however, already weighed down their budget. It often happened that a *soma*'s client would postpone a sacrifice due to a lack of money, especially when a second round of sacrifice was required. One could argue that the poor in southern Mali become victims of *soma* when they fall into the emotional web of the occult. I would add an ethnographic nuance. People in Bougouni do not question the occult; on the contrary, the occult has always been part of their lives. What matters is how they relate to the nonhuman forces that constitute this field. Do they consider them to be an 'acting power' in their [human] lives? If yes, how do they try to influence their acting power?

When Alou and Salif entered the emotional web of the occult, they allowed their respective psychological despondency to become a social hurdle, which could thus be overcome externally (see Favret-Saada 2009). In this regard, *somaya* can also be explored as a kind of therapy. The occult here can also be "one way of interpreting the opening up of new horizons and new opportunities" as a deeply selective process (Ciekawy and Geschiere 1998, 6). In the edited book *Postcolonial Subjectivities in Africa*, Richard Werbner invites the reader to analyze "modern subjectivism" as "constituted by artistic self-fashioning, globally driven consumption, and the struggle for control of identity, autonomy and explicit consciousness" (2002, 7). In her analysis of the occult in Mali, Schulz explains new opportunities as a source of conflict: "New images and goods of consumption inspire in women (and men) new ideals of greater individuality and a 'modern' life orientation. These wishes are diametrically opposed to the scarcity of economic resources; they translate into numerous daily conflicts over material issues between husband and wives, among co-wives or between friends" (2005, 103). Jean Jansen further argues that Mande sorcery had become a "prerequisite for successful participation in the modern market economy" (2009, 111) since the impact in the Malian economy of the 1980s Structural Adjustment Programs (SAPs) imposed by the International Monetary Fund.

I agree with their lines of inquiry insofar as the access to money in Bougouni, seen as the unavoidable key to achieve consumerist aspirations, was considerably unequal in 2010 and has become more so since the SAPs of the 1980s and the post-1991 neoliberal reforms in Mali (Soares 2005, 77–78). Social inequalities in town were therefore domesticated by the poor in the shape of accusations of egoism and jealousy toward bad persons who act secretly against their aspirations. As Francis B. Nyamnjoh rightly wrote, "In general, if people had what they merited, and merited what they had in liberal democratic terms, there would be little need for a hidden hand of any kind, real or imagined. But because nothing is what it seems, the invisible must be considered to paint a full picture of reality" (2001, 37). Following a more existential perspective, I would add that, for *aventuriers, the impression of going nowhere fast, despite the efforts to move forward in life,* stressed the anxiety to be motionless as much as the need to be in forward motion on the earthly path. In this perspective of lives in motion, the nature of tomorrow was determined by occult forces that could be solicited through experts in esoteric sciences (e.g., Touré and Konaté 1990). Among occult forces, however, Muslims acknowledged God as the Almighty mediator of their destiny (*dakan*) on earth.[20] How, then, does God intervene in their existential motions?

DESTINY AND HUMAN RESPONSIBILITY

In Bougouni destiny was a common topic of daily conversation. Destiny was also a classic topic of Malian traditional music and, more recently, of the Malian film and music industries.[21] For Muslims in town, destiny was more than a mere idea or a belief; it was an important component of their faith. Literally *da.kan* (creation.word) or *na.kan* (coming.word) refers to the Word that creates, animates, and determines their fates as human being—in other words, God.[22]

I noticed that destiny was embedded in Muslim life in three main themes. The first theme was the Almighty Will of God. Muslims often exclaimed *Ala ka bon* (God is the greatest) or *Ala ye a latigɛ* (This is the Will of God) when an event stunned them. The Almighty Will of God here stresses fatalism. In Mali, Muslims refer to this theme to explain the inevitability of sudden misfortunes, such as car accidents. Death is the fact of God par excellence.

Rare are the relatives who ask for the intervention of human justice in lethal car accidents, because Malians think that the causes of such tragic outcomes dwell beyond human reach. Muslims also refer to the Almighty Will of God in public to disengage themselves from a tricky conversation or a misfortune (e.g., disappearance of money or livestock). Lamine, a local entrepreneur, used to argue that "when Muslims say, 'God has decided it,' here exactly ends personal reflection." Others simply mention God as a statement of ignorance. I once argued with *touts* in the bus station of Sikasso due to a system of rotation that distributes clients among bus companies. They wanted me to buy a ticket for an old bus that was about to leave, but I wanted to take a later one that looked much newer. An elder who was waiting for the bus to be filled then told me, "Old or new, a bus is a bus. It does not matter. Engine is good. God, and not the bus, decides whether you will reach your destination or not." In Bougouni, Muslims often referred to the Almighty Will of God to stress the divine fatalism of misfortunes, to acknowledge their ignorance, and to deny or cover their responsibility in a given troubling event.

The second theme was kinship. People in Bougouni said that *wolola yé dakan yé* (birth is destiny) because, as stressed by one of my research assistants, "you do not choose your legacy, your parents, your brothers and sisters, your country, and your town." This theme resonates with Robin Horton's (1961) personality theory based on the impact of parents and ancestors upon individual destiny. An individual belongs to a descent group through birth; by coming into the world, individuals are imprinted all their life with their descent group's genealogical legacy. This aspect of destiny is relevant for the exploration of the transmission of *barika* between generations of Muslim saintly lineages, for instance. It also partially explains the local figures of "the blessed child" (*dubabu/barika den*) and "the cursed child" (*danga den*), which I explore in the next chapter.

The third theme was human responsibility. For Muslims, the destiny of a human being is certainly in the hand of God, but God lets him or her select among various paths. Each path is set in motion by specific causes that a human being has to uncover. Here destiny involves a conception of the future that is expressed through the subtle word *sababu*. According to Charles Bailleul, *sababu* originates from the Arab word *sabab* (cause, reason). *Sababu* generally means "cause" and can in specific contexts signify "origin," "reason," or even "secret" (1996, 345–46). In lay settings, *sababu* refers to a cause-and-effect way of thinking proper to human rationality. In religious settings *sababu* becomes more complex, concealed, and ethical. In other words, human beings can prepare their future, seen as a field of possibilities, by seeking the causes that support the possibilities they will opt for—in other words, their destiny. These causes are mysterious in the sense that their effects have a divine origin but their actuation is of an ethical (human) origin; this divine origin is profound in the sense that it is more than the perception of God as the Witness of all the Creation, such as the One who sees all interactions between human beings and the direct consequences of these interactions in the coming interactions. In this regard, its temporality is surprising, hence unpredictable. This latter set of meanings echoes the Arab word *sabab* when it precisely denotes a cause that may influence someone's destiny. *Sababu's* linkages with destiny are deciphered in the next two sections.

"THE SECRET NAME OF GOD IS *SABABU*"[23]

As a reminder, going off on *tunga* is to face the unknown through hardship, novelty, and the hope of migration. In other words, *tunga* is about uncertainty. Instead of taking uncertainty as "the grounds for action" (see Cooper and Pratten 2015), however, I am intrigued by the fact that, for *aventuriers*, the only certainty that accompanies them along the tortuous path of *tunga* is God. What does "the certainty of God" mean in practical terms in their quest for a prosperous life? Here I would like to demonstrate that this certainty of God is potentially creative insofar as it may give rise to virtues that set *aventuriers* in motion and consequently make them move forward in life. To be in motion here requires seeking *sababu*.

I often noticed the phrase *sababu man nɔgɔ* painted on big trucks passing by Bougouni and public green vans called *sotrama* or *duuru-duuruni* in Bamako.[24] This phrase literally means "[finding] the cause is not easy." In existential terms, Malians understood it as "moving forward in life is not easy." Working in public transport in overcrowded and polluted Bamako, for instance, was known to be tiring, dangerous, and not well paid. Moving forward in such a risky business was deemed not obvious. People's *sababu* are deemed secret and hidden to themselves because, as Malians say, "Tomorrow is in God's hand." Nevertheless, they can partially uncover their future on earth by seeking their *sababu*. To do so, they search for the underlying causes that unfold their destiny. Destiny here indicates that people's lives develop along a chain of causes and effects: human beings are responsible for their causes, and God is responsible for their effects.

During the second half of my stay in Bougouni, I often exchanged thoughts with *aventuriers* about the linkages between *sababu* and *dakan*. Once, while waiting for clients at the mechanical mill, Kassim explained to me that God has reserved for each person two earthly paths: a prosperous path, which unfolds through *sababu ɲuman* (good cause), and a failed path, which is provoked by *sababu juguman* (bad cause). In an occult lexicon, Kassim would most likely translate "prosperous" into "blessed" and "failed" into "damned" (see chapter 6). A prosperous path manifests itself in a creative trajectory, whereas a failed path means a destructive trajectory. Human responsibility comes into play through the ethical quality of the *sababu* one uncovers. Kassim continued his explanation by stating that when you act correctly, God will bless you and hence help you to uncover your *sababu ɲuman*. This creative (forward) motion will allow you to achieve prosperity on earth. Heaven will probably be your fate after death. On the other hand, in case you do not act correctly, God does not help you to uncover your *sababu ɲuman*. God might even curse you through the uncovering of *sababu juguman*. Your life on earth will then be filled with afflictions. Hell will probably be your fate after death. God basically acts upon people's lives through a system of rewards and punishments that stems from their attitude on earth. In reality, however, people uncover both kinds of *sababu*. Over the life course, their earthly path becomes characterized by a mixed trajectory. This point again demonstrates that in life evil and good do not stand in clear-cut opposition.

The meaning of seeking *sababu* also depends on how the home community defines earthly prosperity. The life story of Salif the tailor exemplifies what prosperity signified for most Muslim *aventuriers* of rural origins whom I met in Bougouni. He lived a typical childhood in southern rural Mali. His father then sent him 500 kilometers away to a traditional Qur'anic school in Segou, where he spent the following nine years. His father died during these difficult years far from home. Salif then went back to his village. Following the local tradition, he settled next to his mother and his big brother. Unmarried and under the close authority of his elders, however, Salif could not build up his life in his own way. He thus left his home village after "one farming season" in order "to seek [his] *sababu*" (*nɛ ka sababu ɲini*). He went off on *tunga* because he wanted "to obtain a respectable social status" (*ka position sɔrɔ*) within his home community. He often compared himself with his big brother, who was settled in the village. For Salif, this big brother—married, a father, a head of family, and a big cattle trader—had already acquired a respectable social status. But Salif, as "unmarried" (*cɛgana*) and still dependent on his family, had not yet achieved such social prestige. For Salif, seeking *sababu* meant getting married (*ka muso furu*), having children (*ka denw sɔrɔ*), taking care of the family (*ka nasɔngɔ di*), and building a house (*ka so jo*). These goals, however, could not be achieved without money. Seeking *sababu* hence implied seeking money. Salif thereby moved to Bougouni in search of money. He interpreted the fact of moving to Bougouni as belonging to the destiny he chose when seeking his own *sababu*.

Aventuriers understood Bougouni as a site full of *sababu ɲuman* and *sababu juguman*. The *sababuw* they unearthed and picked determine their ups and downs in their quests toward better lives. But how exactly does someone find his *sababu*? What does religiosity mean in this specific context? All of my Muslim friends responded to me by stating that one must face hardships with a distinctive culture of work.

"WORKING IS WORSHIPPING"[25]

Once, in the late afternoon, I met Fousseini the carter in a *grin* next to the working place of Shiaka the seller of tapes. Madou, a friend of Shiaka, who worked as laborer, was also present this day. Madou was an *aventurier* from central Mali. Shiaka was born in Bougouni. He had returned home from *tunga* in Côte d'Ivoire a couple of years earlier. I then initiated a conversation on how someone seeks and finds his *sababu*. Shiaka replied by saying, "If you only sit, how can you gain *sababu*?" Madou, pointing his finger at a big can of water next to us, added, "*Sababu* is in God's hand. Look at the big can. If you push this heavy can, God will help you [to push it farther]. But if you do not push it, God will not help you [the can won't move]." Incriminating the laziness of people who spend their days in *grins*, sitting, drinking tea, and gossiping, Fousseini said, "If you do not sit and you stand up and go looking for a job, and accept a difficult job, God will give you a hand." He then added, "God created human beings, and work is their father and mother."[26] They all agreed that seeking *sababu* was about standing up, being active, and working, in contrast to just sitting, waiting, and being passive. The "work ethos" they put forward precisely stresses the importance of working hard,[27] as jokingly suggested by my friend Moussa the *bogolan* maker:

> If you hold the tail of the lion and you ask for help, nobody will come. However, if you hold the head of the lion and you ask for help, people will come and will help you to bind and immobilize the lion [*laugh*].

This work ethos entails the following religious motivation: sooner or later hard workers will receive help from God in their life. But they should not expect anything from God quickly. On the contrary, good Muslims—those who seek sababu *juman*—should always act with patience, courage, and endurance.[28] The practice of Islamic precepts was certainly important for *aventuriers*, but the virtues that constitute this work ethos were even more important in order to become a good and prosperous Muslim away from the security of home.

Near the end of my stay, I once met Kassim, who by this time ran a cement-built shop servicing mobile phones. He was listening to an Islamic radio program while fixing a mobile phone. A sermon of the popular Islamic scholar Chérif Ousmane Madani Haïdara was being broadcast on the local station Radio Bediana.[29] Addressing the hypocrisy of public Islam in Mali, Haïdara was arguing that a correct attitude in life preceded regular praying in the making of a good Muslim. Kassim agreed with Haïdara. He was equally skeptical about the sincerity of public Islam displayed by heads of family in Bougouni.[30] Kassim was rather an observant Muslim, but he told me that he preferred to remain humble (discreet) in his regular practice of Islamic precepts. He then added some comments that highlighted the virtues that move *aventuriers* in Bougouni:

> Certain people pray and ask God for 100,000 FCFA [US$200] at the end of the month. If they do not obtain this amount, they stop—Affaire de Dieu.[31] Praying is not that! Look at your bicycle [pointing at my bicycle]. If you feel confident that your bicycle can bring you to Bamako, whatever the cost, you will get it. If you feel already discouraged and you do not trust your Chinese bicycle . . . , you will never reach it. You should never expect something from praying. You should trust God. This is it. Sooner or later, God will help you. God will thank you.

Yacou comes from a village near the town of Bla (central Mali). He used to work as a farmer for his paternal uncle. A few years ago he decided to go off on *tunga* in Bougouni. He could no longer stand to work for free for his uncle, a patriarchal constraint explored in the next chapter. Away from home, he therefore had to find a work as a houseboy. He once expressed this work ethos in a more direct way: "Regular praying is important, but it does not put food on your plate." For these *aventuriers*, people who sit idly all day and just stand up for taking ablution and praying and fasting during the holy month of Ramadan will not find *sababu juman* in their life. By contrast, those whose hard work is moved by patience, courage, and endurance please God. All of their efforts will be rewarded at some point in their quest toward a prosperous life. The local saying "working is worshipping" expresses a certainty of God that comes into being through the practice of these virtues. Conceptions of piety, whose keystone is based on work ethos as a means to earthly prosperity (hence salvation), have been observed elsewhere in Africa, such as among members of the Muridiyya (Ebin 1996). They also resonate with Max Weber's (2001) famous book on the protestant ethic and predestination.

I also heard Bambara proverbs (*zana*) in Bougouni that express how work ethos goes hand in hand with religious motivations. For instance, one proverb said, "If you manage to hold your calabash up to your ankle, God will help you to raise it up on your head."[32] Bambara proverbs are allegedly ancient. Locals said they date back from the historic Mande period. Their references to items of traditional farming (e.g., *daga*) and today's missing wild animals (e.g., lions) do not contradict the ancient historicity of these local recollections. Subject to further investigation, I would argue that these linkages between work and religiosity stem from a long-standing conversation between local ethics, hardships in life, and the Islamic figure of God Almighty. The "practical occult" that pulls the string of this conversation resonates with the ancient Mande feature of the twofold nature of power: the genuine root of what is observable lies beneath it, the spiritual (occult) power; what is observable, the manifested power, provides an ethical glimpse of what is beneath. As demonstrated by Michael Jackson (1988) in his chapter called "In the Thrown World: Destiny and Decision in the Thought of Traditional Africa," the dialectic interplay of destiny is prior to Islam in Africa, a point that would deserve to be further explored in other works.

Fousseini, Shiaka, and Madou all stressed the importance of working hard in the search of *sababu*. The verb *ka baara kɛ* means "to work." The work can also be analyzed as a relational ethos when it embodies a specific set of power relations around the search of working opportunities. Fousseini and Madou were *aventuriers* of rural origins. Shiaka was a child of a modest family of Bougouni. All three had livelihoods that barely allowed them to save enough to finance other life projects. In this financial hardship, their work ethos also expressed the relationship between social inequalities and access to the job market in town. Below, I insert this analysis of discourses about work ethos into the concreteness of the kind of economic hardships these *aventuriers* found in town in order to elaborate a more existential approach to this issue.

"*SABABU* IS PUTTING PEOPLE TOGETHER"[33]

In August 2009 I visited Moussa the *bogolan* maker in his village, which was located 30 kilometers south of Bougouni. At some point we traveled to a nearby weekly market and made some purchases for his family there. When we were about to return to Moussa's village, it suddenly started to rain heavily. We ran to shelter in a nearby mud house. Once inside the house we realized that we were not alone; a dozen people had retreated to the house for the same reason. We greeted them and found somewhere to sit. People were talking as well as exchanging ideas, advice, and contacts. Moussa was debating with two young men over the meaning of praying in the mosque. They thought that praying in the mosque was important because it allowed people to accumulate the necessary *baraji* for entering Heaven. Moussa was telling them to view the mosque as an important meeting point where news and knowledge circulate and solidarity is created. In another corner of the room, a Fula man was giving the recipe for a Bambara medicine for backache and kidney pain to a farmer who complained that his wife was suffering from a severe backache. Other people were preparing the usual tea that accompanies talks in Mali. These exchanges continued for more than an hour until the rain ended (even longer for some). Before departing, the Fula entertained the crowd by cordially exclaiming, "Thanks to God who made us meet up together today. Rain came. We could not go. Each of us took refuge here [*laugh of approval from the crowd*]." This very day, our encounter was not understood as a random event. People who took refuge in the shelter perceived the fact of coming together in this mud house as the outcome of God's will, which manifested itself through a sudden heavy rain.

Aventuriers often stated that "*sababu* is putting people together" because another important practical dimension of *sababu* was networking. Turning points in *aventuriers'* lives were often of a social nature that they interpreted as divine interventions, and this especially in contexts of poor (or absent) established networks. Similar to what Ferguson observed about central and southern Africa, "The production of wealth . . . is understood to be inseparable from the production of social relations" in West Africa (2006, 72). Many studies have further demonstrated the importance of networks in the construction of migrant careers, as illustrated by Senegalese (Riccio 2001, 2005; Schmitz 2006) and West Africans (Schmitz 2008) moving to Europe. Well-established Soninke migrant networks in France have significantly supported transnational migration as the main path to adulthood for young men from northwest Mali during most part of the post-Independence period (see Man-chuelle 1989, 1997; Jónsson 2008). Contacts were also crucial to the economic integration of *aventuriers* into Bougouni. However, in contexts of poor (or absent) established networks, *aventuriers* sought contacts through different strategies. One of them was the economy of charity.

THE ECONOMY OF CHARITY

In Bougouni biographies of *aventuriers* often developed along key encoun-ters. A relative or a friend already settled in town could provide shelter and food to the newcomer, but further networking was crucial for securing a de-cent livelihood. The realization of such earning aspiration mostly depended on patronage in an urban economy characterized by high unemployment.[34] More importantly, access to this economy was often rendered possible by members of the local elite—who acted as gatekeepers of sorts, able to hire *aventuriers*, to finance them, or to recommend them to other employers. As elsewhere in Africa (Chabal and Daloz 1999), personal links took precedence over institutional links in most daily affairs. More than resources themselves, what was crucial is the *access* to resources (Foeken and Owuor 2006). This issue of access generated a specific moral economy characterized by patron-age and clientelism. In such circumstances, seeking *sababu* was about striving for being connected with powerful individuals who could help you to access the local job market. Below, I flesh this point out through the work-seeking trajectory of Kassim the former handyman and mill worker who managed to start a small business with the patronage of a local civil servant.

Kassim had settled in Bougouni a few years earlier with the help of his "Ivorian aunt," an older woman with whom he shared the same regional identity. She had moved into town years ago with her husband, a native of Bougouni who undertook *tunga* in Côte d'Ivoire. Because of her local con-nections, this aunt found Kassim work as a houseboy, lumberjack, farmer, and handyman for various better-off families. These jobs certainly provided Kassim room and board, but with a monthly wage of 5,000 FCFA (US$10) he could not save money. Kassim remembered this period of *mɔgɔ baara bolo* as shameful. *Mɔgɔ baara bolo* literally means "working on someone's hands"—in other words, to work for a patron. As he said to me, "When I came back home from the field, I was so dirty. The daughters of my patron looked at me as if I was not a [human being] man!" After one year of *mɔgɔ baara bolo*, Kassim eventually found a job in a gasoline-powered mechanical mill after a neighbor put him in contact with the owner of the mill. I met him when he had been working there for nearly two years.

In the mill Kassim earned a monthly wage of 20,000 FCFA (US$40). At that time, he rented a single room that shared a courtyard with other families. He ate with a neighboring family by paying a food contribution. Although single, the challenge posed by such a wage was how to cover daily life expenses and still be able to save money. Over time Kassim aspired to undertake a small trade project. When *aventuriers* managed to save a little amount of money, they were often inclined to purchase prestigious items (e.g., mobile phones). They were then tempted to finance what young men called *l'amour commercial* (commercial love) in the fortunate case of having their savings not already "eaten" by *le social* or spent on *ordonnances* (prescriptions).[35] Kassim worked from morning to late afternoon in the mill, but his hard labor did not allow him to amass any considerable savings. How, then, could he move forward in life? He decided to make some extra cash by selling cigarettes, sugar, chewing gum (*cigarɛtitigi*), coffee, tea, and egg sandwiches (*shɛfantigi*) in the evening. To do so, he needed an initial investment of 30,000 FCFA (US$60) so as to buy a table, a bench, and a chair, as well as the required merchandise to make food and the stock to sell. He therefore embarked upon various strategies to reach this ambition.

Kassim was not satisfied by his wage in the mill. He nonetheless kept working hard but not only to secure this job. More importantly, in working hard he was also hoping for a generous gesture from his patron. He was a faithful worker who had stayed loyal to his patron when other workers left. He had also trained other co-workers of the mill. He thought that sooner or later his patron would be thankful for his hard work. In order to counteract the eroding effect of *le social* over his wage, he also joined a *tontine* under the cover of a female friend.[36] He was investing 5,000 FCFA every month in this *tontine*, hoping his reward would come soon. Kassim also visited local saints to receive their blessings, such as the descendant of a renowned *maraboutic* lineage settled in the village of Kologo. He also visited experts in Bambara esoteric sciences. He told me that all of these visits aimed to improve his luck (*garijɛgɛ*). In Mali luck is never a random phenomenon. It is God's favor and spirits' protection that accompany "the blessed child" (*dubabu den*; see chapter 6) throughout the unfolding of a person's earthly path.

Time was passing but Kassim's savings were not growing. He therefore activated what I call the "economy of charity" by asking a wealthy contact for financial help (a loan or gift). The key to this strategy is to become the protégé (a sort of client) of a patron. In this particular case, however, the patron-protégé relationship is not based on a business venture, such as what happens among Wahhabi merchants of Sikasso. In this latter case, "protégés work for a continual flow of goods and credit which give them the opportunity to make profits themselves" (Warms 1994, 118).[37] The patronage I explore here was also the outcome of a slow process through which someone gains "a reputation for seriousness" (*mɔgɔ sɛbɛ*), but this process was not primarily based on "successful repayment of small debts and devotion to religion" (109). The economy of charity involves a patron-protégé relationship resulting from an asymmetric friendship characterized by submissive behaviors of respect through which the protégé slowly becomes considered as a *mɔgɔ sɛbɛ* by the patron. *Sɛbɛ* signifies "reliable" in general; its precise ethics is hence situational. For instance, *sɛbɛ* can stress an attitude of politeness toward elders. In the economy of charity, it emphasizes the qualities of diligence, loyalty, and respectful submission. Whereas a patron-protégé relationship among traders aims at mutual prosperity, the case of Kassim illustrates how this relationship gradually brings access to financing for the protégé and reinforces the status of the patron as a good Muslim and a *mɔgɔ.ba* (big man) in town. I was well placed to analyze this dynamic because I got along well with both Kassim and Ibrahim.

The patron of Kassim had a close friend, Ibrahim, a civil servant who worked in a decentralized state service. Every working day Ibrahim spent lunchtime and late afternoon on the threshold of the mechanized mill, where its owner hosted a *grin*. He often encountered Kassim at his workplace. Ibrahim told me that Kassim had greeted him with politeness and respect by shaking hands while looking down since their first contact. Each time Ibrahim arrived at the *grin*, Kassim would come out of the mill, greet Ibrahim, offer him the best seat, and then swiftly return to work within the mill. While waiting for bags of grain to grind or during breaks, Kassim often sat behind Ibrahim and prepared tea for the members of the *grin*. The cup of tea circulated first between the patron and his friends and thereafter between the workers (when in sufficient quantity). When Ibrahim engaged in conversation with Kassim, Kassim never interrupted Ibrahim and listened to him carefully. When Ibrahim ate at the mill and invited Kassim to join him, Kassim always found an excuse to eat after Ibrahim. When Ibrahim needed something, Kassim went on an errand for him. Kassim's daily practice of a set of submissive conducts of respect toward Ibrahim turned into an asymmetric friendship through which Ibrahim progressively started to perceive Kassim as a *mɔgɔ sɛbɛ*.

Ibrahim was not just anyone in Bougouni. He held a key position in a powerful state service. He earned a considerable amount of money and had contacts with influential members of the local elite. He was the oldest brother of a local family and covered most of the expenses of his parents and siblings. In parallel, Ibrahim managed to build a cement house and to buy a laptop, a new Jakarta motorbike, and several building plots in Bougouni (among other minor prestigious items) in one year. Owing to his local status of "big man," Ibrahim faced a particularly intense flux of requests (*le social*) coming from kin, friends, and the neighborhood within the context of severe economic inequality.[38] As a Muslim, he prayed regularly and fasted during the holy month of Ramadan. In the evening he also sometimes listened to public Islamic sermons organized in town. As a prosperous Muslim, moreover, he felt affected by what the scarcity of money provoked around him. Reflecting upon his privileged position in town, he once stated, "The value of man is to learn a profession, to find a job, to earn money, and to feel pity for others." He had to deal with what Malians called *hinɛ*, a word that expresses both pity and compassion. *Hinɛ* is an important dimension of *adamadenya*, the local (Mande) notion of humanism. In this case Ibrahim felt *hinɛ* as a call for "solidarity" (*ɲɔgɔndɛmɛ*) toward those who were less privileged than him. *Hinɛ* is also regarded as a virtuous sentiment that local Muslim scholars related to the third Islamic pillar (*zakat*/alms, charity). In Bougouni *hinɛ* simultaneously informed local perceptions of good Muslim and big man.

Ibrahim nevertheless had to be selective about whom to financially support. In case he refused all requests from people in need, he would most likely be denigrated in town as selfish (*ɲegoya*), or worse, a cursed child (*danga den*).[39] Witches were known to be drawn by such disparagements. On the other hand, Ibrahim could not reply positively to all requests from people in need because, despite a communal context of limited income, he cared for his own interest as well. Like most big men in Bougouni he had to carefully balance his investments between his person, family, and extra-familial contacts (e.g., friends, neighbors, colleagues). In a system of patronage characterized by the continual search for mutual help and a "win-win" situation (Bayart 1989; Bayart, Mbembe, and Toulabor 1992), the charity of Muslim patrons does not work randomly. This charity foremost benefits those whom big men consider to be reliable persons. Here we can argue that "pragmatic instrumentalism and pious sincerity" coexist within the same person (Osella and Osella 2009, 216).[40] In addition to the work ethos described in the previous section, *mɔgɔ sɛbɛ* in the case of Kassim signifies the hard worker who demonstrates submissive behaviors of respect to a big man. These behaviors symbolically determine who is the reliable person in need and who is the compassionate patron to praise. This kind of friendship is certainly asymmetric in terms of social status and money; however, both persons give and take. The compassionate patron gives money to a hard worker in need who, in return, publicly praises (*ka mɔgɔ tɔgɔ fo*) this patron as a genuine *mɔgɔba* in town. The hard worker might also help the patron in the future by rendering multiple services. This patron-protégé relationship can also develop into a business venture over time.

A few months had passed since Kassim's first mention of his ambition of starting a small evening trade business. Despite all of his efforts, Kassim confided to me that he felt that his life was stagnating. He was still not able to finance his trade project, but during a dinner we shared in a *gargote*, he told me that he still kept trust in God. A few days after my last conversation with Kassim, Ibrahim confided to me how Kassim aroused his *hinɛ*: "Kassim is really courageous. He is a hard worker, and he respects me too much! I feel pity for him." A week later I learned in town that Kassim had opened a small evening trade selling *cigarɛtitigi* and *shɛfantigi* after receiving financial help from Ibrahim. In this regard, Shiaka the seller of tapes meaningfully told me, "*Sababu* is the fact of meeting people who feel pity for you because, although you work hard and you gain your life through the sweat of the brow, you do not move forward in life." As Ferguson highlighted about the market in Africa, Kassim's example of an economy of charity also illustrates that "economic facts are moral" in southern Mali (2006, 82). When traditional networks of solidarity were not present in town, *aventuriers* prepared the ground for solidarity by waiting for patronage to turn up in an active way. In Bougouni stories of financial help from patrons to *aventuriers* explained most of the forward motion of *aventuriers* on their earthly paths. In fact, such stories of financial help are widespread in Mali. This economy of charity, in return, legitimates discrepancies of wealth and prestige between townsmen. Docile *aventuriers* in search for *tunga* away from home praise the generosity of local big men. These asymmetric relationships assume social inequalities in Mali.

THE OBVIOUS MYSTERY OF ALMIGHTY GOD: TOWARD A KALEIDOSCOPIC NOTION OF DESTINY

Bruno Riccio's Senegalese informant says, "The migrant does not have a precise global project; he is an adventurer. . . . Only the signs of prosperity can be aimed at as a general goal" (2005, 105). Young Muslim men who left their rural homes knew the social expectations placed on their shoulders, but the rest was in the hands of God. They were *aventuriers*. For them, *tunga* initially meant leaving home in search of money. They also knew that such decisions brought them on a demanding path toward prosperity (or failure). Thus, they were putting their honor and shame at stake. Thereafter they lived *tunga* as a deeply challenging school of life (a kind of *rite de passage*) along which the consequences of their actions were in the hands of Almighty God. Instead of being the product of a "prescribed faith" (Marsden 2009, 60), their Muslim faith was questioned, tested, and reconstituted in their struggles toward a prosperous destiny. Their arduous search for *sababu*, the ground of their religiosity, did not express the slogan "Islam is the solution" as an uncritical reality.[41] Rather, it stressed the obvious mystery of Almighty God as *the* transformative axiom of their ethical life on earth. What does the phrase mean in terms of religious experience?

As a reaction to the above question, I would like to conclude this chapter with my thoughts on the phenomenology of Almighty God. These thoughts shall be taken as a laboratory whose main ingredients are observational and conversational materials collected among the dozen of *aventuriers* with whom I shared friendship in Bougouni. For these *aventuriers*, piety was not reduced to a scriptural solution put into practice in the shape of a project of self-formation. Piety concerned a field of experiences in which the unfathomable presence of Almighty God in their lives was ethical by nature. From a phenomenological perspective, I argue that the "lifeworld" of *aventuriers* comes into being through their relationship to God (Desjarlais and Throop 2011, 91–92). In parallel with its Islamic orthodoxy, Muslim life should also be understood as a complex, concealed, and moral path whose destiny lies in the hands of the relationship that a Muslim cultivates with God. The field of piety here concerns a Muslim's relationship to God, which ideally must be unmediated. In ethnographic terms, this ideal is lived by Muslims through the ups and downs that punctuate the unfolding of their life on earth. The religious experience of *aventuriers* is hence explored as much as a tortuous path to uncover as it is the practice of a prescribed solution ready to use. Kassim, for instance, told me that he perceived Ibrahim's gesture as the fact of God. In other words, his encounter with Ibrahim was the *sababu juman* that at some point manifested as the financial help that allowed him to start a small evening trade. Ibrahim's act of charity was the very moment in which Kassim felt the presence of God at the forefront of his life. Kassim did not imagine God in this very moment. He intimately recognized the immanence of God as Almighty just as he would recognize the hardness of a stone as solid. Such experience remains momentary in its recognition because Kassim, like numerous *aventuriers*, perceived God as an obvious mystery. It is why most of the time God was felt as being present in the backdrop of their lives or even as not felt at all.

Most of the time it is indeed the constant flux of phenomena, although ephemeral and changing, that catches the attention of Muslims. Living within phenomena is like a wandering. Finding one's way in this wandering is to meet God—in other words, to accept, connect with, and come closer to the Unity of the Creation. What matters in this faith is to be and remain actively patient and thankful for the divine gift of life through virtues (e.g., work ethos, *mɔgɔ sɛbɛ*) so as to acknowledge the transformative presence of God in one's life.

Paolo Gaibazzi, in his inspiring article on fate, fortune, work and the unexpected among Gambian Soninke hustlers, shows that their "'quest for luck' conjures up a kinetic notion of destiny" (2015, 228). In Bougouni the *aventuriers'* struggle to move forward in life also illustrates a kinetic notion of destiny. The practical meanings of Almighty God in their lives, moreover, make me think of a kaleidoscopic notion of destiny. I use the metaphor of the kaleidoscope to analytically depict their religious experiences. Kassim, for instance, makes the kaleidoscope turn through his actions. God adapts its transforming presence to the ethical resonances of Kassim's actions. The resulting dynamic—life as it emerges—is what one perceives in the kaleidoscope: an ever-changing flow of colorful geometrical shapes. Human interpretation of this dynamic will always be multiple because *sababuw* are complex, concealed, and ethical. The recurrence of geometrical shapes stresses traces of past actions and future consequences in the present. Their shifting colors illustrate that bad and good are not clear-cut in life. A person's gaze mostly circulates between specific colorful geometrical shapes. This visual wandering means that one's presence is the phenomenon. To wander (seeking God) is the dominant norm in religious life. Those who are wandering emphasize that one's presence is not aligned with the central axis around which all colorful geometrical shapes turn: God. The alignment with this central axis, however, can happen, but like a flash. Then "stop wandering and recognize God as Almighty," they said.

CHAPTER 6

The Resilience of Mande Figures of "Humanity"

The courtyard of my host family overlooked a sandy street that connected the town's center with the *brousse* in a straight line. Bordering two districts, Massablacoura and Heremakono, this street was an important residential lane that featured numerous shops and workshops on its façade. I bicycled on this street every day. Over time I came to know most of its occupants that operated from the tarred crossroad announcing the town's center to the courtyard of my host family. I used to stop by an electrical repair workshop to greet Abdoulaye. There we chatted for a while and sometimes drank tea with his fellow workers. Abdoulaye was born in a village near the small town of Garalo, 50 kilometers south of Bougouni. He moved to Bougouni in the early 1990s so as to find a cash job. He became an electrician and later married in town. When I first met him in 2009, Abdoulaye, in his late forties, was the head of a large family. Like most of his contemporaries, the 1991 Malian coup d'état brought him hope of a better life. However, twenty years later, his feelings about the future of Mali was mixed. Every month he was still having difficulty making ends meet. He also complained about the *dégradation des moeurs* (moral decline) hitting contemporary Mali, especially the decrease of the authority of elders in general.[1]

Once he looked daggers at a young man standing in front of the workshop. This youth was sticking out his chest a few meters away; he was showily smoking a cigarette while looking at activities on the street. He then loudly hailed a passer-by: "You! Come here!" Abdoulaye grumbled, "Democracy arrived. But many people and the youth have only understood it as—you can do what do you like—[*pffff*]."[2] Like many Malians who have lived through the civic changes brought by the events of 1991, Abdoulaye supported the democracy but regretted that many Malians, especially the youth, had understood it as a mere laissez-faire attitude. Many Muslim elders felt nostalgia for the respect for authority that they portrayed as characteristic of the authoritarian regime of the overthrown Moussa Traoré (1968–91).[3] For Abdoulaye, youths smoking cigarettes in front of their elders without embarrassment meant "the strength of *adamadenya* has diminished."

Abdoulaye's nostalgia for how the power of elders worked in the epoch of Traoré's regime mirrors a "crisis of meaning" (Ferguson 1999, 14) of traditional authority in post-1991 Mali (Chappatte 2018b, 236–39). On the other hand, youth's challenge of elders' authority seems antediluvian in this part of Africa, not to mention that the categories of youth and elder are not fixed for good. As documented by Brian J. Peterson (2011), for instance, Islamization in southwest Mali has been the progressive outcome of mobile social groups (freed slaves from 1910, colonial soldiers, migrant workers from 1920) who returned to their homeland and introduced prayer into their villages. Most of these groups were made up of youth. For them, "Islam provided an alternative moral framework through which young men critiqued their elders." In justifying their break with tradition, "Islam provided the perfect edge" (Peterson 2011, 205, 198–207). Abdoulaye's nostalgia for the traditional power of elders is a recurring generational phenomenon that is new in intensity but not in nature. Focusing on "mille-feuille" ethical formation, this chapter probes the resilience of Mande figures of humanity found in Bougouni's social life.

Aventuriers exemplified "simply Muslims" raised and educated in generic Islam. They learned rudiments of Islamic dogma and rituals during their late childhood and youth. Then they practiced generic Islam with various degrees of diligence. But generic Islam does not indicate how a Muslim should ethically act in social life. How, for instance, should a Muslim behave in between prayers? In Bougouni the ethical life was shaped by the Mande figures of "the noble Muslim" (*silamɛ ye hɔrɔn ye*; literally, "the Muslim is a noble") and "the blessed child" (*barika/dubabu den*). The exploration of these traditional figures of humanity demonstrates that Islam and Mande culture together are indissociable elements of *laada* (custom).

REMEMBERING AN EPIC LIFE

In the old district of Dougounina, at three-minute walk from the house of the chief of the village, stood a crossroads with no homes. Brick walls enclosed an imposing isolated tomb erected, next to a *balanzan* tree, in the middle of an empty square. Members of Bougouni's traditional chieftainship informed me that it was the tomb of Diakassan Moussa Diakité (DKM),[4] one of the most famous ancestors of the founders of Bougouni. In 2010 it was the only tombstone that stood outside the main cemetery of Bougouni located in the district of Medine. Before a visit to this tomb, I greeted Kaka Diakité, the traditional chief of Bougouni (*dugutigi*), in his nearby courtyard. He told me the life story of DKM, a great Diakité warrior who left his mark on local history because of his epic life.

DKM lived in ancient times when the *kafo* of Bougouni was a vassal of the kingdom of Ségou (17th–19th centuries).[5] Beginning in his childhood, DKM drew attention to himself by virtue of his precocious maturity. Kaka Diakité stressed his deep sense of *hɔrɔnya* (nobleness), the ethical disposition of the noble. Consequently, his elders sent him to Ségou as the representative of the *kafo* of Bougouni. During his stay in the royal town, DKM became renowned for his military prowess. In parallel, he also learned the Arabic language, converted to Islam, and became a fervent Muslim. Later, DKM returned to Bougouni accompanied by a Muslim scholar. He then brought Islam to Bougouni and ruled the *kafo* with rightness and justice. On his deathbed, he implored God to immortalize his earthly achievements through a noble tree. His wish was fulfilled: a majestic *balanzan* of Abyssinia, the emblem of the city of Ségou, emerged next to his burial place. The feats of DKM were still remembered in Bougouni more than a century after his death. His descendants had maintained his burial place with an imposing tombstone.[6] The original *balanzan* tree was destroyed by lightning in the late 1980s; the traditional chieftainship replaced it with the current *balanzan*. The path leading to the place of the tombstone was repaired in 2009 by the Diakité chieftainship, an investment that illustrates the contemporary importance of what is considered as a historical *patrimoine* (heritage) of Bougouni by its founding families. The travel guide *Le Petit Futé Mali 2012/2013* considers this tomb as the main tourist attraction of the town.

In 2010 this historic heritage was not confined to a tombstone and the narration of an epic life. Locals cultivated it through a sort of hero cult. On the last Sunday of every month, members of Diakité families gathered around DKM's tombstone to praise their illustrious ancestor. For them, God greatly blessed DKM because he acted according to the *hɔrɔnya*. Consequently, locals used to say that DKM's tombstone was a place invested with *baraka*—in other words, God's favor. In this blessed place, *baraka* manifested in a specific way. According to locals, when a woman has difficulty in giving birth, she come to the tombstone and asks through prayer for the delivery of a healthy child. In case God fulfills the request, the family of the newborn must give an offering (*saraka*), such as a cock, goat, cow, or amount of money, to God via the intermediary of the chief of the village, the sacrificial officer. If the newborn is a boy, his parents will give him the name Moussa. If the newborn is a girl, her name will be Diakassan. Locals came to this blessed place with other requests as well. The life story of DKM and his hero cult supported the legitimacy of Kaka Diakité's family as the town's traditional chieftainship. The story also integrated this powerful family into the distinguished history of locals who achieved early conversion to Islam. The commemoration of this local hero aims to anchor Bougouni, a town notorious for its backward (un-Islamic) activities, in the national history of contemporary Mali as a Muslim country. In doing so, it also illustrates the Diakité chieftainship's strategy to retain its power in a context of growing decentralized power (see De Jorio 2016, chapter 1). As explored in Bougouni's hinterland (Chappatte 2018c), this tombstone commemorated *hɔrɔnya*, a traditional ethics that was present in people's lives in a diffuse way.

THE HEIRS OF *HORONYA* IN SOUTHWEST MALI

In 2010, in the roadside village of Sido (30 km north of Bougouni), I saw in the home of a teacher a campaign poster of the political party Rassemblement Pour le Mali (RPM) for the candidacy of IBK (Ibrahim Boubacar Keïta), who had run in the presidential election of 2007. The poster, a head-and-shoulder portrait of IBK, who became president of Mali in the next presidential election, depicted IBK in front of a microphone and wearing a rich *boubou* and a small Muslim cap. Under his famous nickname, "IBK," one could read the word *kankelentigi*. This Bambara-composed word (*kan.kelen.tigi*), the owner (*tigi*) of one (*kelen*) language (*kan*), finely touched the core of *hɔrɔnya*: a man of his word. As a political slogan, moreover, this composed word resonated well with the (immaculate) white color of the candidate's garments, which in this context indexed the purity of Islam, and his illustrious family name. Keïta, literally "[the one] who has taken (all) things" (Dieterlen 1955, 40), is an important *hɔrɔn* family name (*jamu*) in Mali because it refers to Sundiata Keïta, the founder of the great Mali Empire. The epoch of Sundiata Keita (thirteenth century) belongs to what is often considered as the golden age of the historic Mande world. This poster, connecting a man holding the *jamu* of a prestigious royal lineage (Turco 2007) with the virtue of being a man of his word, implied in such a way that by voting for IBK as president of Mali, southern Malians do not vote only for a man of *hɔrɔnya*; they also vote for the legitimate heir of *hɔrɔnya*. This campaign poster brought my exploration of *hɔrɔnya* back to the historic Mande world.

The term *hɔrɔn.ya* refers to ancient local structures. The societies composing the historic Mande world were structured into multiple groups, a complexity that became codified during the colonial period under three main vocational statuses: the *hɔrɔn* (free man, noble),[7] the *jamakala* (artisan), and the *jon* (slave).[8] This "tri-partite corporate group" (Perinbam 1998, 8) has since been known as the "Mande caste system" (Conrad and Frank 1995, 7).[9] Each of the three groups, structured into distinct statuses,[10] was bound to specific activities that conferred resources, power, prestige, and identity upon the group. The unity and continuity of the historic Mande society was based on the complementarity of each group in the division of work. Members of different groups interacted in village life but followed strictly endogamous rules of marriage.[11] In addition to illicit exogenous intercourses, a breach of the system was produced when someone encroached on the fundamental activities of other groups. The *hɔrɔnw*, the freemen and nobles of Mande communities, were farmers, herders, and warriors. They also held political offices. The *jamakalaw* were the artisans of Mande communities: blacksmiths (*numu*), griots (*jɛli*), cobblers, potters, leatherworkers, and so on. As the etymology of their name indicates (*jama.kala*), they were known to be experts in the manipulation of *jama*, a sort of impersonal energy that inhabits all matter and all beings.[12] In the Bamanan zone, they were also the guides of initiation societies such as the *komo*. The *jon* was not necessarily a status ascribed by birth. The slaves were usually former *hɔrɔnw* enslaved through capture in battle. They could regain *hɔrɔn* status through the purchase of freedom over the years. However, most slaves who gained freedom did so as house-born slaves (*woloso*). Slaves of second generations were usually not sold, as they developed special ties with their master's household. These ties eased the accumulation of wealth necessary for the purchase of freedom; on the other hand, slavery by birth reinforced slave status via education and memory by creating slave lineages.[13] Slaves were usually the housemaids, servants, and workers of the two other groups.

A breach of the system, monitored by the feeling of shame, was also produced when someone acted in a way that was inappropriate to someone's social (vocational) role. Being a *horon*, for instance, was as much a matter of vocation as a matter of attitude. This interpenetration of vocation and attitude also worked for the artisans and the slaves. In Bambara the dimension of attitude is brought by the suffix *ya*, which conveys the state (or condition) of being of what is named. The linguistic scope of *hɔrɔn.ya* therefore brings us beyond its classic scholarly definition as "statutory condition of free lineages" (Berger 2010, 149–50) to express the ethical disposition of the noble. Hence, the linguistic term *hɔrɔnya* points to the *adamadenya* of the noble.

Mande statuses still exist in the contemporary Mande world; however, these statuses have been regionalized in complex sociohistoric ways that shape the localized exploration of their contemporary meanings. For instance, the Malian decentralization has brought new political offices into communities by election. In some communities, inhabitants refused to elect a *jamakala* as mayor because, for the majority of them, only a *hɔrɔn* can accede to a political seat. In other *communes*, locals chose a non-*hɔrɔn* as their mayor.[14] Besides the regional histories of Mande statuses, descendants of *horonw*, such as IBK, cultivate on the national level the traditional perception of *horonw* as politicians by vocation (among other traditional perceptions). Despite the force of regional histories, we need to bear in mind that different meanings of Mande statuses coexist with different intensities in a given region.

In southwest Mali, the history of *horonw*—hence *hɔrɔnya*, the *adamadenya* of the noble—is particular in this regard. In the region of Bougouni, aristocracy by birth (*horon*) did not manifest much in social life. The criterion of origin was certainly relevant in local elections and land access issues. However, locals who claimed local ancestry did not feel of higher status by birth than foreigners whatever their Mande statuses. In southwest Mali, traditional statuses were also much less significant in marital issues, in contrast to the north of Mali.[15] Causes of this discrepancy are historical.

During the nineteenth century, the region of Bougouni was part of a buffer zone between bigger political units (e.g., the kingdoms of Ségou and Kenedougou) (Peterson 2008, 263). This borderland was characterized by a series of decentralized societies, with small slave holdings, which were frequently targeted by bigger political units for enslavement (89). Its inhabitants, moreover, suffered from a short period of mass enslavement (ten to fifteen years) under the yoke of Samory Touré in the late nineteenth century (24–57). This West African savanna was an important area of enslavement via raids until the end of legal slavery also due to the polytheistic identities of its inhabitants. In the decade following the end of legal slavery in 1905,[16] "southern French Sudan was the single largest recipient of former slaves," according to colonial documents (89). These formerly enslaved people were able to downplay the social consequences of this brief but shameful past for three main reasons: they were not born into slavery, so they knew who they were before being enslaved;[17] as they moved away from their former masters to return to their region of origin, their statuses were not shaped by former master-slave social ties (by contrast to the Sahel); and nearly all local families were hit by this Samory-led slavery.[18] This massive but transitory period of enslavement left insignificant traces in the birth statuses of the descendants of these former enslaved people, mostly because all families suppressed what happened during this forced exile. As Peterson observed, however, slavery and its idioms would remain a "cultural artefact of the mind" for describing any unequal social relations (154). I argue the same minded imprint for nobleness. When local families started to convert to Islam in the late colonial period (154), the Islamic stance of the equality of all Muslims in front of God arguably further dismantled the traditional Mande status of the noble from its ethical disposition. The heritage of *hɔrɔnya* is thus peculiar in this savanna because it is loosely linked to the birth status of the noble (*hɔrɔn*). *Hɔrɔnya* became, above all, performative because this region was shaken by a specific history of mass enslavement that abruptly dismantled the ethical disposition of the noble (*hɔrɔnya*) from the status of noble through a collective suppression.[19]

"THEY DO NOT KNOW *HƆRƆNYA*"

In the district of Massablacoura, Fousseini the carter rented a two-room flat in a decrepit mud house reinforced with cement rendering. There he lived with his wife and two small children. His family shared a courtyard with two other families of rural origins. Living in similar housing conditions, they had also moved into town in search of a prosperous life. One head of family worked as a farmer for various better-off families, the other as a builder for a local entrepreneur; both complemented their low income with petty trades in town. This peculiar context of neighborhood, commonly called *cour commune* (common courtyard) in Mali, designates the crowded living conditions that characterize poor urban districts in French-speaking West Africa.[20] As is customary, when a wife cooked, all were invited to eat. The parents used to courteously decline the sharing of the meal; the children would come to eat if they were hungry. One of the three families would then make tea for the whole courtyard. Daily life in the courtyard was rhythmed by the sharing of meals when all children would often come together. I used to pop into the courtyard to meet Fousseini and to greet the families there.

Once, during a visit, Fousseini sneered and said, "They do not know *hɔrɔnya*," while staring at a child who was chewing on a piece of meat in the threshold of his family housing. Fousseini's wife muttered, "This family, when their meal is rich, they eat inside." Then the mother of the child swiftly moved him back inside the house. Fousseini explained to me that it was not the first time that he had caught this family eating alone when the meal was generous in meat. He and his wife regretted that such an attitude undermined the custom of sharing meals in this *cour commune*. I then asked him what he meant by "they do not know *hɔrɔnya*." Traditionally, "the behaviour of an *hɔrɔn*, according to the Guinean *hɔrɔn* scholar Sory Camara, is distinguished by its 'sense of honour, restraint, respect of convention in all daily behaviours,'" in contrast to the exuberant, energetic and shameless behavior of the *griot* (for instance) (Hoffman 2000, 87). In contemporary southwest Mali, *hɔrɔnya* shared a similar sense of dignity. According to Fousseini, *hɔrɔnya* was about being honest (*mɔgɔsɛbɛ don*): "You do what you say."[21] Thus, someone who follows *hɔrɔnya* cannot act undercover on purpose.[22] For Fousseini, when you share a meal, it is the act of sharing (and not the meal itself) that fosters *ɲɔgɔndɛmɛ* (solidarity) among the inhabitants of the same *cour commune*. But when the quality of the meal becomes more important than the act of sharing to a point that you discreetly eat inside when your meal is rich, your mind does not follow *hɔrɔnya*; it follows *ɲɛgoya* (selfishness).

In Bougouni to be named *hɔrɔn* or accused of being devoid of *hɔrɔnya* referred foremost to the ethics of *hɔrɔnya*. More precisely, this reference to *hɔrɔnya* was often associated with Islam through the idiom *Silamɛ ye hɔrɔn ye*,[23] which I translate as "the noble Muslim." *Aventuriers* coming from regions belonging to the contemporary Mande world often assessed Muslims' attitudes that happened in between prayers via moral discourses, the values of which expressed *hɔrɔnya*. I later asked Fousseini about the connection between Islam and the ethics of *hɔrɔnya*. He stated, "Islam brought prayer and fasting here but nothing else! In terms of morality, we still live the way our ancestors did." Fousseini's emotional exclamation of "nothing else" expressed his mistrust of Muslim scholars in general. Beyond this emotional tone, his opinion illustrated a widespread understanding of the roots of Muslim ethics in southwest Mali: local social ethics were deemed of Mande origin.[24] Fousseini's opinion also stressed that contemporary Muslims in Mali do not learn good manners by reading the Qur'an. The learning of good manners takes place on a daily basis from a very young age. Children are immersed in the ethics that shape social life in their family courtyard and the neighborhood and on the streets of their locality. This everyday education is an intrinsic dimension of social life that transmits traditional values proper to southwest Mali's cultural backdrop.

As illustrated with the vignette of sharing meals in the *cour commune*, the term *hɔrɔnya* stressed a specific set of attitudes within the field of *adamadenya* at large. In Bougouni *hɔrɔnya* now had no blood; it was open to all. *Adamadenya*, as informed by Mande ethics, was also linked to the speech act of blessing.

"YOU BECAME BAMANAN!" ON ETHICAL BLESSING

In 2008 I lived two months in Bamako, where I attended intensive Bamanan classes. Knowing my interest in Muslim life, my teacher, Mohamed Larabi Diallo, devoted specific lessons to the vocabulary of the religious. Approaching the end of the language training, he once told me that he wanted to teach me how to bless someone (*ka dubabu kɛ mɔgɔ la*) in Bambara. He argued that blessing (*dubabu*) is crucial to the Muslim society of Mali in many ways. He added, "You will discover in the course of your sojourn in Bougouni that blessing is omnipresent in Malian social life." We then spent an entire morning studying how and when to bless someone. I was not highly motivated by this specific lesson, because this practice seemed quiet alien to my etiquette. I moved to Bougouni shortly after this somewhat boring lesson.

Six months later, however, I realized in the midst of a greeting to an elder that I routinely blessed people whom I met and encountered in Bougouni. Professor Diallo was right! Oddly, I did not know when I had started to behave so. Why did I not notice it before? Part of the answer lies in the fact that the act of blessing belongs to the quotidian of Malian households. Geert Mommersteeg stressed that in the town of Djenné (the center of Mali) "blessings . . . recur throughout conversations and throughout the day" (2009, 74). Illustrations of blessing in Bougouni were similarly numerous. As this speech act slipped into the unremarked phenomena of social life, it became to my mind a quasi-natural obviousness due to its ubiquity.

After breakfast, for instance, parents gave blessings to their children. They asked God to give their children a safe way to school, to grant them success in their studies. When members of a family were about to travel, elders of this family asked God to give them a smooth and safe journey home. During a visit, blessings punctuated final farewells. The host and visitor exchanged blessings for health, peace, and prosperity toward their respective families. Each morning, I greeted my host family before leaving the courtyard. Adults present replied, "May God gives us lots of pleasure today,"[25] or, "May God gives us a smooth day."[26] I then concluded with "May God grant your blessings."[27] Practices of blessing were commonly uttered during visits, greetings, and comings and goings. Locals were often amazed to hear a white foreigner giving blessings in Bambara. They would exclaim, "You became Bamanan!"[28] Or "You became Malian!"[29] These locutions illustrate the centrality of blessing in local etiquette. In retrospect, my involvement in this customary practice of blessing eased my integration into the local Muslim community. This customary practice was constitutive of local ethics, hence it shaped politeness, good manners, and pious disposition. In the same vein as the above analysis of *hɔrɔnya*, the speech act of blessing informs *adamadenya*.

INVOKING THE POWER OF THE INVISIBLE (OCCULT)

God is visible and intervenes on earth, but God has no contour. (Youssouf, hip-hop singer)

The domain of blessing, unlike *hɔrɔnya*, does not necessarily involve an act that connotes a pious disposition. To give a blessing is the speech act through which Muslims make requests to God. In a conversation, when the speaker starts with *Ala ka* (May God) and then his or her interlocutor answers *amiina* (amen),[30] you can be pretty sure that you are in the presence of a speech act of blessing. Muslims can also pronounce blessings alone in a room, such as in *maraboutic* and Sufi practices (e.g., Chappatte 2021). In both cases, the speech act of blessing involves three agents: the giver of the blessing, the receiver of the blessing, and God. The last agent, God, brings blessing its invisible dimension. In this regard, the speech act of blessing can be explored as a humanistic ritual (Rappaport 1999). By "humanistic" I mean that the speech act of blessing informs us about human ethics of the invisible. According to Islamic dogma, God is beyond any representation. Any worldly reproduction of God (e.g., image, statue) is thus prohibited as an act of idolatry. In southwest Mali, this prohibition did not mean that God is out of reach. On the contrary, Muslims, like Youssouf, stressed the presence and practical meanings of Almighty God in their lives.

Youssouf grew up in a village located in the Wassoulou region of Mali. Attracted by "urban music" broadcast on the radio, he went off on *tunga* in Bougouni. In 2010 he was involved in petty trade in town while developing his passion for hip-hop. In the late afternoons, Youssouf used to stop by the *grin* of Salif the tailor, where we sometimes met. I appreciated conversing with him because of his thoughtful mind. He once told me that "God is visible . . . but . . . has no contour." For Youssouf, God is beyond any representation because his presence is beyond any limits. God, therefore, cannot be encapsulated in delimited forms, hence he has no contour, but still God is visible on earth because his presence is felt and asked for in people's lives. Youssouf's locution expressed that the existential presence of Almighty God is an obvious mystery, a perception shared among Muslims in town. It is through the very speech act of blessing that Muslims ask for God's favor on earth. These requests mean that the interventions of God on earth are concrete, hence visible. They also mean that these interventions are God.[31] In other words, the origin and the concrete manifestation of such an intervention are both divine. As the origin of these interventions is linked to the "underneath" nature of God, the speech act of blessing refers to *the* power of the invisible that can decisively alter people's lives.

In Bougouni, Muslims pronounced blessings to summon the power of the invisible to their side, especially in life-cycle rituals because of their pivotal influence in people's life trajectory. An Islamic baptism, for instance, always concludes with the ritual of blessings. Typically, a crowd of men (regular prayers, neighbors, friends' parents) gather in the *carré* of the parents of the seven-day-old newborn after the first Muslim prayer of the day.[32] Muslim scholars sit on carpets. Around them, men sit on benches and chairs rented for the occasion. The male crowd listens to Muslim scholars who recite the appropriate *sura* in Arabic for the religious baptism. At this moment, the newborn receives a Muslim name and thus enters the Muslim community. As soon as the name-giving ceremony is over, a designated man stands up and announces in a loud voice, "We are now going to make blessings."[33] A silent ambiance of concentration takes over the crowd. Men place their palms in front of their face to get ready to receive blessings. The leading Muslim scholar then pronounces a long series of blessings in Bambara. This series is punctuated by the *amiinas* of the crowd.[34] Some men devotionally touch their forehead during the collective *amiinas*. This body language expresses a focused mind and shows where blessings are supposed to enter the body. The blessings are made for the newborn as well as for the attendant congregation of Muslims. The leading Muslim scholar asks God to protect the newborn against illness, misfortune, and the work of Satan. He also asks God to grant health and prosperity on earth for the Muslims who have made the joint effort to attend this baptism. Such a ritual of blessings solicits God's protection and favor on the earthly path.[35] Invoking the power of the invisible can also be more personal. Muslims, for instance, utter personal blessings during moments of uncertainty and suffering:

> Islam is about blessing; I mean not in the Mosque but alone during the night between you and God when everybody sleeps, and nobody disturbs you. Me, I know how to use the *wurudi* [Islamic rosary]. Each evening after the prayer I pronounce blessings to find *sababu juman* [divine cause].[36] . . . All the good things I got in Côte d'Ivoire, I got them thanks to blessings. (Amidou, carpenter)

Amidou grew up in a village next to the small border town of Manankoro. He spent his late childhood in Bamako before going off on *tunga* in a town of southern Côte d'Ivoire. He rushed back to southwest Mali when the Ivorian crisis burst. In early 2009 I wanted to buy a small wardrobe for my room. On my bike, I went looking for a carpenter workshop in town. I stopped by a workshop that was located along a street façade in the district of Medine and met Amidou. I then used to visit him in his workplace from time to time. Besides carpentry, Amidou farmed in the town's vicinity. He did not earn much money, but he lived in his own cement house. He used to thank God for what he had learned in traditional Islamic schools.

In his late childhood, Amidou spent six years in a traditional Islamic school in Bamako. He was initiated to a transmission of esoteric knowledge and secrets (Ar., *sirr*) between master and disciple through which he learned *maraboutic* practices,[37] such as a long series of blessings uttered at night following Islamic numerology (Chappatte 2021). Amidou had since kept performing maraboutic practices of blessing on a regular basis. For instance, he "prepared [his] *tunga* in Côte d'Ivoire by nights of invocation of the power of the invisible." He was thankful and not surprised when he obtained "a well-paid job" within the first year abroad. He then built a cement house in Bougouni, the bigger town of his home region, thanks to this job. The power of the invisible, Almighty God, can be invoked by and can act through human beings as a gift of grace called *barika*.

The etymology of *barika* stems from the Arabic term *baraka* (or *barakah*). It is a prominent Sufi concept related to blessing that means the "gift of grace" or the "power of sanctity" (Schimmel 2011, 82). Numerous studies have focused on the charismatic and institutional characteristics of *baraka* to make explicit the linkages between the saintly quality of grace and the worldly privileges (wealth and power) of Sufi religious authorities in West Africa (Brenner 1984; Cruise O'Brien and Coulon 1998; Schmitz 2000). In the edited book *African Islam and Islam in Africa*, for instance, *baraka* is defined as a beneficial force of divine origin that is the source of power and authority of saint lineages in Africa (Rosander and Westerlund 1997). These analyses of *baraka* among Muslim elites are relevant, but they do not entirely capture the implications of *baraka* for Muslims at large.[38] In Bougouni the concept of *barika* was intrinsically linked to the Bamanan figure of "the blessed child."[39]

INTRODUCING *"THE BLESSED CHILD"*

In Bambara "the blessed child" is called either *barika den* or *dubabu den*. Both terms (*barika* and *dubabu*) mean "blessing." In local discourses, some people do not distinguish between them; others do so in terms of their origins. This nuance stresses the relationship between God and human beings. In this regard, Salif the tailor used to tell me that *"dubabu* and *barika* are linked like rice and sauce." Whereas *dubabu* is voiced by human beings, *barika* is only granted by God. Boubacar the small trader in *yuguyuguw* explained to me that "people give blessings. God may transform their blessings into *barika*."[40] He added, "Blessing is the path where *barika* lays."[41] What makes God transform a blessing into *barika* then? Muslims in Bougouni used to tell me that God turns a deaf ear to blessings uttered by someone without *barika*, because only a good Muslim can attract God's favor. Put differently, *barika* was linked to local conceptions of a good Muslim. In this way, a *barika den* is automatically a *dubabu den* because God has granted people's blessings upon him, thanks to his piety. However, a *dubabu den* is not necessarily a *barika den* because people's blessings may not be fulfilled by God in case they are not pious. *Dubabu* expresses the social dimension of blessing, and *barika* its invisible (occult, underneath) dimension. Ultimately, only God can put a child on the blessed path:

> If you do not have *barika* and someone gives you millions of francs, you will not be able to build something. You will only waste your money. However, if you have *barika* and you possess only one pack of cigarettes in your shop,

step by step your trade will prosper. Sooner or later, you will be rich. (Ablaye, manager)

As explained by Ablaye, a former student at the IFM of Bougouni who is lengthily introduced in the next section, a blessed child is a person whose earthly path will be prosperous. All that a person undertakes in life blooms because God has blessed that person. How, then, do Muslims detect the presence of this blessedness? Often, they refer to "the blessed child" when a lucky phenomenon occurs.

I used to spend late afternoon in the *grin* of Salif the tailor. There we chatted, drank tea, and gazed around. On one occasion, Salif suddenly exclaimed, "Ehhhh!" We all looked at him. He had a big smile on his face while passing his mobile phone from one hand to another. He then told us, "I just received 1,000 FCFA of mobile credits just like that! [snapping his finger]." The sender of these mobile credits most likely dialed Salif's number in error. But one of his friends blurted, "You are a blessed child!" because gaining mobile credits in this way does not happen every day. On another occasion, we were observing traffic on the tarred road around midday. A group of policemen were systematically checking all motorbikes passing by. From the *grin* we noticed that riders often quarreled with police officers. A member of the *grin* joshingly said, "Even if you follow the law, a policeman searching for a small banknote will show you the contrary!"[42] Another rider was coming. We were all about to feel pity for the driver's expected fate. Policemen looked at the rider . . . but did not ask him to stop. They ignored him. The rider continued on his way freely. Salif commented in a stunned voice, "This guy is a blessed child! Luck is with him!" In Bougouni, *garijɛgɛ* (luck) is never a random phenomenon. *Garijɛgɛ* is God's favor that accompanies the blessed child throughout his life. It is therefore said that God protects the blessed child and grants him prosperity in life. The blessed child therefore avoids misfortune and moves forward toward prosperity.

OBEDIENCE TO TRADITIONAL FAMILY

I first met Ablaye in early 2009 when I was searching for a place to eat around Bougouni's bus station. In a juxtaposing street, I curiously entered an indoor restaurant in a town where most eating spots were mere *gargote*. These small restaurants were rudimentary: a front bench, a table with cooking pots and plastic cutlery on it, a female cook behind. In this indoor restaurant, however, the clientele could sit on proper chairs and eat at clean tables while watching TV. Moreover, this upgraded restaurant offered local dishes for the same affordable price as *gargotes*. Thanks to its central location, comfort, and affordability, this restaurant was often full during lunch and dinner times. Its clientele also appreciated the warm welcome they received from the manager, Ablaye. Over the months, I became friends with Ablaye, a young man in his mid-twenties who grew up in a village of the Wassoulou region. After obtaining his DEF, he moved to Bougouni to pursue his studies at the IFM. But Ablaye had ambition; he did not want to waste time in a school that was considered to be a professional dead end. "How could a primary school teacher become rich?" Ablaye sniggered. After a while, he dropped out of the IFM to manage the former *gargote* of his "older sister" Oumou. By "older sister" Ablaye meant a daughter of a paternal uncle who was his elder. His *tunga* in Bougouni was therefore not totally away from home.

Like Ablaye, local Muslims originated the path of the blessed child first within the traditional family and second in the local community. The blessed child is, above all, a "child" (*den*). A child is dependent on its parents by filiation. In this way, the figure of the blessed child reminded Ablaye that he belonged to a specific line of descent. His person was marked by the history of his lineage. For him, the way ancestors lived influences the lives of their descendants. This hereditary principle is a sort of blood momentum that is transmitted and shaped from generation through generation via kinship.[43] In this way the living generation also shapes this hereditary principle. Here, the attitude of a wife toward her husband is of the utmost importance.[44] Local men and women of all social statuses used to say that God blesses children if their mother obeys (*obéir*) her husband. This popular belief reinforced the traditional submission of wives to husbands. Locals especially stressed that a *dubabu den* cannot be a *barika den* if his or her mother did and does not respect (*bonya*) her husband.[45] On this subject, Ryan Skinner wrote, "Through her dress and gesture, the woman embodies the pious obedience of the Mande wife" (2015, 43). This peculiar path of blessedness, moreover, extended to Bougouni's social life. It was said that blessed children seek blessings of people in general. More eagerly, blessed children seek blessings of their parents and elders. God indeed listens more carefully to the blessings uttered by parents for their children and to the blessings uttered by elders for their juniors. Behind this widespread belief lay the idea that elders are closer to God than juniors because pious disposition matures with age. This belief also reinforced the traditional obedience of children toward their parents and elders. Obedience as a kind of *bonya* was also translated into politeness, gift giving, and esteem.

I once accompanied Ablaye to visit his relatives who lived in a village behind the small town of Yanfolila. Since his move to Bougouni, he had regularly paid visits to his native village. Shortly after our arrival, Ablaye sought out his elders. He first looked for the head of his family (*gwatigi*). We found him in his house. Kneeling and looking down, he greeted us and gave him 1,000 FCFA. The old man thanked him with a series of blessings. He then looked for another elder of the family, an uncle who had raised him after the early passing of his father;[46] he again performed an esteem greeting ritual. Finally, he greeted his mother and gave her 2,000 FCFA. She blessed him at length. Ablaye told me, "The strength of a man comes from his source. . . . The elders will be pleased with me and will bless me." Such esteem greeting ritual toward kin elders by a junior was typical in southwest Mali. In this way, the traditional authority of the elders was strengthened via the occult power of their blessing. In parallel to seeking elders' blessings, the juniors avoided confronting them because they feared their curse. The curse (*danga*) is the opposite of the blessing. Like blessing, the curse can be pronounced by human beings, but it is only given by God. By contrast to the blessed child, the cursed child (*danga den*) is blamed as uneducated, impolite, lazy, and selfish. It was said that such persons would encounter only misery and misfortune on earth. Hell would most likely be their fate after death. Narrations about the consequences of such curses were frequently voiced among the inhabitants of Bougouni:

> Blessing is the respect by and the acceptance of your parents, your elders. It is a life principle. It is a philosophy. It is deep. It is the fact of God. If you follow it, your life will be eased. It is like that here. If you refuse to help your parents, they will get irritated. They can even curse you. If you run away from them, you will only collect misfortune there. (Ablaye)

During this visit Ablaye also added, "The mother is sacred in Mali. We fear disobeying her because we fear her curse." His thought joined what numerous people in Bougouni told me: the curse as well as the blessing of the mother is stronger than those of the father. Cheick Mahamadou Chérif Keïta explains that in the traditional Mande (polygamous) family, the father-child relationship is marked by competition, whereas the mother-child relationship is marked by love (1995, 135–37). In this regard, Fousseini the carter confided to me that when he expressed to his parents his desire to go off *tunga*, they disagreed over this matter. His father wanted him to keep on fishing where his ancestors had always fished: in the river next to their native village. On the other hand, his mother supported his desire to leave. Fousseini tried to convince his father to change his mind but without success. He later decided to go on *tunga* in Bamako anyway, since he had at least secured his mother's blessings. Fousseini had no doubt that the fact that the blessing of his mother was more powerful than the possible curse of his father. The traditional path of the blessed child has been a gatekeeper of how power works in Mande society between wives and husbands and elders and juniors. In the traditional family, this path has also been a gatekeeper of the mother's prominence over the father in securing invisible protection for the aspirations of their grown children.

OBEDIENCE AND ASPIRATION:
WHEN THE VALUE OF WORK MATTERS

Clients of Oumou's catering business often told me, "Ablaye, he is a junior who has done well."[47] When Ablaye became the manager of his older sister's restaurant, her restaurant had been a *gargote* for years. She earned some money but never plowed it back into the *gargote*. Ablaye came with a new ambition. He convinced Oumou to invest more money in her catering business in order to attract more clients. He then supervised the construction of a small cement house with a wooden extension that included a small terrace furnished with newly purchased tables and chairs as well as a secondhand refrigerator and TV set. He then decorated the building with colorful paintings. Outdoor at the entrance, Ablaye also installed a large board where potential clients could read the menus and fixed prices from the street. The first time I entered this restaurant, I was captivated by its cleanness and its friendly atmosphere. Not surprisingly, the renovated restaurant quickly became popular in Bougouni. Ablaye's business acumen turned Oumou's petty trade into a story of prosperity. The turnover of diners in the restaurant multiplied by five.

In accordance with custom, Ablaye did not ask his older sister for a wage. Hoping for a later generous gesture from his older sister, he instead displayed an attitude of respect, courage, and patience.[48] While Oumou prepared food at home, Ablaye managed the restaurant from late morning until the evening. Helped by two younger sisters of Oumou, he welcomed the clients, took their orders, served them, accepted their money, and cleaned the place. The following morning of each working day he gave the previous day's takings to Oumou. Months passed. When working at her former *gargote*, Oumou's earnings were just enough to handle daily expenses. Because of the success of the renovated restaurant, however, within a few months she bought new clothes for her children, a building lot in town, and a new motorbike (among other items). She also opened a bank account to place her savings. After a year in this working context, however, Ablaye's patience reached a critical point.

Observing the new prosperity of his older sister, Ablaye was not happy, because Oumou had not yet made a gesture to thank him for his daily hard labor in the restaurant. Arguing that he was the true *promoteur* (instigator) of the current success of Oumou's catering business, he confided to me, "Without my help, her [Oumou's] business would still be the same petty *gargote!*" As months passed, he progressively lost patience. He then broke the silence by asking Oumou to help him buy a secondhand Jakarta motorbike. She sidestepped his demand. He insisted. They quarreled over his demand for a month. Their relationship deteriorated. His older sister did not change her mind. Ablaye consequently left the restaurant, a move that he considered as a *grève* (strike). The decline in clientele was felt rapidly. Ablaye's business acumen no longer enlivened the restaurant. His older brothers in town then intervened. They firmly told Ablaye that as Oumou's younger brother, he should not contradict her. On the contrary, he should go back to work in her restaurant. Ablaye listened but did not obey them. Oumou therefore asked their *gwatigi* (family's oldest uncle) to settle their conflict. Ablaye was summoned back to his home village by the old man.

I visited Ablaye shortly after his return. Three months had passed since he had left the restaurant. I undertook a small detour to the restaurant before heading to his room, which was located in the vicinity of the bus station. I noticed signs of poor maintenance. A table and a few chairs were cracked, the terrace was dusty, and a pile of rubbish was openly juxtaposed to the restaurant. I then crossed the road to meet Ablaye in his room. He told me that back in his home village, his uncle had lectured him about the importance of birthright between generations in keeping the family united. The old man also warned him that young people should not show the way to their elders. Reflecting upon the traditional control of elders over the youth's workforce, he told me, "All these rules are linked to our environment. They are *inventeries* [*laugh*]. But without these *inventeries* the social life here would be difficult."[49]

The slang term *inventeries* had a negative connotation. Ablaye explained to me that *invent.eries* combines the French words *invention* (invention) with *connerie* (crap). He recognized that traditional rules of filial duty aim to prevent dissension within families, but he blamed elders' abuse of these rules for being detrimental of the emancipation of their juniors. For Ablaye, when elders are abusing these rules, the path of the blessed child becomes mere *inventeries*. He did not contest the authority of his older sister per se; she was the patron because she financed the business. He just thought that work (*travail, baara*) must be rewarded even within the family. He did not accept that birthright justifies free work anymore. He added:

> Someone who is more than 70 years old has no *avenir* [future]. Someone who is young has an *avenir* that needs the help of people to be built. I have seen so many talented older brothers upon whom our elders put pressure. They [talented older brothers] obeyed and now they are poor.

Finally, Ablaye did not obey the elders of his family. Nor did he reconsider his decision, because his older sister kept refusing his demand. Two months later, he moved to Bamako to work with a friend who was involved in the business of interior decoration and events. I came back to Bougouni a few years later to find that Oumou's catering business was back at it had been earlier: a mere *gargote*. As for Ablaye, he found a well-paying job in an NGO operating in the region of Kaye.

Ablaye's conflict with his older sister around the value of work in the context of a family business illustrates that in the Bougouni of the early 2010s, juniors understood the path of the blessed child as based on the following interpretation of *adamadenya*: juniors' obedience toward elders' status goes hand in hand with elders' care toward juniors' future. Such conflicts were common in Bougouni. Most juniors did not question the ancient nature of this obedience; rather, they argued with elders about the temporality of the reciprocity involved in this social deal. By resisting juniors' wish to decrease the temporality of this reciprocity, elders inclined juniors to go off on *tunga* away from any family ties.

"Mande Islam": The Politics of Labeling Local Ethics

The anthropologist Roy F. Ellen (1983) argued that the difference between *adat* (custom) and Islam in Southeast Asia highlights the existence of an unclear and thick boundary made of highly complex, intertwined, reinterpreted, and reordered integrated elements of *adat* within Islam and vice versa. What is understood as Islamic practice by some people might be understood as the perfection of *adat* by other people of the same local community. Similar arguments are made by Louis Brenner concerning Muslim identities in Mali (1993a) and by Anne Doquet (2007) concerning Islamic knowledge and non-Islamic knowledge in Mali. Tal Tamari (1996) shows how most Islamic education in Mali is delivered in local languages and among individuals still engaged in what is interpreted as Bamanaya practices. My analysis of how Mande humanism (*adamadenya*) is embedded in the local figures of "the noble Muslim" and "the blessed child" also demonstrates that a sharp distinction between a sphere of custom (*laada*) and one of Islam is dubious. In the Bougouni of the early 2010s, Islam was constitutive to experience and not simply an order imposed upon experience. Instead of questioning the Islamic nature of a practice, the analyst should investigate the dynamics through which Islam is evoked.

In Bougouni the Bamanan way of life was alive, active, and ubiquitous on the street. Its ubiquity, however, was difficult for locals to realize, because the human mind does not notice the obvious. It is there, period. In public conversation, the evocation of this way of life was even contested, especially by observant Muslims. Bamanaya, the Bamanan way of life, was still too much associated with the un-Islamism. The term "Mande," moreover, was not used to label the origin of local ethics. Locals sometimes referred to *facε* (the legacy of the father) but mostly in terms of Bamanan occult practices (see Peterson 2011). The labeling of local ethics was being Islamized, although values and virtues that shape Muslim life stemmed from mille-feuille formations of Mande ethics in different domains of social life even if these processes were not mentioned, denied, or confirmed. Part of this process of labeling shall be understood within the post-1991 revival of Muslim expression in public Mali.

In 2009 the Malian Assembly voted for a *nouveau code de la famille* (new family code). Muslim associations and some political parties organized demonstrations against this code in Bamako as well as in most provincial towns of Mali. They denounced a *nouveau code de la famille* that went against Islamic precepts. Eventually, the president refused to give his approval to the *nouveau code de la famille* and requested a revision from the Malian Assembly. The modified version of the code, called the *Code des Personnes et de la Famille*, was eventually ratified in December 2011. Western media criticized the Islamist tone of the modified version of the new code and deplored the fact that the Malian Assembly had ceded to conservative Muslim forces.[50] In parallel, Islamic media criticized the Western influences on the first version of the *nouveau code de la famille* and praised the ratified version as a victory for Islam.

What I observed in Bougouni, however, differed from these media analyses. I ate in a *shefantigi* catering place overlooking a main tarred road of the town when the demonstration against this law was passing by. I saw Salif the tailor in the crowd of demonstrators. We greeted each other and he rejoined the crowd. I met him later and we spoke about the issue of the *Code des Personnes et de la Famille*. Like many of my local friends, Salif was against the code because some of its changes did not correspond to the (traditional) Mande family. Instead of "wives must obey their husband,"[51] the *Code des Personnes et de la Famille* framed gender relations in term of "mutual respect."[52] Moreover, the new code extended the rights of inheritance to children born out of wedlock. Beside a minority of educated families living in urban areas, most Malians opposed this reform. More importantly, many Malians acted so with little reference to Islam. Salif told me, "This has nothing to do with Islam; it is our culture, that's it." He demonstrated because he felt that this reform scorned one of the bases of Mande family: patriarchal authority.

In the evening, I raised the issue of the *Code des Personnes et de la Famille* in the *grin* of the shopkeeper just off the courtyard of my host family. A local teacher told me that Islamic associations recuperated this popular discontent. For him, these associations managed to become the standard-bearers of the discontent in the media to turn this grassroots claim for the respect of local customs into an Islamic agenda, although Malians knew that the content of what demonstrators defended was not Islamic per se. Another member of this *grin* moved the conversation to the rights of inheritance for children born out of wedlock. A woman of a next-door *gargote* jokingly added, "Men are involved in extramarital relations. Then they are afraid that the child is not theirs. They do not want to recognize the child. They wonder, 'The child of the goat comes from which ram?'" To her mind, what was at stake was to safeguard the Mande patrilineal society. Western as well as Muslim media "Islamized" this popular claim, whereas most inhabitants of Bougouni first criticized the *nouveau code de la famille* as irreconcilable with a way of life based on local norms and practices of social ethics, which were widely interpreted to be of Mande origin. Islam is well and truly a local religion, but making it as *the* marker of the local culture remains simply some people's claim. In southwest Mali, locals understood Islam as being within Mande culture.

CHAPTER 7

Social Motions
Chinese Products and Material Modernity

Many *aventuriers* were engaged in a new livelihood: small traders of Chinese goods. They installed stallholders known as shops *par-terre* (literally, "on the ground") in busy locations, such as in and around the bus station and on the street façades of main roads of the town center. Others circulated deep into residential areas as street vendors who hawked a set of fantasy accessories (e.g., toys, caps, club flags) and daily items (e.g., tissues, batteries, padlocks) to those (e.g., wives, elders, children) who remained at home during the daylight.[1]

Aventuriers who could invest a bit more money in trading sold more valuable Chinese goods, such as mobile phone items, Western-like clothes, and kitchen utensils. As these goods were markedly cheaper than Western-manufactured goods, start-up costs for trading became much lower than during the epoch of Moussa Traoré. In the 1990s most traders in town were still selling expensive Western-manufactured products; to be a trader meant to be among the local better-off, since only a minority of Bougouni's dwellers could save enough money to start a trade. Following the privatization of the Malian market after 1991 and the liberal opening of China under Deng Xiaoping, trade between these two countries has been boosted considerably since the turn of the century. Thanks to the new opportunities to gain business visas offered by China, Malian wholesalers located in Le Grand Marché and Marché Rose of Bamako have been able to supply the Malian market with cheap manufactured goods by making short business trips, especially to Guangzhou, the "centre for African migrants and itinerant traders" in China (Haugen 2011, 166).[2] In 2010 local traders bulk-bought these Chinese goods in Bamako to then retail them in provincial towns through the country.[3]

In Bougouni I quickly noticed that Chinese goods, which were flooding local markets, shops, and households, contributed to an urban way of life based on material prosperity, and this was especially true among *aventuriers* in search of *tunga*.[4] This chapter explores the possible social mobility brought by the consumption of Chinese goods in town. In this classic sociological perspective, the existential motion is studied in relation to the whole social structure. In contrast to utility theories of consumer behavior, it attempts "to supply a motivational structure to consumption" (Friedman 1994, 6) by articulating consumption to an urban lifestyle and upward mobility. The first part of the chapter studies the consumption of "things" as a process central to the creation of status (van Binsbergen 2005) that constantly redraws "the lines of social relationship" (Douglas and Isherwood 1996, 39). It especially illustrates how *aventuriers* consumed made-in-China goods to display a material prosperity that they associated with a modern urban identity.[5] Due to their low quality, these goods were nonetheless denigrated as cheap and short-lasting imitations of Western products. The chapter then addresses the ambivalent feelings generated by the consumption of Chinese goods: while responding to *aventuriers'* aspirations to upward mobility in terms of consumption as a way of life, these cheap goods often gave them not more than a second-rate modernity.

THE AFFORDABILITY OF CHINESE PRODUCTS

Aïcha grew up in the small town of Yanfolila, the administrative center of a neighboring *cercle*. Five years ago, she moved to Bougouni to attend the nearest secretarial school from her hometown. Her uncle also lived in the main town of southwest Mali. Afterward, as she did not find paid employment, she started running a small *pharmacie par-terre* (street vendor of medicines) on a street façade at the center of Bougouni. Waiting for clients, she used to sit in the morning and late afternoon on a small wooden stool while looking after a pile of boxes, tablets, and pills displayed on a mat in front of her. Like most street vendors, she killed time by greeting, teasing, and chatting with passers-by and neighboring vendors. I sometimes stopped by her point of sale on my way to the big market. Once, while we were taking news from our respective relatives, two young men came and asked for four *comprimés* (tablets of paracetamol). Aïcha replied, "Which ones? You want French or Chinese tablets?" They asked the cost. She informed them that one French tablet cost twenty-five francs (US$0.05), and two Chinese tablets cost twenty-five francs as well. They finally opted for the Chinese tablets, bought them, and continued on their way. Aïcha then began to grumble about the French tablets. They were not expensive compared to other Western tablets, but she would not buy them again because of the difficulty of selling them. "Although the quality is not the same, people prefer the Chinese ones because they are cheaper!" she argued.

During the first months of my stay in Bougouni, the lock on my next-door neighbor's door broke. This distant relative of my host family had recently moved into town to work as a hotel attendant. A locksmith came and replaced the lock with a new Chinese-made lock. However, that one broke after only two weeks. My next-door neighbor then told me that he preferred to buy a Chinese lock for 1,250 FCFA (US$2.50), which could break at any moment, rather than buy a made-in-France Vachette lock for 7,500–10,000 FCFA (US$15–20), which would last for years. With what little money he earned, he simply wanted to buy other things as well: mobile phone credits, a new T-shirt, and small batteries for his flashlight. The locksmith came back and managed to fix the Chinese lock without changing it. After having listened to one of our conversations about the lock issue and Chinese goods in general, an old woman who was visiting the mother of my host family this day jokingly told us:

> Chinese are very clever. They adapt themselves to your money. Tell them how much you possess and then they fabricate you a good corresponding to your budget. For instance, if you have 2,000 francs for a lock, they will give you one worth 2,000 francs. If you have only 200 francs, they will manage to manufacture one worth 200 francs [*laugh*].

For most inhabitants of Bougouni, prices of goods mattered more than their quality insofar as opting for lower prices multiplied the consumption. These people therefore took the risk of buying cheap Chinese goods because this strategy of systematically consuming goods with lower prices allowed them to make further purchases. They wished to gain access to the "society of consumption" to take part in "globalization" today, not tomorrow (Bredeloup and Bertoncello 2006, 208). In other words, they perceived the consumption of foreign-manufactured goods as an up-to-date way to be connected to the wider world. This was especially the case when they could consume regularly and buy sophisticated goods. Chinese companies have well understood this African niche, so in Bougouni their cheaply manufactured goods covered most contemporary material demands, such as beauty products, household items (e.g., plates, thermoses, cups), clothes, medicines, accessories (e.g., sunglasses, jewelery, toys), everyday electronic products (e.g., radios, flashlights), spare parts for light engineering (e.g., cables, bulbs, batteries), hardware, bicycles, motorbikes, and, most recently, cars. Whereas most scholars have studied the increasing presence of China on Malian soil in terms of investments, buildings, and men (Bourdarias 2009, 2010; Sanogo 2008), I realized that in 2010 it was through things called *produits chinois* (Chinese goods) by Malians themselves that China had recently managed to enter deep into all Malian households. Cheap Chinese goods, moreover, allowed *aventuriers* to accede to a wide range of formerly as well as new prestigious manufactured goods.

"CHINESE *ONT VULGARISÉ* THE VIDEO RECORDERS"

Late during my stay in Bougouni, I heard of the existence of a *cinéma* (movie theater). Intrigued by what I oddly felt as a belated discovery, I decided to visit this place. Instead of a thriving movie theater, however, I discovered a rather run-down and deserted building attached to a vast enclosed area invaded by wild vegetation. In a corner I encountered a TV and DVD player repair shop. Two young men who were watching a kung fu movie on a TV set informed me that the movie theater had to close during "the time of Alpha" (1992–2002), the former president of Mali, because it showed "only old movies." They added that these movies were still shown for children but only during Muslim celebrations. Not totally convinced by their responses, I left the place with a question in my mind: Why was this movie theater closed in what had been a fast-growing town since the early 1990s? Nouhoum Doumbia, who was the first mayor of Bougouni, later elucidated the reason for its closure in a conversation we had about the development of Bougouni during the last two decades.

> In 1985 I was mayor. You needed the authorization of the mayor for plots and building permits. A friend came to me with a file. He wanted to build a movie theater behind the Siraba Togola Auditorium. . . . I advised him to build a hotel instead. He asked why. I said that in ten years nobody would go to the movie theater. He replied that this was impossible. I argued that the Chinese

would soon make them [TVs, video recorders, and cassette movies] *à vils prix* [cheap prices] and that people would buy the cassette movies they want in shops and watch them at home with their family. . . . Chinese *ont vulgarisé* [have popularized] the video recorders. Who wants to pay for a seat in a movie theater now?

Cheap Chinese goods have made accessible to Malian masses what were formerly prestige goods, such as TV sets and DVD players. This opening in sophisticated consumption abruptly ended the movie theater business in Mali. Provincial towns still bore the scar of this *revolute* epoch: run-down and deserted buildings of former movie theaters. In 2010 the only movie theater still in operation in Mali was the Babemba Cinéma in Bamako. Nouhoum's idiom *à vils prix* for cheap prices is thus meaningful because the adjective *vil*, in addition to emphasizing the very low cost of such products, connotes the rapid devaluation brought about by such prices to what were formerly prestigious products of "distinction" (Bourdieu 1979). The Malian society was not perceived as being divided into social classes in a Western sense. But still the possession of prestigious goods distinguished people moving forward toward prosperity from those who felt poor and were stuck in poverty. Similarly, his idiom "Chinese *ont vulgarisé* the video recorders" stresses that when expensive products become cheap, hence accessible to all, they tend to lose their prestige. In other words, these formerly expensive goods become *vulgaire*, which means "common," therefore banal and hence valueless in terms of social distinction. These cheap Chinese goods brought changes in the material culture of the inhabitants of Malian provincial towns. These changes have caused a genuine turning point in terms of a consumption motivated by social distinction and access to mass consumption. In the 1980s most manufactured goods, the so-called *France aurevoir* or *Europe aurevoir* goods, were expensively imported from the West and exclusive to a tiny urban elite only. Two decades later, however, *aventuriers* could be poor but trendy in urban Mali thanks to these Chinese goods.

BEING POOR BUT TRENDY IN PROVINCIAL BOUGOUNI

Boubacar the *yuguyugu* trader left the traditional Qur'anic school during his late teenage years to work as a hawker in the nearest town from his native village: Mopti, the capital of the central north *région* of Mopti. He decided to turn away from the traditional occupation of *sɛnɛkɛla*.[6] For him, money (*wari*) was a mundane necessity that he interpreted as the principal door leading to a prosperous life. Back in his native village, he also felt the weight of the wild fluctuation in food production caused by the environmental degradation in the Sahel as well as the land-farming pressure created by the region's demographic growth. As Mopti was already full of hawkers, he then moved south to the big town of Ségou and thereafter to Bamako for similar reasons. In expensive and sprawling Bamako, he also faced difficulties to make ends meet. Hearing about new trade opportunities related to the growth of Bougouni,[7] he learned that in Bougouni one could easily find a spot to start a small trade. In less than two years he indeed became an established stallholder who benefited from a fixed trading spot in the central market. With his little bit of savings, he also managed to build a small sheet metal hut where he sold Chinese-made *yuguyugu* clothes previously bought in the Marché Rose of Bamako. Despite his ascending prosperity, his monthly income was no more than 50,000 francs (US$100). In his daily life, he was slightly above being able to make ends meet.

Boubacar used to wake up shortly before the first regular daily prayer. He ate a light breakfast with his wife, Aminata, and their two young boys. He then walked fifteen minutes to reach the central market. Afterward, he spent all day in his rudimentary shop trying to sell enough *yuguyuguw* to cover at least "the family's daily food expenses" (*nasɔngɔ*). His wife popped in at noon to bring him lunch. Boubacar worked for several more hours before closing the shop at dusk and then going home with his daily receipts in hand. Aminata was preparing the family's dinner, and he saw his two boys playing together in the common courtyard with kids from the neighborhood. During daylight Aminata used to sit at the threshold of the courtyard's entrance, where she sold salty pea fritters and sweet-potato chips to passers-by. On market day she operated as a street vendor of seasonal fruits. Boubacar encouraged his wife's petty trade. As head of the family, Boubacar took on the family expenses, but he welcomed his wife's financial support, especially when his daily sales were low.

Their financial situation did not allow them to rent a *maison à étages* (multistory house) made of bricks and cement and equipped with modern equipment, such as showers, Western-style toilets, and air-conditioning units. Such houses were an important sign of prosperity in urban Mali (see Choplin 2020, 157–60). Luxurious houses had recently started to appear in Bougouni among the numerous traditional mud houses with thatched roofs and enclosed by mud fences, which were, by contrast, increasingly associated with village life. The former president, Amadou Toumani Touré (nicknamed

ATT), even promoted the cement villa as the habitat of modern urban Mali through the social housing project called *ATT-bougou* (ATT town/village).[8] In 2010 an *ATT-bouguou* area made of a few dozen cement villas was under construction at the exit toward Yanfolila. But Boubacar's family was too poor to be considered for a social housing project that was designed for specific modest families: lower urban employees with regular incomes, such as public school teachers and police officers (low-ranking civil servants). They did not live in a mud house reinforced with cement rendering and equipped with roofs of sheet metal, the standard housing built by slightly better-off urban households. Instead they had to be content with a rented room in a crumbling mud house within a *cour commune*. Their housing overlooked an unlit narrow, sandy, and particularly uneven street of the old town. Their room was modestly equipped with a couple of mats, cookware, and bags where they put their clothes, private items, and a few valuable goods.

As a married man, father, and a small trader established in the town's center for a couple of years already, Boubacar was nonetheless respected by *aventuriers* who had recently settled in the town, such as Yacouba, a young single man from a village near Youwarou (a small town of northern Mali) who had moved to Bougouni two months earlier. I often met Yacouba in the early evening at Boubacar's home. Wearing clothes covered by reddish dust, Yacouba always looked exhausted. Since his arrival he had lived a daily struggle to seek money as a hawker of cheap watches and sunglasses made in China. For this, he had to walk all day across the town in search of customers. A couple of other newcomers in the town also regularly visited Boubacar and his wife during the evening, where they relaxed before heading home. I used to find them at around 8 p.m. on mats Aminata had placed in the common courtyard just off their room. There we all sat around the teapot we typically shared together along with various jokes, exchanges, and debates. At some point during our conversations, Aminata brought us some finger food and traditional Malian dishes, which we cheerfully shared together.

During these evenings of conviviality Boubacar acted as a host, a respectful traditional status in the West African Sahel (Whitehouse 2012). This type of respect, however, has a cost. Unlike his guests, Boubacar could afford to regularly provide sugar and tea for them. And due to his household's little savings, his wife was also able to cook extra food from time to time. After a day of hard labor, new *aventuriers* in Bougouni often felt empty stomachs, and Aminata's salty pea fritters and sweet potato chips enlivened the conviviality within the group. But it was especially on the evening of the Muslim sacred day (Friday) that Boubacar's family provided prestigious food and service for his visiting friends. In addition to the usual tea and sugar, Aminata often cooked a generous plate of *riz-sauce* (rice served with various sauces), a valued meal in Mali because rice was an expensive cereal associated with urban life and feast days, compared to millet, the basic cereal of rural Mali. The plate of *riz-sauce* was further complemented with a generous portion of meat, a rare luxury in poor families. At the beginning of the evening, moreover, Boubacar entered his room and took out from a big bag one of his most precious possessions: a secondhand TV made in China that he had recently bought in Bougouni. He had also purchased a secondhand car battery, which he attached to the TV set. As his housing was located next to a secondary street that was far away from the local electricity network, Boubacar opted for the battery instead of buying the costly electric wires and meter necessary for connection to the two big generators run by the EDM Mali Company in town. He still had to pay for loading the battery up during the days he wanted to make the TV work. Then, together with his family and friends, we watched the popular TV program *Top Etoiles* on ORTM, in which musical clips of Malian artists were broadcast, while drank tea, joked, and chatted about various issues. Later, although most people did not watch it, the TV remained switched on to provide a proper sense of hospitality. Two decades ago people had to buy their seat in front of the couple of TV sets and two cinemas found in Bougouni. But since the arrival of cheap Chinese TV and DVD players, this line of business was now finished for a few years already. In the 2000s the TV set became an appliance found in many urban familial compounds while still being rare in rural Mali.

Boubacar and Aminata each also possessed a mobile phone, which they placed on mats next to them during these evenings of conviviality. Their mobile phones were on display for practical and particularly ostentatious purposes. Boubacar and Aminata could answer calls quickly, but this happened rarely. Friends, who often had no mobile phone, would regularly manipulate the hosts' mobile phones either by playing games or by discussing their features (e.g., ringtones, music, radio, pictures) and prices. With the recent arrival of Chinese-made mobile phones in Mali, Boubacar and Aminata were able to buy secondhand phones. Both praised Chinese goods because they allowed Malian masses to get access to formerly expensive technologies. As in numerous other African countries (see Hahn and Kibora 2008; Archambault 2010, 2011, 2017), in less than a decade the mobile phone had evolved from a luxury product (early 2000s) to an affordable item among urbanites (early 2010s). In early 2000 only new and secondhand *France aurevoir* mobile phones were found in the country. Malitel, the state company that monopolized the market, sold expensive SIM cards and mobile credits that were accessible only for rich people living in a couple of big towns connected to the mobile network. The market in communication was liberalized in early 2000. Two years later, Ikatel (affiliated with France Telecom and renamed Orange Mali in 2006) expanded quickly in Mali, partly through ambitious marketing strategies that have completely transformed the market in mobile phones there. The price of SIM cards and credits for Orange Mali became affordable to ordinary Malians; in a few years, it tumbled from more than 200,000 francs to less than 500 francs. In parallel, the mobile network reached most small towns and big villages. Such fast and far-reaching changes were further facilitated by the arrival of cheap Chinese-made mobile phones, which accelerated the bankruptcy of the market for traditional telephone boxes in Mali.

However, Boubacar's and Aminata's mobile phones did not have the trendy options that Malian urbanites were looking for at that time. They did not have, for instance, the money to buy the new Chinese-made mobile phone that had recently arrived in the Malian market. This mobile phone was in vogue among better-off families in town due to its double chip system, slot for memory card, fancy façade, Bluetooth, music, video, and photographic and TV services. In urban Mali the mobile phone turned into an accessible prestigious item subject to routine upgrades, exchange, and bargaining. In this regard, the mobile phone particularly marked the dynamism of its owner. As a recent technological, clothing-like, item of ostentation, the mobile phone was *the* accessory for those who wanted to be considered *à la page* (trendy). Even with their school education, Boubacar and Aminata were not able to write text messages. But with the invention of the *zɛrɛ* (watermelon) *orange*, a mini–Orange Mali top-up credit of 100 francs (US$0.20) available on the market since 2008, they could call and have a short mobile conversation with friends in town or relatives in Mopti, for instance. But they rarely did so because the *zɛrɛ* Orange service could quickly burden their already limited budget. In case the communication was not about an urgent matter, they preferred beeping people, hoping these people would call them back. Apart from listening to music, their mobile phones were rarely used for what we initially used to consider as the mobile phone's primary functions: calling and texting. In the liberal context of post-1991 Mali, consumption as a marker of status has strengthened. For their guests, Boubacar and Aminata's consumption of a few trendy goods illustrated a "civilized" material culture. In other words, they were moving forward toward a desired urban (modern) way of life that most *aventuriers* aspired to.

In Mali, Boubacar faced years of hardship in *tunga* in big towns and the capital. In the provincial town of Bougouni, however, he felt that he was finally getting on the right track. Boubacar's family started to enjoy a sense of moving forward toward prosperity. Helped by his devoted wife, Boubacar was able to cope with the daily expenses of his family and to buy a few trendy goods made in China while prospecting for the purchase of other valuable Chinese goods. One prestigious good he was lacking was a motorized means of transport. Boubacar could afford to buy a bicycle. However, the once-prized bicycle, bought with money earned on the plantations of Côte d'Ivoire during the 1960s in southern Mali (Peterson 2011, 197–98), had become old-fashioned since the turn of the century. In Bougouni urbanites sarcastically associated the bicycle with a *broussard* (bushmen) way of life. In 2010 it was the motorbike that was the type of vehicle in vogue in town. Because of the then-recent arrival of Chinese motorbikes in Africa (Khan Mohammad 2016), the price of a motorbike was cut by 75 percent in less than a decade compared to the expensive Japanese and French motorbikes that have for decades been in the hands of a tiny local elite. Above all, Boubacar aspired to buy a Jakarta, a colorful and easy-to-drive scooter-style vehicle with low fuel consumption and automatic gears, which is made in China by KTM.[9] New Jakartas were mostly bought by better-off families. It was Boubacar's hope, therefore, to purchase a secondhand Jakarta for less than 150,000 francs (US$300) within the following year.

Boubacar and Aminata's hosting evenings of conviviality documented the ways *aventuriers* of rural origins were employing Chinese goods to enjoy new forms of material prosperity. They perceived modernity as an urban way of life based, importantly, on the consumption of prestigious technologies. *Aventuriers* understood provincial towns like Bougouni as open doors toward wider trends coming from *là où ç'est évolué* or *là où ç'est civilisé*, such as African capitals, Europe, the United States, Mecca, since the early 2000s Dubai, and now China.[10] Thanks to the arrival in the 2000s of this Chinese-made material culture in Mali, *aventuriers* in town thought that one can be poor (earning a bit of money) but trendy at the same time insofar as the consumption of these manufactured products, although cheap, granted them access to a "civilized" (urban) way of life. In parallel, *aventuriers* who still followed a rural way of life were mockingly called *broussards* by long-standing urbanites.

The short life expectancy of Chinese goods, however, reminded Malians that such items were, as they said, "bad imitations" of Western goods: "They [Chinese goods] are of poor quality." The consumption of these cheap goods therefore also brought them a new dilemma about this modernity. While the affordability of such goods allowed the masses to accede to "civilized" lifestyles, they were simultaneously experienced as only a second-class modernity because they did not last, an ambivalence explored in the next section.

TRANSFORMATION IN THE LOCAL HIERARCHY OF GOODS

I met Alou on a busy street corner of the district of Torakabougou where we were both bargaining for cheap sandals at the same stallholder. Thanks to our initial complicity carved around this bargain, he invited me to his home, a small cement house that he rented from a local entrepreneur. I occasionally visited him at his home thereafter. Alou was a married man and secondary school teacher in his mid-forties. He grew up in a village near the town of Kaye. At an early age he moved to Kaye, where he was raised with an aunt's family. Avoiding the farming activities of village life, he was able to pursue his studies in town. Having successfully completed his own education, he later became a public school teacher. After winning his spurs as a teacher in rural Mali, he was then transferred to Bougouni, where he settled with his family. Since that time, he had worked in one of the state secondary schools. As a civil servant of the Ministère de l'Education Nationale du Mali, he benefited from a stable job, hence a regular income. As a schoolteacher with experience, he earned a monthly wage of roughly 100,000 FCFA (US$200),[11] a low amount of money compared to civil servants working in *ministères* where *les affaires* were more lucrative.

One late afternoon, I found Alou at the threshold of his courtyard moaning about a recent purchase that proved to be a bad deal. Although it had been made in China, Alou had spent a considerable 50,000 FCFA (US$100) to acquire what was not a simple device but the new generation of double-chip mobile phones. Acquiring such a trendy mobile phone was a noticeable mark of material distinction at that time and would continue to be until the next generation of Chinese mobile phones was released in the Malian market. Alou was not the kind of man who was running after material distinctions all the time; he had a family to take care of. Living by possessing a few such goods that shape this distinction, nonetheless, meant being a respectable head of family in southwest Mali. The day he bought this fashionable mobile phone was therefore a good day. Two weeks after this long-awaited purchase, however, some of the phone's keys had already started to weaken. Worst of all, a third of the screen turned to a complete blur. Grumbling about the poor quality of his mobile phone, he commented, "We like French or European goods, but they are too expensive. If someone offers you a modern mobile phone for a very low price, what can you do?"

Alou admitted that systematically opting for the lowest prices might not be the best strategy in the long term. However, he often felt compelled to buy cheap Chinese goods because they were the only goods that gave Malian masses affordable access to a modernity based on the consumption of manufactured products, trendy services, and sophisticated technologies. This access, however, lasted for only a short period of time. Within a month the product often started to deteriorate, if not to break. Alou then spent money to fix it, but how long would the repairs last until it broke forever? Sooner rather than later he knew that he would need to replace the good with a new one so as to reestablish what he considered an up-to-date lifestyle that connects Malians in technological mode with the wider world. Alou lamentably added, "Chinese are more capitalist than Europeans because their products are *à usage unique* [single-use]; they do not last at all! You'll need to buy a new one soon." Malians often complained about the poor quality of the so-called *produits chinois* by saying *c'est de la pacotille* (it is cheap junk).[12]

While watching two young guys tearing down the road on a Chinese-made Sanili motorbike, Alou commented that after the arrival of Chinese motorbikes in the early 2000s, many young farmers have spent their farming loans granted by the Compagnie Malienne pour le Développement des Textiles (CMDT) on such motorbikes instead of on fertilizers for cotton:

> Many of them [young farmers] are in debt now. They hang out in town and neglect farming activities. Look at them! Instead of going to bed so as to get up early for taking care of cotton fields, they show off on their motorbike until late in the evening. This is not all! Petrol costs money. . . . The worst is that many of these cheap motorbikes are rotting in the courtyards. They break down quickly, and people do not have the money to fix them. . . . Chinese have spoiled the area.

Does access to a cheap albeit trendy material culture of Chinese manufacture turn ordinary Malians into modern (connected to the wider world) consumers? Due to the affordability of such goods, inhabitants of Bougouni were able to enjoy a "civilized" material lifestyle, but this pervading consumption simultaneously seemed to be experienced as only a second-class modernity, because Chinese goods did not last long. Moreover, an enduring access to an up-to-date lifestyle through these cheap goods remained costly because it required continuous repair and purchase of such goods in order to be maintained over time. Alou blamed the fact that "the Chinese are eating [people's] money!" Cheap Chinese goods tended to drag ordinary Malians into a sort of vicious circle of quick consumption and regular repairs and then purchases that impoverished those who could no longer do without this popular material culture. Alou illustrated this situation by mentioning a neighbor who could not wait to replace his mobile phone, which had just broken, and shortly after had to beg for money in town when his daughter felt sick. So the consumption of cheap Chinese goods was lived as a mixed experience among ordinary Malians insofar as this consumption only *temporarily* fulfilled their aspirations to a material modernity. Soon, they knew, they would have to fix and replace these goods if they wanted to prolong their somewhat ephemeral modernity. And this ended up being costly over time. However, better-off Malians also bought such cheap goods.

"HE! IBRAHIM IS A PATRON!"

Ibrahim, a wealthy civil servant introduced in chapter 5, was a good example of better-off Malians who settled in Bougouni following new work opportunities generated by the recent growth of the town. He grew up in the town of Kita and then studied engineering sciences at the University of Bamako. After a period of unemployment, punctuated by various small jobs in Bamako and Kaye, he managed to pass the very competitive yearly *examen de la fonction publique*.[13] He was fortunate enough to start a career in one of the state decentralized services. After a couple of years as a junior civil servant in Timbuktu, he was transferred to the office of Banamba. Five years later he received a promotion and moved to the office of Bougouni, where I met him with his family. Malian provincial towns, which were turned into administrative centers of *cercles* under the reform of *la Décentralisation*, had hosted many civil servants from most parts of Mali since the late 1990s. They settled in provincial centers for a couple of years, following the logic of transfer set by the government of Alpha Oumar Konaré (1992–2002) to fight against the regionalization of a state career. Besides Bamako,[14] civil servants often retired to the provincial town where they ended their career or where they grew up or came from. Ibrahim belonged to a growing but tiny local elite composed of civil servants, big traders, entrepreneurs, and qualified workers whose monthly *affaires* exceeded 200,000 FCFA (US$400).[15]

As the eldest son of his family, however, Ibrahim had to cope with numerous expenses. He took care of his aging parents. He also financed the studies of his younger siblings. In his neighborhood he was considered as a big man—in local terms, a *mɔgɔba*. He therefore also helped the inhabitants of his district financially, such as paying for the prescription for a neighbor in need. In other words, he responded to *le social*.[16] The considerable amount of money he gained through *les affaires* was nonetheless not infinite. Ibrahim had to spend his money wisely. If he refused all demands, people of the local community would label him a "selfish" (*ɲɛgoya*) and "cursed child" (*danga den*).[17] Because of the affordability of Chinese products, he was nonetheless able to make gifts to those around him, such as the TV set that he bought for his parents. His father used to bring this TV set out every evening on the family courtyard for the enjoyment of modest families from the neighborhood. Ibrahim had recently offered a trendy double-chip mobile phone to his fiancée. That year he had also purchased a new Jakarta motorbike for his younger brother, who studied at the University of Bamako. In parallel, he sometimes managed to buy expensive Western products for himself. I remembered that once he came to the *grin* at the threshold of Kassim's patron's mechanized mill with a Hewlett Packard laptop computer in hand. He sat on a chair, switched it on, and turned on a video clip. Members of the *grin* gathered around him and scrutinized this new acquisition. Intrigued by the rollicking bunch of onlookers, Kassim also came out of the mill. He observed Ibrahim and his computer for a few seconds and then exclaimed, "He! Ibrahim is a patron!" Besides the fact that Ibrahim was able to handle this sophisticated device that uneducated people used to call a *kabako masini* (surprising device), the consumption of such expensive sophisticated products of Western manufacturing concretely communicated to the other members of the *grin* Ibrahim's status of *mɔgɔba*. Ibrahim later confided to me that he had received this Hewlett Packard laptop as payment for an administrative service he provided for a local entrepreneur.

In the epoch of the Independence (1960s), Malians were materially divided between a tiny elite, who possessed Western products, and the masses, who barely had access to secondhand Western products. However, since the

2000s, Malians have remained materially divided into three categories: the tiny elite who enjoy Western-branded products, the many who are limited to the so-called Chinese products, and the many who barely buy any foreign sophisticated goods because of the lack of means. Although Chinese goods have been flooding markets of Malian provincial towns, we cannot state that they have replaced the so-called *France aurevoir* goods. Rather, these cheap goods have added an affordable intermediary level to the hierarchy of goods in Mali. With their higher value, itself based on their quality and the long-standing reputation of their trademark, Western goods have remained the most desirable, and hence prestigious, items that distinguish big men from the masses, such as the *aventuriers*.

A CONCAVE MOBILITY MADE IN CHINA

In 2010 Ibrahim had already worked a couple of years as a civil servant in Bou-gouni. He knew that sooner or later the Malian state would order his transfer to another administrative center of provincial Mali. As for a transfer to Bamako, he did not even think about this pivotal possibility, because he did not have the right relations to make it plausible. In fact, he was not in a hurry about this coming transfer. A year after my stay in Bougouni, he confided to me over the phone, "*Les affaires* have prospered here." His two former positions were less lucrative than the current one. In Timbuktu Ibrahim kept a low profile due to a recent violent past that hit the north of Mali: the 1990s Tuareg rebellion. As he worked in a state service linked to urban planning, *les affaires* did not flourish there because of a weak construction market. Against the backdrop of a post-Independence accelerating rhythm of cyclic insecurity hitting northern Mali, many locals were erecting houses in Bamako instead. Ibrahim's next transfer, to Banamba, a provincial town 120 kilometers north of Bamako, was even worse. Banamba was a small provincial town far away from any international tarred roads. But his transfer to Bougouni was revealed to be lucrative. He discovered a fast-growing town where the construction market was in expansion. After a few years in Bougouni, Ibrahim managed to finance his wedding and the construction of cement houses for himself and his new wife and his aging parents, besides the couple of Jakarta motorbikes, Chinese mobile phones, and TV-DVD sets (among other trendy goods) that he bought for members of his family and a few protégés. He also acquired an expensive building plot in Bamako, where he planned to build a multistory cement house for his retirement. He was also saving money for the purchase of a secondhand Western car. Ibrahim belonged to the growing but still tiny elite of Malian provincial towns whose residents were looking for Western goods for themselves and offering Chinese goods for their network of protégés.

Alou, the secondary school teacher, benefited from a state, hence stable, job. But he regularly faced hardships to save money for making purchases beyond his family's daily expenses. A year after my stay in Bougouni, he told me over the phone that "*le social* was eating [his] money!" He therefore still had to make do with cheap sophisticated goods made in China in order to live a material modernity that he lived as "connected" to the wider world. Nevertheless, because of his regular income, Alous was able to secure a loan from a bank to buy a building plot in a new district of Bougouni. His plan was to gradually, over the next decade, build a one-story cement house for his retirement. He had already constructed a well, without which an empty plot could still be sold to someone else. Then the groundwork would be planned, thereafter the walls, and eventually the roof, with an optional iron structure for the second floor. Alou belonged to the growing but still minor group of low-paid employees of Malian provincial towns who struggled for years to achieve the construction of a modest cement house while making do with a second-rate modernity made in Asia.

With the 2000s arrival of a Chinese-made material culture in Mali, *aventuriers* like Boubacar thought that one can be poor (earning a bit of money) but trendy at the same time insofar as the consumption of these manufactured products, although cheap, granted them access to a "civilized" way of life. As an established small trader of the central market, Boubacar enjoyed a respectable status among new *aventuriers* in town. His acquisition of a few sophisticated goods made in China provided a tangible form to this status. But what can we say about his social status beyond these migrants of rural origin? Apart from getting married and becoming a father, Boubacar did not really move upward in terms of social mobility since he had left central Mali. Thus, the consumption of Chinese goods granted him a concave mobility. In other words, the pleasure of handling Chinese goods gave Boubacar a kind of material plenitude that soon shrank into "cheap junk" when these goods started to deteriorate. Beyond hosting *aventuriers* for evenings of conviviality, Boubacar's earthly path did not allow him to move upward in the social structure of contemporary Malian society.

Beyond the study of *aventuriers'* lives in motion in Bougouni, existential motions brought by the consumption of Chinese goods—the feeling of moving forward toward a prosperous life—were not openly understood by the whole Malian society as genuine social mobility. *Tunga* often turned out to be a mixed set of experiences marked by transience, a point that is explored in the concluding chapter.

CHAPTER 8

The Mercy of the Savanna

Since the turn of the twenty-first century, the discipline of anthropology has been marked by a focus on macro-changes that are deemed inevitable, such as modern forms of globalization (Eriksen 2007), speed (Ho 2006), and neoliberalism (Comaroff and Comaroff 2000). The pivotal status given to these macro-perspectives has also been made possible by the sharp historical line implied in "post-theories" (Kipnis 2008, preface). Consequently, the study of Muslim life has explored transversal transformations, such as new media (Eickelman and Anderson 2003), modern education (Launay 2016), and capitalism (Tripp 2006; Rudnyckyj 2010). Anthropologists, as fellow human beings, have equally been caught by popular global concerns, such as climate change, intercontinental immigrations, and international trade. In Malian studies of religiosity, it is telling that in the 1980s and 1990s, anthropologists (e.g., Amselle, Hoffmann, and McNaughton) explored how Mande traditions frame religiosity, whereas from the 2000s on, a new generation of anthropologists (e.g., Holder, Schulz, and Soares) has examined how democratic opening, new media, and neoliberalism have shaped contemporary religiosity. Although unintentional, the juxtaposed reading of these studies reveals a rupture, as if the cultural (local) forces that originate from the historic Mande no longer shape religiosity. *In Search of "Tunga"* demonstrates otherwise.

Riding across Bougouni on a bike, I encountered *aventuriers* who conceive, like most local Muslims, the conduct of a Muslim life as a multidimensional phenomenon. I especially explored the ethical ramifications of their twofold conception of piety. A pious conduct certainly involves Islamic precepts, the observance of which is framed by a set of rituals, signs, and moral discourses. This observance thus marks public life. By granting civil liberties (freedom of press and association), the post-1991 democratic and liberal processes in Mali have promoted the diversity and visibility of activism in public. Religious actors have embraced this renewed activism to promote the prescribed dimension of religious experience in public. In the first part of the monograph, "Navigating Street Life and Public Islam," I explored how since the 1990s newly legally founded Muslim associations have inclined the vast majority of Muslims, the self-described "simply Muslims," to perform public expressions of Muslim piety. In Bougouni the conduct of Muslim life has therefore been marked by a public Islam (acute display of outward signs of piety), especially for Muslims who were traditionally expected to be respectable (good) Muslims: elders and heads of family. To look Muslim and to practice Islamic precepts in public, in a way, has increasingly been partaken in the building of a prosperous (Muslim) life.

The nature of this religious ostentation, when understood within communal life, is not Islamic per se. It is fostered by the open setting and centrality of street life in the daily plot of urban Mali. The traditional built form of spaces of sociality, where social life and business intermingle, nurtures a pervasive public gaze during daylight. The Islamic renewal observed in contemporary Mali has strengthened the authority of Islam in public through moral evaluation based on sight. For *aventuriers*, in parallel to public Islam, the conduct of Muslim life also involves an inner force that informs someone's personality, maturity, and *barika*. Besides building trustful ties with *aventuriers*, the appreciation of this ethical dimension was both the fruit of linguistic and ethnographic engagement, what I call "an informed bike tour" of the town. This empathic engagement enabled me to tackle the obviousness of ethics. By "obviousness" I mean the cognitive tendency of the mind to conflate interactions that are omnipresent, such as ethical interactions, into the unquestioned "natural" banality of daily life. In other words, this omnipresence renders the ethical dimension difficult to pinpoint analytically because our initial perception of this dimension is everywhere and nowhere at the same time. The analyst therefore tends to confuse the appreciable social contours of this dimension. Apprehending forms of social life from words to values and from these values to people's attitudes month after month, however, I became able to distinguish the contours of these ethical interactions. It then became clear that *aventuriers* related this inner force to Mande values. This monograph thus demonstrates the metamorphic resilience of local ethics deemed ancient, which are explored as sociohistorical articulations; their transformative processes take the shape of mille-feuille formations.

These two dimensions, prescribed and ethical, however, do not necessarily overlap. The "simply Muslims" understood piety as both the practice of

Islamic precepts and self-discipline (virtuous ethos), the interplay of which is not imperatively spontaneous and straightforward. This twofold nature of piety reminded *aventuriers* of public Islam's moral ambiguity in their search for a prosperous life. Public expressions of Muslim piety, supported by Muslim currents, their associations, and members (scholars and followers), shaped someone's reputation of being a good Muslim but did not necessarily index pious intentions. When moral failings were involved, Muslims responded to the discourses of "truth and ignorance" of Muslim scholars and the moralization of public life supported by their followers through discourses of "sincerity-hypocrisy," such as with those they nicknamed "zigzag Muslims." As a thread running through local ethical life, this twofold nature of piety enabled me to recognize the centrality of Mande humanism in the conduct of Muslim life, what locals called *adamadenya*. Exploring the human condition as inherently ethical, I then took Paolo Gaibazzi's invitation (2018) to undo the power making that informs Mande ideas of humanity.

Sociohistorical analyses of oral tradition in West Africa have stressed the close connection between spiritual (occult) and physical (material) power in the unfolding of people's lives during the historical Mande epoch. More precisely, this oral tradition stipulates that the genuine root of what is observable (the tangible power) is beneath (the spiritual power), and what is observable provides an ethical glimpse of what is beneath. In a nutshell, what is observable is the ethical manifestation of the occult power. This monograph explores the metamorphic resilience of this ancient Mande perspective as a mille-feuille formation. Sharing the quotidian with young male Muslim *aventuriers* of rural origin who moved to Bougouni in search of *tunga*, I discovered that their attempts to build a prosperous life on earth stemmed from their engagement with *the* underneath root of existence: *Almighty God*. Islam has been a constitutive factor of the Mande world since its arrival in the continent in the eleventh century. Mande people have therefore considered God (godlike figure) as *the* original bottom of this existential root from time immemorial. Following an existential approach to religiosity, I have thereby documented the "practical meanings" (Jackson 1996) of God as *the* occult force whose presence was felt like "an obvious mystery" by these *aventuriers*. None of them denied the existence of God, but still their awareness deciphered God's Almighty presence in erratic moments that were imponderable to the intellectual mind. In addition to concrete achievements, prosperity in this existential approach becomes a feeling of creative forward motion or a dynamic of "being on the right track," with "being" meaning moving forward in life. The second part of the monograph, "Motions and Ethics on the Earthly Path," examines how *aventuriers* perceived God as *the* occult force that sets in motion human lives via specific ethics. I demonstrated how they performed submissive work attitudes that they lived as an active conception of destiny. I also illustrated the contemporary Mande figures of the noble Muslim and the blessed child that grounded their practical meanings of God in the traditional ethos of family obedience. By contrast to anthropological works, which stress local interpretations of macro-changes in terms of novelty, I probed the metamorphic resilience of Mande humanism by describing its mille-feuille formation in local ethical life. This monograph thus documents how in 2010 the twofold nature of power, an ancient Mande feature, still informed how *aventuriers* perceived the motion to prosperity and its underlying occult propulsion in contemporary Mali. This existential motion is further translated into social mobility in terms of the recent surge of consumption made in China. I showed that this affordable mass consumption, while granting *aventuriers* access to a modernity based on new sophisticated goods, was not understood as genuine social mobility in wider social circles. Western products remained the product of distinction par excellence. Social mobility was articulated to a social scale, whereas existential motion expressed a social aspiration.

Within a year after my departure, most of the monograph's main characters left Bougouni following different decisions and perceptions of fate. What does the transiency of *aventuriers'* stay in Bougouni teach us about current transformations in West African mobility? As a concluding call, I now introduce how the transiency of Salif the tailor, Kassim the handyman and mill worker, Boubacar the small trader of *yuguyuguw*, and Fousseini the fisherman and carter invites scholars of contemporary Africa not only to question the status of the sedentary urban home in light of changes in the forms of social inequalities based on mobility but also to reconsider the allegedly marginality of the savanna in West Africa.

NEW NOMADS

Salif's master tailor craftsman did not want to teach him the lucrative craft of embroidery, so Salif started his own sewing workshop. But he found it difficult to save money because he offered only ordinary sewing services. One of his friends, employed by a local NGO, then suggested he work on a new gardening project. After a promising start, however, the project collapsed because of mismanagement. With his reputation of being a good farmer, Salif then agreed to farm for a family of civil servants so that he could save enough money to eventually start a trade in the seed business. The head of this family promised him a "substantial sum of money" at the end of the harvest. However, neither the yield nor the generosity of his patron proved to be as he had hoped. Salif felt stuck. For him, "bad persons" did not want him to move forward in life. He then began to visit a *soma* in order to remove occult hurdles from his earthly path. Ultimately, Salif became disheartened after years of hardships in Bougouni. Shortly after my departure, Salif made an important decision. Still single and without savings, he eventually yielded to what he had attempted to avoid since moving to Bougouni: an "outdated" rural way of life closely regulated by the authority of elders. Salif then settled back in his village of origin next to his traditional extended family. There, he farmed and made extra cash by offering his services as a tailor during the weekly market of Garalo. A year later, the head of his *gwa*, his big brother, suggested a bride for him, and the two became engaged. His big brother, an important cattle trader of the area, financed Salif's wedding. He also gave him an amount of money to settle his household. Salif became a married man. His wife soon became pregnant. However, he henceforth had to accept his position as a subordinate son and little brother. His moving forward in life followed the customary way: it was granted by his elders.

Near the end of my stay, Kassim the handyman quit his job as a mill worker to take over a cement-built shop servicing mobile phones. Kassim made a deal with the former occupant of this shop, who moved to Bamako. This latter let Kassim run his business in exchange for a monthly remittance. As years of *tunga* had turned him into a skillful handyman, Kassim quickly learned how to fix mobile phones on the job. From this opportunity on, his financial situation was considerably improving. For the first time in years, he was thinking about plans for a wedding and the purchase of a secondhand motorbike. He was also able to imagine the prospect of making an honorable return to his native village in Côte d'Ivoire in a few years. I then left Bougouni. A couple of months later, I tried several times to call Kassim, but nobody picked up the phone. I therefore called his former patron, the owner of the mill, with whom Kassim remained on good terms. This patron explained to me that Kassim left the town following an "unfortunate event." Apparently, Kassim entrusted his neighbor with a considerable amount of money so as to conclude a big purchase. Kassim wanted to sell mobile phones. But the neighbor spent Kassim's money on personal needs instead. This financial loss undermined Kassim's business project. He felt betrayed and was gutted. He therefore left the town. Kassim moved to the neighboring town of Yanfolila. There he made a living by fixing mobile phones in a small shop *par terre*. A year later I heard that Kassim was in Guinea taking his chances with a gold-panning site.

After years of hardship in *tunga*, Boubacar the small trader of *yuguyuguw* felt that he was finally getting on the right track. His family started to enjoy moving forward toward prosperity—in other words, toward a desired urban (modern) way of life that most *aventuriers* aspired to. Helped by his devoted wife, Boubacar was able to achieve more than simply coping with the daily expenses of his family. He regularly hosted his friends and bought a few trendy goods made in China. One day near the end of my stay, he beeped me a few times. Boubacar's insistence surprised me because this was not his habit. I called him back. He then urged me to come to where he was living. I found him anxious. He told me that he had just spent a few days in jail. The previous week the local police had conducted a roundup in the big market. They arrested several small traders of *yuguyuguw*, accusing them of selling stolen goods. The police put all of these small traders in jail, where they were soon joined by other small traders. The jail was filling up hour after hour. As small traders were complaining about what was, for them, "false accusations," they learned that bail for each of them was 100,000 FCFA (US$200), about the same as the monthly wage of a public school teacher in Mali. Boubacar managed to borrow from friends or relatives to pay the bail, but now he had to pay this money back. This was the only instance when he asked me for financial help. He seemed to be frightened and humiliated at the same time. Boubacar and his family left Bougouni a few days later. He did not want to pay more for a crime for which he believed he was wrongly accused. The police's roundup among small traders fed conversations in *grins* for a while in town. Gossip said that the head of the town's police, an old man from the *région* of Koulikoro, was about to retire. He therefore had abused his power by making false accusations against a number of small traders to quickly make easy extra cash in preparation for his coming retirement. People in *grins* knew that most of these small traders were *aventuriers*, hence powerless persons away from their native homes. They also stressed that the head of the police could act so because his place of retirement was most likely not Bougouni. A month later I had a call with Boubacar. He was back in Ségou, selling *yuguyuguw* there but not in the big market. For a start he made do with a shop *par terre*. He concluded our exchanges by remorsefully saying that before moving to Bougouni, people had warned him about the notorious reputation of the town: "Bougouni is full of bad persons who do not want you to move forward in life!"

During the second half of my stay, Fousseini the fisherman and carter faced consecutive months of poor fishing. For him, his lack of luck caused his daily catch of fishes to be meager, so he started to be more regular in his utterance of blessings. He also asked a *marabout* to improve his occult diagnosis, but still his luck did not improve. He therefore abandoned fishing to momentarily retrain as a full carter in the center of Bougouni. Because the job of carter was physically demanding and poorly paid, he was on the lookout for other work opportunities. Six months after my departure, I heard that Fousseini had moved a bit north to the small town of Selingue with his family. He explained to me over the phone that he made this decision because a friend who settled in this locality two years ago told him that fishing in the Selingue lake was lucrative. In early 2012 Fousseini told me that he had recently started to work as a digger in a nearby Guinean gold-panning site while his family remained in Selingue. As he argued, "I would like to take my chance with gold." When I called him in July of that year, his family was preparing to live with him near this gold-panning site.

Most *aventuriers* who gave life to this monograph settled in Bougouni for a few years. They then left Bougouni following different decisions and perceptions of fate. In addition to concrete achievements, prosperity in this study of lives in motion has been examined as an existential feeling of creative forward motion. As a study of Muslim life, moreover, it probes how and to what extent God is perceived to set human lives in forward motion. In a longitudinal perspective, hinted by what happened to Salif, Kassim, Boubacar, and Fousseini within a year after my departure, *aventuriers* in southwest Mali can also be explored as a kind of "new nomads." The condition as nomads does not stress freedom. On the contrary, it reveals that in West Africa, periodical moves or itinerant homes are a way to cope with hardships—in other words, a sign of poverty. The image of an *aventurier* in search of *tunga* features a wandering with a disconnected start and end, whereas the image of a prosperous person features a series of star-like shapes that both start and end in their center.[1]

The latter image depicts planning, hence order; the former depicts drift, hence disorder. What do we know about the thousands of new nomads who, in and out, stimulate, despite themselves, urban growth in West Africa? Are we facing a recent development of mobility within West Africa in which having a (permanent) sedentary urban home is becoming a privilege? These questions remain unanswered because of the lack of studies of intra–West African migration, a corollary of the extreme media attention and political failure to stop the tragic South-North migration across the Mediterranean. Moreover, by contrast to the 1950s, when Jean Rouch filmed *Jaguar*, this intra–West African migration does not only occur toward forest and coastal areas. The West African savanna is increasingly becoming a migratory destination.

RETHINKING THE POLITICAL GEOGRAPHY OF THE SAVANNA

I left Bougouni in April 2010. Two years later the peaceful period that Mali had enjoyed since 1991 abruptly stopped. In the aftermath of the fall of Muammar Gaddafi (October 2011), the north of Mali was conquered between January and April 2012 by the Mouvement National de libération de l'Azawad (MNLA), allied with the so-called Islamist insurgent factions according to international vocabulary. The MNLA resulted from an accelerating rhythm of post-Independence Tuareg rebellions in northern Mali (see Lecocq 2010; Lecocq and Klute 2018). In Western media the qualifying term "Islamist" crystallizes the post-9/11 revival of a fear of an "evil" pan-Islamism which is also nurtured by the current Global War on Terrorism (see Galy 2013). African media especially are using the term "terrorist" to stress the cruel, hence un-Islamic, motivations of such insurgent factions. Following a logic of provocation with Western powers and African states, the insurgent factions also seek to maximize their media presence by stressing their Islamic identity.

These insurgent factions also illustrated recent forms of transnational banditry that flourish in porous border zones or territories with a weak governance, such as the Sahel (Daniel 2014).[2] A group of Malian military men led by Captain Amadou Haya Sanogo, contesting the political handling of the military operations on the ground, overthrew the Malian president Amadou Toumani Touré by a coup d'état on March 22, 2012. This coup d'état happened a month before the planned presidential election. After a three-week power contest between the military junta and the international community (particularly the Economic Community of West African States, or ECOWAS), the deputy and head of Mali's national assembly, Dioncounda Traoré, became the interim president of Mali. The Islamist insurgents then ousted the MNLA from key localities of northern Mali by the end of June 2012. They thereafter progressed southward toward the town of Mopti, a strategic crossroad between north and south Mali. As the Malian army kept losing ground, French troops stopped the insurgents' progression in January 2013 at the request of the interim government of Mali. The Malian army helped by deploying foreign forces,[3] then reconquered most of northern Mali within two months. Ibrahim Boubacar Keïta (IBK) won the presidential election in July 2013 and a second presidential mandate in August 2018. But the situation in northern Mali has remained troubled and unstable. The United Nations Multidimensional Integrated Stabilization Mission in Mali (MINUSMA), which supports the stabilization of Mali, has since its inception in July 2013 been the deadliest UN peacekeeping mission of the last fifty years. Insurgent factions, claiming to be of Islamic allegiance (e.g., the Movement for Unity and Jihad in West Africa [MUJAO], the other Ansar Dine,[4] and Al-Qaeda in the Islamic Maghreb [AQMI]), have regularly launched attacks against Malian and UN troops. Other armed factions, moreover, emerged in central Mali, where they have kindled ethnic tensions since 2015. These attacks are deemed "terrorism" by the Malian state and the international community. Another group of Malian military men led by Colonel Assimi Goïta, in the wake of civil demonstrations led by the M5-RFP,[5] overthrew the Malian president IBK by a coup d'état on August 18, 2020. The Malian state has since been run by the Conseil National de la Transition, a both civilian and military committee that is supposed to prepare the next presidential election in 2022. As I am revising this conclusion on May 28, 2021, the Conseil National de la Transition is being hit by what media are calling "a coup d'état in a coup d'état." The Malian state is again being destabilized by Assimi Goïta and his military men.

At the end of March 2012, when I called my host family in Bougouni to ask how they were doing, the mother replied, "Here, there is nothing. It's quiet. It is in Bamako that it gets heated."[6] In Africa as elsewhere, most coups d'état are barely, if never, felt outside the capital. She added, "In Mali, when it bursts, only Bamako [the capital] is hit. People in the rest of the country carry on their quotidian [lives]. The governments change. We remain." Within the capital, moreover, only strategic buildings (e.g., parliament, national broadcast company buildings) are directly targeted by the coup d'état's henchmen. But the conquest of northern Mali by insurgent factions hit entire territories to finally provoke a coup. The insurgent factions' twelve months of ruling northern Mali left deep traces among the local population. These traces have impinged on the return of the rule of the Malian state. Faced with a longstanding predatory state (Darbon 1990; Hamidou 1996) whose civil servants tend to work first for their interests before any sense of wider common good (Bayart 1989), some locals have been seduced by insurgent factions' allegedly stricter but fairer administration of justice. Others, especially the youth,[7] see in these factions and new forms of transnational banditry job opportunities that propel them beyond the elders' traditional constraints over their being adults in waiting. Turning ancient rivalries between Bambara and Dogon farmers and Fula breeders into political claim, the Macina Liberation Front (MLF) came to prominence in January 2015 by claiming a series of attacks in central Mali; it has subsequently chased away numerous civil servants to take control of entire territories of the *régions* of Koulikoro and Ségou. The Malian state, despite the support of the MINUSMA, has since faced difficulties in securing rural areas of central Mali. In 2021 this instability persisted.

As the instability of central and northern Mali endures, locals' incentive to migrate is being reinforced. Nesting in the long-standing state failure to provide fair and efficient social services to local populations, this instability has accelerated the general southbound migration observed in West Africa since the 1980s Sahelian droughts. Besides the important minority of the population living in this economy of instability, famers and breeders who have been hit by this volatile situation have increasingly moved to safer areas of the savanna in search of *tunga*. In Mali this savanna covers the administrative *région* of Sikasso, the only *région* of Mali that has not been directly hit by the post-2012 violence. In early May 2021, Moussa the *bogolan* maker told me over the phone that "numerous Dogon families have since [2015] settled in the village [in Bougouni's hinterland]." These families have fled the interethnic violence that recently hit central Mali to take refuge and even rebuild their lives in southwest Mali.

The emergence from oblivion of this former buffer zone between ancient Mande empires and kingdoms, and thereafter marginal area of French Sudan, is here to last due to the recurring political porosity of the Sahel, and its post-Independence ecological degradation and high birth rate. The cases of Boubacar the small trader of *yuguyuguw* and Fousseini the fisherman and carter exemplify this West African southbound migration from the Sahel toward the network of provincial towns located in safer and more fertile areas of the savanna. Boubacar grew up in a village near Mopti. In this rural area, farming opportunities were getting scarce. After taking his chance in Mopti and Segou, Boubacar moved south to Bougouni with his wife and two young boys, word of mouth having stressed this urban locality's "sweet climate" and growing trade opportunities. Fousseini grew up in a Bozo village along the river Niger not so far from Mopti. He left his native village a few years ago with his newly married wife because fishing became too competitive there.

He tried his luck in Bamako as a carter, but that did not work out. The capital was already overcrowded with carters. He then moved to Bougouni, where he fished in the nearby Ba River in the morning and worked as a carter in the afternoon. For a while, this working combination provided an assumable livelihood. Fousseini was not able to save much money, but at least his livelihood could cover the daily expenses of his family.

In parallel, the provincial towns of the *région* of Sikasso have also attracted *aventuriers* who go off on *tunga* in the *chef-lieu* of their region, such as Salif the tailor. By elevating small towns to administrative centers, the Malian decentralization has accelerated this provincial urban migration from the hinterland. Salif wanted to start a household in full independence. He did not want to remain in the political bosom of his family, waiting for his elders to finance his wedding. For this he needed to become more than self-sufficient: he had to save money. Salif therefore moved to Bougouni, where he did an apprenticeship to become a tailor. In 2010 a former mayor of Bougouni told me that the administrative *cercles* of Kolondiéba, Yanfolila, and Bougouni were pushing for the creation of a new *région* with Bougouni as its capital. Recently the *région* of Bougouni became the eleventh *région* of Mali, an administrative promotion that certifies the rise in importance of southwest Mali in the country. In 2021 Bougouni hosted more than 80,000 inhabitants.

Besides the southbound migration of Sahelian people and the provincial urban migration from the hinterland, urban growth in the West African savanna can also be marked by the political contingency of coastal countries. Kassim the handyman and mill worker, for instance, grew up in northern Côte d'Ivoire. Attracted by the economic dynamic of southern Côte d'Ivoire, he went off on *tunga* on the Atlantic coast. After a few months in the town of San Pedro, he became a dockworker in its deep seaport. At that time his moving forward in life was slow but constant. The Ivorian crisis then erupted. Due to his northern identity, he fled to take refuge in Mali. He could not come back home with empty hands. He first worked a few months as a gardener in Sikasso and then a few days as a carter in Bamako. He then encountered his "Ivorian aunt" in Bougouni during a greeting visit. She helped him to find jobs as a houseboy and handyman for better-off families. Establishing his own network in town, he then found a job as a mill worker. Later, a local big man financially helped him to start a *shɛfantigi* at night.

For *aventuriers* encountered in Bougouni, the decision to go off on *tunga* in the "crossroad of southwest Mali," according to the popular Malian singer Nahawa Doumbia, illustrates the existential attraction that shapes what I call in a narrative way "the Mercy of the savanna." By contrast to studies that build on the classic historical connections between the Maghreb and the Sahel (e.g., Mokhefi and Antil 2012), the Mercy of the savanna expresses *aventuriers'* existential perception of the coming to the fore of the savanna in contemporary West Africa. This ethnographic observation invites social scientists to also value the scholarly under-considered historical connections between the southern shores of the Sahara (Sahel) and the lands south of these shores (see Lecocq 2015). It thus asks for a new political geography of the savanna, a political geography that reckons the savanna as a strategic crossroad between the Sahel and the forest and coastal regions of West Africa. The savanna is increasingly becoming all but not marginal.

NOTES

CHAPTER 1

1. All amounts of money in francs refer to the West African CFA franc or XOF (ISO 4217 code); US$1 was worth roughly 500 West African CFA francs in 2010; 1€ 650 CFA.

2. Except for public figures, all names mentioned in this monograph are pseudonyms.

3. By "Ivorian aunt," Kassim referred to a married and older woman who came from the same region as he did.

In southern Mali, kinship terms are not only used between biological siblings. For instance, *balimakɛ* (brother) and *balimamuso* (sister) are well-mannered expressions used for an acquaintance or a foreigner. People of this part of West Africa cultivate a view of themselves as belonging to the same large family; however, they do so with different degrees of closeness.

4. All translations are by the author.

5. Dyula (Jula; Fr. *Dioula*) is an important trade language of West Africa, spoken in Côte d'Ivoire, Burkina Faso, Mali, and Guinea by millions of people as a first or second language. Dyula contains many French idioms, whereas Bambara is perceived as more authentic.

6. *Je suis un aventurier.*

7. The equivalent English terms ("adventure," "adventurer") have been less explored because their use is rare among English speakers in Africa.

8. For instance, see Barley (1984).

9. In the neighboring Soninke language, *tunɲa* means "exile" because migrants live elsewhere (Gaibazzi 2015, 59).

10. "They came to the Gold Coast or to Côte d'Ivoire to look for money, but also to search for adventure."

11. In the regions of Bougouni, a head tax of one franc was introduced in 1895. Taxes increased incrementally over the next several years (Peterson 2011, 67).

12. I opted for the term "prosperity" rather than "success" because *tunga* means more than seeking money. I do also use "prosperity" and "better life" interchangeably.

13. *ailleurs fantasmé.*

14. See http://www.infomigrants.net/fr/post/3644/ces-migrants-africains-qui-ne-veulent-pas-venir-en-europe (retrieved February 1, 2021).

15. There is no equivalent term for "town," "city," or "urban" in Bambara; a community is called *dugu*, a large community is a *duguba*. The common Western concept of the urban (demography, density, differentiation) hardly fits societies of precolonial West Africa.

16. For a sociohistorical outline of the question of the female adventurer in Africa, see Bredeloup (2014, 113–30).

17. Isabelle Bardem explored young men and women in situations of precarity in Ouagadougou. She named young men *aventurier*; she did not name young women *aventurière*. She observed that these women ran away from familial duress (1993). In this study, young men sought for familial blessings before going off on tunga (chap. 6).

18. For a social history of the circular migration system in West Africa, see Cordell, Gregory, and Piché (1996).

19. *Tunga kalanso dɛ don.*

20. Exploring itinerant Mouride traders in North America and Europe, Victoria Ebin equally stresses the educational dimension of travelling (1996).

21. Locals employed *danbe* and *honneur* interchangeably.

22. In 2010 "maidens, meal and money" were still among key elements of prosperity in rural Mali (Meillassoux 1981).

23. On the ambivalent representation of "heroes or tricksters," see Riccio (2005).

24. "*Sini bɛ Ala Bolo*" (Bambara). The Bambara language (*Bamanan.kan* or *Bamana. kan*) is the lingua franca of Mali.

25. Ethics is more a sensibility of conduct that is socially cultivated, and morality is a personal conduct with social consequences; nonetheless, I use them interchangeably. From now on, by *aventurier* I mean Muslim *aventurier*.

26. In West Africa the *marabout* is a type of traditional Muslim scholar expert in Islamic esoteric sciences.

27. British administrators in Africa thought in similar ways, see Seesemann 2011 (Introduction).

28. The colonial administrations in British, Portuguese, and German West Africa were also concerned with pan-Islamism but to a lesser extent.

29. In West Africa political shifts happened in Mali as well as in Benin, Burkina Faso, Cameroon, Côte d'Ivoire, Niger, and Togo.

30. In 1981 the military regime launched the country's sole officially authorized Islamic association called AMUPI (Association Malienne pour l'Unité et le Progrès de l'Islam). This organization was an instance of regulation of conflicts between reformist Muslims and Sufi orders and an instrument of coordination of the "petrodollars" coming from Arabic countries in the 1980s (Brenner 1993a); Soares 2005, 228–29). In 2010, AMUPI was not a state association anymore, but it is still considered as such.

31. Ar. *Tajdid*. Islamic revivalist dynamics are not new; they "are a response to and an expression of Muslim modernity" that can be traced back to the "reform" movement of the Prophet. These dynamics resurge when Muslims face changing political, social, and economic conditions (Lapidus 1997, 444–48, 456–57).

32. *Nɛ yé silamɛ yé.*

33. *silamɛ dɔron.*

34. Charles Hirschkind argues that the contemporary emergence of "political Islam" is also due to "the contemporaneous expansion of state power and concern into vast domains of social life previously outside its purview, including that of religion" (1997).

For an overview of the Islamic Reform in Senegal, Mali, Nigeria, Niger, and Chad, see Loimeier (2016); for Nigeria, see Kane (2003) and Thurston (2016); for Niger, see Sounaye (2016). For an overview of political Islam in sub-Saharan Africa, see Gomez-Perez (2005).

35. Michael Gilsenan (1982) already critiqued the preoccupation of Western politics and media with the idea of the "Muslim mind" as the key to understanding the essence of the people of the Islamic world.

36. This tendency can be strengthened by the power of *allodoxia*, which is the super-imposition of the dominant discourse with the appearance of reason and the authority of science (Bourdieu 2004; Wacquant and Bourdieu 2000).

37. In an article about the encounter between lay Jains and environmental activists in the Animal Liberation movements, James Laidlaw (2010) questions the idea of ethical traditions as immutable by showing how ethical choices are embedded in "the contingency of the situation."

38. Samuli Schielke wrote that "there is too much Islam in the anthropology of Islam in the sense of a lack of balance between the emphasis on religious commitment and a not always sufficient account of the lives of which it is a part" (2010, 2).

39. Michael Lambek would specify that taking a meal is a practice because it is a relatively open phenomenon, whereas the uttering of *b'ismillah* that punctuates the practice of meal taking is a performance because it is a discrete, finite, precise, and completed phenomenon (2015a, 34).

40. René Otayek and Benjamin Soares express the contemporary reformulations of Islam in Africa as the emergence of an *"islam mondain"* (2007). The study of *"islam mondain* does not privilege Islam over anything else, emphasizing instead the actual world in which Muslims find themselves" (Soares and Osella 2009, 12). Magnus Marsden and Konstantinos Retsikas, through the concept of "articulation," invite the analyst to study how the religious phenomenon is constantly "produced, reproduced and transformed in particular social and historical contexts" (2013, 3), and this happens in mutually constitutive dynamics and often unpredictable ways.

41. The *jɛli* belongs to the caste of artisan. For more information on the Mande caste system, see chapter 6.

42. For a similar relation between aging and devotional Islamic practice among the Tuareg in Niger, see Rasmussen (2000).

43. Rather than examining their epistemological statuses.

44. For other approaches to explore God as a social reality, see Schielke (2019).

45. See Comaroff and Comaroff (2000).

46. Ar. *baraka* (the gift of grace), see chapter 6.

47. Material or monetary gifts.

48. For a comment on the penetration of neoliberal forces in the Mande world in terms of emerging individualism, see Conrad 2005.

49. "Mande is the linguistic and civilizational space that descends from the medieval Ghana and Mali Empires, covering much of the westernmost part of the Sahel and extending up to the Upper Guinea Coast" (Gaibazzi 2018, note 3).

50. On the epic of Sundiata Keita, see Niane (1960).

51. For more information on the Mande caste system, see chapter 6.

52. Robert C. Newton explores the Mande culture as a "reinvention which breathes the life of shared cultural traditions into the circumstances of the present" (1999, 315).

53. A ruler was also called a *kɛlɛ.masa*, literally a warlord (Bazin 1988b). The *faama* of the *kafo* (a political unit) of Bamako in precolonial times was also known as the *muru. tigi*, the master (*tigi*) of the sabre (*muru*) (Meillassoux 1963, 197, 218).

54. Bougouni was initially "a commercial outpost of the Bamana Segu state" (Perinbam 1998, 206).

55. On the Bamanaya religion, see Dieterlen (1951). "Bamanaya" became a generic term for "un-Islamic religious practices of local origins" in Mali.

56. A precise dating is complicated due to the orality of the sources (Meillassoux 1963, 186–87).

57. In Mauritania and Mali during the nineteenth century, "economic behavior was the second most common issue examined by Saharan [Muslim] jurists after theological or purely sacred matters" (Lydon 2005, 128).

58. In the 1950s and 1960s in Mali, Bamako hosted an important minority of Wahhabi wealthy traders. For Amselle, these traders significantly turned Islam into an "*idéologie bourgeoise*" (1977, 251).

59. In a study of economic change among the Giriama of Kenya, David J. Parkin (1972) investigated the undermining consequences of capitalist development for customary egalitarianism.

60. From the Arabic *Amir al-Mu'min*.

61. In postcolonial Minyanka areas of Mali (Jonckers 1990, 164), the term *faama* became associated with politicians and wealthy traders.

CHAPTER 2

1. Since the 2000s, the size of a courtyard in Bamako has considerably been reduced due to increasing demand and property speculation.

2. The bicycle became a new, hence trendy, item of consumption in between the two world wars; see Peterson (2011, chapter 4).

3. See figure 3. All photographs in this monograph are by the author unless credited to others.

4. In Mali, out of 46 localities of more than 15,000 inhabitants, only 6 localities hosted more than 100,000 inhabitants in 2009; see http://www.citypopulation.de/Mali-Cities.html (retrieved May 14, 2021).

5. See Misanthropic Anthropologist, PhD, "Knowing the City by Bike," *Fieldwork at Home* (blog), https://themisanthropicanthropologist.blogspot.de/2008/03/knowing-city-by-bike.html (retrieved May 14, 2021).

6. I also had a bigger notebook where I ritually wrote notes about what happened during the last twenty-four hours every day after lunch. In total, I wrote one thousand pages of field notes.

7. This elitist status is more pronounced in rural Mali, where farming and household chores often lead students to drop out of school early.

8. Dating back to the mid-seventeenth century (Perinbam 1998, 107).

9. "Buffer zone" is Peterson's expression (2008, 263).

10. On the wars of Samory in south Mali, see Peterson (2011, 24–57); Person (1970).

11. On colonial head tax (*nisɔngɔ*), see Peterson (2011, 66–67).

12. The French moved their local administration from Faragouaran to Bougouni in 1894 due to a water shortage.

13. For an overview of the importance of Sufi orders in the spread of Islam in West Africa, see Hiskett (1994, chapter 4).

14. Interviews by the author with Mamadou Traoré, Bakary Diawarra, Ablaye Diarra, Youssouf Coulibaly, Bougouni, June 6, 2009.

15. In the historic Mande world, age grades and adulthood were marked by rites of passage. The neighboring village of Kola still hosted a cult of *kɔmɔ* in 2010, but many young people did not attend it. On *kɔmɔ* cults, see Dieterlen and Cissé (1972). On Bamanan institutions of initiation, see Colleyn (2001).

16. Interview by the author with Nouhoum Doumbia, Bougouni, November 17, 2009.

17. Interviews by the author with Mamadou Traoré, Bakary Diawarra, Ablaye Diarra, Youssouf Coulibaly, Bougouni, June 6, 2009.

18. For instance, Lallama Sylla of Bamako who settled in Bougouni in the early 1950s.

19. From the noun *dugu.ma* (soil) and the verb *ka kalan* (to study); basically, in these traditional Islamic schools (or Qur'anic schools) students (Ar. *talibe*; Bam. *garibu*) sit directly on the ground and learn the Koran by heart (*ka durusi kɛ*).

20. The declaration of religious identity in front of fellow villagers during the colonial census paved the way to the profession of a public Muslim identity so as to avoid mockery, shame, and other negative connotations associated with Bamanan identity (Peterson 2002, 2011, 207–10).

21. At the back of the book it is stated that El-Hajj Ladji Blen entrusted Mamadou Sissoko with the "*mission sacrée*" of writing the book.

22. In 2010 Bougouni hosted seven *médersas*.

23. Bougouni also hosted a minority of Christians, Protestants, and Baha'i followers; non-Muslim communities did not turn out to be major actors in my fieldwork.

24. Bamanaya certainly diminished; as these religious practices were mostly hidden, I had difficulty assessing their presence.

25. *Mɔgɔ bɛɛ donna silamɛya da a la.*

26. *Hali ni ɛ bɛ ɛ da ko kosɛbɛ, ɛ bɛ min dun, kasa bɛ a la.*

27. The town of Kolokani had a similar reputation in Mali.

28. For more information on the RN9, see Chappatte (2016).

29. In 2010, except for adults of local origin, most young people and strangers did not know about the original context of this play on words. They just associated it with the general backward character of Bougouni.

30. Interview with Nouhoum Doumbia, Bougouni, November 17, 2009.

31. For an extended study of such youth festivals, see Arnoldi (2006).

32. Part of southwest Mali, Wassoulou is a historical Mande region known for its music.

33. For an analysis of children's voluntary migration in West Africa, see Hashim and Thorsen (2011).

34. *Coupé-décalé* is a popular Ivorian dance music associated with youth culture, consumption, and success; see Kohlhagen (2006).

35. Teacher Training Institute (IFM), a state school attracting more than a thousand students from all over Mali.

36. "Jacobin" refers to the highly centralized state (French style).

37. The Malian state attempted to involve, through the GREM/GLEM (Groupes Régionaux/Locaux d'Etudes et de Mobilisation), the participation of each level of the society in the constitution and goals of new territorial collectivities that would receive delegated powers (Kassibo et al. 1997).

38. In 2016 Mali was divided into 10 *régions* and the District de Bamako, 56 *cercles*, and 703 *communes*.

39. Communal councillors, mayors, representatives of *cercle* and *région*, the Haut Conseil des Collectivités Territoriales.

40. In 1982, 19 localities were recognized as having the status of Commune Urbaine, among them, 13 became Commune Urbaine during the colonial period (in 1955) (see Kassibo et al. 1997); the Commune Urbaine de Bougouni is composed of 7 districts and 21 villages.

41. Small hospital.

42. BNDA (Banque Nationale de Développement Agricole). In 2018 the town hosted four banks.

43. After 2010 the Total company built what is now the biggest gas station of Bougouni.

44. Four radios were operating in 2010; two other radios were planned.

45. Interview with Nouhoum Doumbia, Bougouni, November 17, 2009.

46. With its 2,000,000 inhabitants, Bamako in 2010 exceeded by far the 250,000 inhabitants of the second-biggest town of Mali (Sikasso). Most inhabitants of Bamako tend to reduce Mali to its capital and an immense homogeneous space they refer to as *la brousse* (bush).

47. For more information on this desiccation, see Agnew and Chappell (2000).

48. Small variations exist between versions, but they do not affect the main plot exposed in this chapter.

49. "*Jatigiya*" refers to the host-foreigner relationship.

50. What Malians call "the extended [patrilocal and patrilineal] family" (*la famille étendue*).

51. See press article, "*Litige foncier. Douze familles saccagées par des Diakité de Bougouni. Le laxisme du Préfet Sankou Touré en cause*," in the Bougouni newspaper *Le Relais*, June 29, 2009, 13, Coopérative Jamana, Bamako, 2–3. *Le Relais* was created in early 2000.

52. See *Lois et Décrets de la Décentralisation*, March 1999, *Mission de Décentralisation et des Réformes Institutionnelles, Présidence de la République, République du Mali, Nouvelle Imprimerie Bamakoise*, Bamako. It is not rare to see kin of the traditional chieftainship holding *communal* political offices when their elders hold the traditional chieftainship (Chappatte 2005).

53. For early writing on joking relationships as reciprocal bonds between two groups in West Africa, see Labouret (1929).

54. Banimonotié is the other name of Bougouni. It means between the rivers Ba and Mono in Bambara.

55. *Kuluba* means "big hill" in Bambara.

56. At Bougouni's exit toward Sikasso, vehicles of all sorts still cross the river Ba over a bridge built during the colonial time. The Malian decentralization divided the national territory into *cercles* that mostly bear the same names and territorial demarcations of those of the colonial period.

57. In his analysis of Brasília as a city without streets, James Holston (1989) compares common Brazilian street corners to outdoor living rooms.

58. The square.

59. Mango trees are well known to have thick leaves that produce fresh shade.

60. Better-off families have bigger houses, but it is rare for a room to be occupied by one person only.

61. On *grins* as spaces of insertion in political activism in Ouagadougou, see Kieffer (2006). For an example of *grins* in northern Côte d'Ivoire, see Vincourt and Kouyaté (2012). On *grin* as element of rural social life, see Jónsson (2008).

62. Bamako Hebdo, "Une particularité culturelle du Mali – 'Le Grin': lieu de détente, de discussions et de décisions," http://www.maliweb.net/societe/une-particularite-culturelle-du-mali-le-grin-lieu-de-detente-de-discussions-et-de-decisions-10586.html (retrieved May 30, 2021).

63. While *grins* are heterogeneous in composition, their members generally share a common marital status (see Schulz 2002, 811). On *grins* as forms of masculine sociabilities in Bamako, see Bondaz (2013).

64. The openness and culture of chat of the *grin* resonates with the sociality found in tea shop *adda* of Calcutta (Chakrabarty 2000, 180–213).

65. Elders often criticize youth in *grins* as being lazy because they prefer to sit, talk, and drink tea instead of working.

66. See *Le Grin* on YouTube.

CHAPTER 3

1. *Ala yé sutara yé.*

2. On infanticide accusation in Bougouni, see *Le Relais*, August 2008, 3; and *Coopérative Jamana*, Bamako, October 30, 2008, 5.

3. *O yé cɛn yé.*

4. Madness in Mali is often understood as incoherent and shameless behavior punctuated by special gifts such as telling the truth and foretelling the future. Mad persons live freely within Malian society, either with their families or on the street.

5. "Some even speculate that many Malians will rub something on the forehead—even a stone—until such a mark appears" (Soares 2004, 221).

6. The ability to shift between contradictory sets of views without being troubled by them. On the illusion of wholeness, see Ewing (1990).

7. *Silame* signifies Muslim. *Mori* means Muslim too, but this latter also refers to *marabout.*

8. Ar. the believer

9. On the Sunni and Wahhabite labels, see Soares (2005, 181–82). For a detailed definition of Wahhabis in Mali, see Soares (2005, 180–209) and Louis Brenner (2001).

10. On modern Salafism or Wahhabi-inclined reform movements in West Africa, see Ahmed (2015), Kobo (2012), and Sounaye (2017). Some scholars call them reformist movements; Loimeier (2016) reminds us that any religious movement is by nature reformist, at least in its inception.

11. "Reformists wrote and spoke forcefully about the need to combat *bid'a* [Ar. Innovation], which means unlawful innovation in Islam" (Soares 2005, 183).

12. On Wahhabis in Bamako, see Amselle (1985). On Wahhabis traders in Sikasso, see Warms (1992).

13. Locals used to tell me that the Wahhabis' expansion in town had stagnated since the 1990s.

14. Muslims of all sides sent their children to *médersa* due to the post-1991 deterioration of the public school. However, *médersa* did not differ from public school in terms of school dropout and absenteeism rates.

15. Muslims adopting Salafi piety in Egypt face "practical problem" and may suffer from "backlash" due to the difficulties of living according to Salafi piety in contemporary Egypt (Schielke 2009, 176–77).

16. Literal Islam.

17. On a detailed analysis of Cheick Soufi Bilal, see Soares (2007, 80–86).

18. Ansar Dine is an Arabo-Bambara expression that means "the guardians/helpers/followers of religion." In post-2012 Mali, the international media associated this expression with the "terrorist" group led by Iyad Ag Ghaly to the detriment of older and popular Ansar Dine (see Peterson 2012).

19. In 2010 this religious association existed in twenty-four countries, mostly in the Bamanan-speaking communities of West Africa and their diasporas settled in the West-

ern world. In Bougouni many sympathizers of Haïdara proudly added "international" to his name. The teaching of Haïdara especially attracted the youth due to its flexible nature with regard to dance and music (Chappatte 2018a).

20. Shahada is the Muslims' declaration of belief in the oneness of God and acceptance of Muhammad as his Prophet.

21. The six promises: "I do not associate anything to God, I do not steal, I do not commit adultery, I do not kill my children, I do not slander, I do not disobey to the Prophet" (Qur'an LX: 12).

22. In Bougouni, Muslim families commonly sent their teenagers to a family of a Muslim scholar for their religious education. They stayed there one to three months (during school break) to learn how to take ablution, how to pray, and for basic moral guidance. Some children received their religious education with an elder of their own family.

23. The secularism (*laïcité*) of the Malian state was inscribed in its constitution at independence in 1960.

24. On an analysis of the category of "world religion" as a historical product, see Masuzawa (2005).

25. The *sura Al-Fatiha* is the first chapter of the Qur'an. Its seven verses stress the lordship and mercy of God. Most Malian Muslims learn *Al-Fatiha* by heart.

26. Similar observations over the unanimity of the five Islamic pillars were made among Muslims in Bobo Dioulasso (Debevec 2012, 36).

27. Christian discourses were also visible through radio and TV programs (e.g., Saturday night Catholic and Protestant programs on ORTM (Office de Radiodiffusion et de Télévision du Mali).

28. I employ the expression "logic of ostentation and dissimulation" to point to the outward/inward identity of a person in public (see Manrique 2015).

29. Broader urban elites (e.g., civil servants, merchants, teachers, doctors, NGO workers).

30. Especially the second prayer time (1:00–1:30 p.m.) and the third prayer time (3:30–4:00 p.m.).

31. *To* is a traditional semolina made of corn or millet. *Gan* is a ladyfinger.

32. *Sɛli* = (Ar. *Salat*). Each prayer contains from two to four *zakat*: a sort of round of prayer that includes bowings and intonations of sura. *Limaniya* = Ar. *Al-iman* (etymology).

33. *Ka sɛli yé ka Ala jigin ɛ kɔnɔ yé.*

34. For an analysis over the cultivation of moral selfhood through Islamic prayer in Indonesia, see Simon (2009).

35. I observed similar interferences in Muslims performing a ritual recollection of God called *zikr* (Chappatte 2018a, 33).

36. Moussa is the main character of my article on "the noble Muslim" in Bougouni's hinterland (Chappatte 2018c).

37. On July 15, 1995, the Muslim Indonesian politician leader Haji Harmoko was accused of having mispronounced the opening verse in the Qur'an, Al-Fatiah, at the end of a *dalang* (shadow puppet performance). His "slip of the tongue" was the subject of

many debates among Indonesian Muslims. Even after his official apology, some of them interpreted his gaffe as proof of ignorance, as if he was, in his heart, more *dalang*-like than Muslim (Bowen 2000).

38. Allah akbar (Ar.).

39. Stories of moral failings of prominent Muslims were also frequently related to charges of corruption and embezzlement.

CHAPTER 4

1. The framework of rural life follows daylight, from 5:30 a.m. to 7:00 p.m. After 8:00 p.m., with no electrical light, nightlife is mostly for sleeping. Other than Bamanan rituals (e.g., spirit cults) and musical events (e.g., local orchestras), except for a few intrepid young people, the entire village community rests by 9:00 p.m.

2. Better-off villagers bought solar panels and car batteries to kindle an electrical bulb and to watch TV for specific occasions (TV news, soap operas, Champions' League football games, etc.).

3. On electric light as a metonym for modernity in rural Mongolia during the Soviet-era, see Sneath (2009).

4. On shame as the concept that articulates honor and respect in Mali, see Holten (2013, 69–71).

5. Bamanan greetings divide the day into four periods: the morning (*a ni sɔgɔma*), the afternoon (*a ni tile*), the late afternoon up to the evening (*a ni wula*), and the night (*a ni su*).

6. Bakhtin employs the mathematician concept of chronotope to stress the indivisibility of space and time in the concrete study of human experience (1978, 237–38).

7. In Hausa the same term means "well-being"; the term *al-afia* in Arabic means "rest" or "time-off."

8. In his study of African religions in Brazil, Roger Bastide (1960) analyzes a situation in which the day belongs to the whites, and the marginal group of former slaves appropriates the night as a time for counter-hegemonic display (*candomblé* brotherhood).

9. In 2009 a TV set was found in most urban *carrés*. On the watching of soap operas in Mali, see Schulz (2006). In Bougouni, people went to bed later on Friday evenings due to the popular music ORTM TV program called *Top Etoiles* (10:15 p.m.—12:05 a.m.); only better-off families bought access to the many TV channels provided by CANAL + TV subscriptions.

10. In the provincial town of Dogondoutchi (Niger), conservative Islamic movements have promoted the seclusion of women as an expression of female piety and as the preservation of a woman's "reputation as a modest and honourable wife" (Masquelier 2009, 97–106). Bougouni was not characterized by the predominance of conservative Islamic movements.

11. In Bougouni some women were involved in bigger businesses. Aïcha, a retired teacher, financed a chicken farm at the outskirt of the town, which produced hundreds

of eggs per day. I often found her husband watching their house from the terrace and saying, "She travelled!"

12. On similar gendered perceptions of mobility and spatial access to the night in India, see Patel (2010).

13. Women should avoid wearing skin-tight or low-cut tops; blue jeans are considered to be sexy clothing. Once, I attended a civil marriage in Bougouni. Most men and women wore lavish *boubou* with jewelry. In the crowd, however, my male friends spotted a woman wearing tight blue jeans and a red blouse. For them, the display of such sexy clothes meant a "loose woman." One of my friends approached her and came back with a mobile number; whether it was hers I do not know.

14. Young unmarried women (*sunguruw*), young unmarried men (*kamalenw*), and children (*denmisɛnw*) were expected to remain within *carrés* after dinnertime. Teenagers and children could, however, go out at night when a mobile discotheque (*balani*) was organized in their neighborhood, especially during traditional celebrations (e.g., Mawlid). When an Islamic public sermon or wedding party took place at night, women, teenagers, and children could also go out without raising suspicion.

15. Local expressions about multiple sexual partners illustrate men's control of women's bodies.

16. In Dogondoutchi the seclusion of women was a sign of upper social status because it required hiring servants to accomplish chores linked to the outside world. Thus, economic hardships might force a husband "to grant his wives greater autonomy and make use of their labor" outside the compound (Masquelier 2009, 100). In parallel, "these secluded wives [were] allowed to visit neighbours and kin after nightfall, when obscurity makes them less likely to be noticed by potential admirers" (98).

17. A wife neglecting household chores would soon become the laughingstock of the local community; such behavior was highly stigmatized in Bougouni, and if repeated led to divorce.

18. At a more pragmatic level, women tended not to go out at night because they were tired from their daily work. Women were the first to wake up the next morning to sweep the courtyard, kindle the hearth, and prepare breakfast.

19. ORTM TV programming end around midnight.

20. An *essencitigi* stallholder is someone who sells gasoline stored in recycled bottles.

21. Similar to Mozambique, "mobile phone communication provides cover similar to the darkness of the night and, as such, brings the possible into everyday life" (Archambault 2010, 130).

22. In Bougouni handling multiple relations at the same time was frequent among unmarried persons.

23. Françoise Grange Omokaro mentions the existence of women's *grins* in Bamako (see 2009, 192); on women's gathering in Mali, see Schulz (2002, 812). *Grins* of women overlooking the street did not exist in Bougouni. Women sat and chatted within *carrés* instead. Furthermore, as they did not come together daily, their visits did not constitute a sort of continuous circle of socialization like the *grins* of men did. The rare women

who spent time in men's *grins* were girlfriends of members of *grins*. Nonetheless, these women avoided visiting men's *grins* regularly because such behavior was ill-regarded. Once, a girlfriend of a member of a *grin* arrived tearfully in the *grin*. Her parents did not want her to be seen in this *grin* anymore. She stopped coming thereafter.

24. *Ne bɛ taa ka na* and *Ne bɛ taa ci la.*

25. *Ne bɛ taa so* and *Ne bɛ taa da.*

26. *Maquis* later became associated with popular uprisings in Cameroon (Prévitali 1999; Sah 2008) and in Central Africa (Cosma 1997, 46–51).

27. I am grateful to Sasha Newell for pointing me to this hypothesis.

28. Sometimes (especially in the capital) a small display advertising a beer brand indicated the presence of a *maquis* in Mali.

29. On how variations of darkness and light affect human experience of space, see Bille and Sorensen (2007).

30. In Odienné, a provincial town of northwest Côte d'Ivoire, half of *maquis* were brothels in the 2010s (Chappatte 2017).

31. Except for me, members of the *grin* never entered Le Vatican.

CHAPTER 5

1. Bamanan proverb: *Tunga man di fugari la* (Bailleul 2005, 247).

2. For a critic of neoliberal prosperity, see Chappatte (2018c).

3. A substantial part of Malian employees' monthly income is made of *les affaires*; there are secret economic takings people collect through gift giving, arrangements, privileges, and *mangement* linked to their work and previous investments in social ties (see (Bayart 1989). Such gifts are not reducible to money and goods. They can be a service, favor, privilege, contact, pull, etc. Moreover, the African saying "the friend's friend is my friend" extends potential recipients of services. Finally, "the system becomes a 'generalised exchange' of services, small and big, which takes officially the shape of illegal favour" (Olivier de Sardan 1996, 105). In absence of networks (that is to say, with a deficit of capital of social ties), the favor becomes a bribe.

4. As it is often the case in contemporary Mali.

5. The American's wife passed away a few years after the wedding. The American decided to finance a new CSCOM in her hometown in the aftermath of her passing.

6. Such strategies were feasible for those who hold privileged positions that were not public (by contrast to politicians).

7. When someone became rich overnight, people pointed to "the devil's money." On accusations of "voodoo economics" toward Babani Sissoko in the United States, see articles in the *Los Angeles Times* at https://www.latimes.com/archives/la-xpm-1998-aug-17-mn-13939-story.html (retrieved May 31, 2021).

8. By "esoteric" I mean a set of secret practices reserved to a small circle of initiated persons.

9. On a comparison between *somaya* and *karamɔgɔya*, see Schulz (2005, 97–101).

10. Or *géomancien païen* (pagan diviner), *thaumaturge* (Kassibo 1992, 546–7); *savant, connaisseur* (expert) (Colleyn 2009, 738); "healer, sorcerer, or diviner" (Soares 1997, 276); "health care and divination expert" (Jansen 2009, 110) in West Africa.

11. Schulz (2005) differentiates *soma* from sorcerer in the same way I differentiate sorcerer as *soma* from sorcerer as witch. My informants used the French word *sorcier* for both categories, while they differentiated them in Bambara.

12. On a rare trial against a *kɔrɔte* accusation attempted during the colonial period, see Méker (1980, 144–45). Such trials never happened during the postcolonial period.

13. Fr. *Poudre.*

14. People referred also to *diɲennatigɛ ka gɛlɛn*, which can be translated as "earthly path is demanding."

15. Her husband left Mali two years ago to pursue adventures in Spain.

16. Jansen did not mention a similar level of discretion in the way a client comes to see a *soma* (Jansen and Kanté 2010, 61) because people often travel long distances to visit a *soma* who does not know their families (Jansen 2009, 119–20). Moreover, Islam as a public force has historically been more an urban reality than a rural reality in the modern history of Mali.

17. Probably objects-power, see Jansen and Kanté (2010, 62).

18. For an analysis of the practice of sand divination, see Jansen and Kanté (2010, part 2).

19. White and/or red.

20. Kassibo states that the "European diviner remains powerless in front of the implacability of destiny," whereas the African diviner, by means of sacrifice, can "ward it off and even master it" (1992, 575) in communities where the *soma* also acts as a priest.

21. In her song called *dakan*, Nahawa Doumbia explains the omnipresence of destiny in people's life and the importance of searching for God's protection on earth.

22. See Bailleul (1996, 70, 286).

23. Bamanan proverb: *Ala dugulentɔgɔ ko sababu* (Bailleul 2005, 10).

24. SO-TRA-MA: Société de Transport Malienne. *Duuru-duuruni* literally means 25 francs, which refers to the price of the first public transport in Bamako during the early postcolonial period.

25. *Baara yé bato yé.*

26. *Ala yé mɔgɔ jigin yé. Baara o yé i fa an i ba yé.*

27. *Ka baara kɛ*: the underlying ethics that inform a given set of practices.

28. On similar understanding of Islamic ethics in terms of "the virtue of patience and endurance" among Moroccan youth in the context of social inequality and social abandonment, see the case of Jawad in Pandolfo (2007, 340–41).

29. On Cherif Ousmane Madane Haïdara, see chapter 3.

30. On the issue of sincerity of public Islam, see chapters 3 and 4.

31. God's business.

32. *Ni ɛ yé daga ta ka se i senkuru ma, Ala bɛ i dɛmɛ ka a sigi kun ma.*

33. *Sababu yé mɔgɔ ɲɔgon yé.*

34. I have used "unemployment" for lack of a better word.

35. Love affairs in Bougouni were important means through which women granted sex to men in exchange for prestigious items (e.g., mobile phones) and money; on love relations in urban Mali, see Schulz (2002, 809–10).

36. *Tontine* is the traditional women's banking system of Mali. Each member of the group chips in a fixed amount of money when they meet over a meal on a regular basis. The total sum is then given to the woman who has been chosen to host the meeting according to a circulatory process. Each member of the association successively benefits from a considerable amount of money at once.

37. A similar logic is observed among Hausa merchants in Niger (Gregoire 1992).

38. In this situation *le social* can lead to an "economy of affection" in which demands arising from a state agent's ties to society generate "corruption" (Villalón 1995, 91).

39. See chapter 6.

40. Trust based on religious identity alone may work within a situation of minority as a marker and maker of a network, such as with the nineteenth-century Muslim trade networks operating in non-Muslim West Africa (Launay 1992). Being a Muslim in Mali is not a sign of reliability anymore because its society is now overwhelmingly Muslim. In such circumstances, trust may instead arise from a shared membership of a specific Muslim movement characterized by a sharp boundary and group solidarity (e.g., Wahhabi identity in Sikasso [Warms 1992]).

41. See Samuli Schielke's analysis of the Salafi piety movements in Egypt, for instance (2009).

CHAPTER 6

1. On post-1991 criticism of the climate of permissiveness, lax morals, and moral corruption made by Muslim preachers, see Soares (2005).

2. *Demokrasi nana. Nka mogow ani dɔgɔw caman yé o faamu dɔrɔn ko "min ka di ɛ yé, ɛ bɛ o dɛ kɛ."*

3. On similar references to nostalgia in Mali, see Soares (2010).

4. Interview with Kaka Diakité, Bougouni, January 2009; paper on local history given by Lassina Diakité, March 2009.

5. On the relations between the *Kafo* of Bougouni and the Kingdom of Ségou, see Samaké (1988).

6. Usually, Muslims do not bury their kinsmen with a gravestone. The so-called Wahhabis especially disapprove of gravestones because they index the act of worship. The Muslim cemetery of Bougouni contained only a few gravestones, mostly related to local notables.

7. "[. . .] transposed from the Arabic *horr*" (Bazin 1974, 135).

8. Most studies of Mande statuses focus on *ɲamakala* (e.g., Camara 1976; McNaughton 1995; Hoffman 1995, 2000) and, to a lesser extent, on the *jon* or slave (e.g., Bazin 1974; Klein 2005, 2009), in which *hɔrɔn* is only referred to, and this mostly by comparison.

9. For a historical and linguistic analysis of caste systems in West Africa, see Tamari (1991).

10. I prefer to speak of corporate groups with distinct statuses rather than castes. Barbara Hoffman, in her study of *griots* (*jeli*) of the town of Kita (Mali), explains that "the Mande caste system does not incorporate an opposition of purity and pollution, but rather a spectrum of differential access to various forms of social and occult power, with the potential pollution arising from inappropriate contact with the powers of other castes" (2000, 247–48). Comparing the Indian caste system with the ranking system of Middle East societies, Charles Lindholm (1985) argued that both systems are primarily based on "oppositional relations" from which social orders emerge.

11. Often the *ɲamakalw* lived in separate districts.

12. On *ɲama*, see McNaughton (1988).

13. The *free* status of the *hɔrɔn* was intrinsically linked to the *servile* status of the *jon*. According to Bazin (1974), their opposition was even central to Bambara culture of the kingdom of Ségou (approximatively 1720–1861).

14. For an illustration of the influences of traditional chieftainship and kinship in the decentralized communal power in southeast Mali, see Chappatte (2005).

15. For this analysis, I consider northern Mali to be at the periphery of the historic Mande world. In Timbuktu, people of slave descent can hardly marry people of noble descent, because the local society still cultivates the endogamous structure based on traditional Mande statuses. Nobleness still means aristocracy by birth. For a study of modern forms of slavery in contemporary Mali, see Naffet Keïta (2012); for a study of the historical evolution of the status of slave descent in West Africa, see Klein (2009).

16. The French administration ended legal slavery by decree in 1905 in the colonies of the Sudan, Guinea, and Senegal.

17. A lack of history over one's own descent system is central to the construction of one's internalized status as slave; see Klein (2009, 36); see also Bazin (1974, 119).

18. Another official observed that because (local) families had "similarly experienced this terrible institution," (the few local) slave owners were more inclined "to understand the sad situation of the slave [hence to let him go] as they themselves await the return of a father or a brother, disappeared since the wars of Samori" (Peterson 2011, 93). For a more general study of slavery and colonial rule in French West Africa, see Klein (1998).

19. Kai Kresse observed a similar performative nobility on the Swahili coast; this performative nobility, however, is based on a local conception of humanity rather than nobility (see 2018, 141–42).

20. *COUR commune* is also an Ivorian soap opera.

21. *E bɛ min fo, e bɛ a kɛ.*

22. In Bougouni's hinterland, *hɔrɔnya* is about *la droiture* (uprightness); see Chappatte (2018c).

23. Literally, "The Muslim is a noble."

24. Gaibazzi's study of Soninke (a westward Mande ethnic group) migrants in Angola demonstrates that a "shared humanity" precedes religious affiliations and differences in terms of "relatedness" (2018, 472).

25. *Ala ka an tile hεεrε caya.*

26. *Ala ka an tile nɔgɔya.* On similar daily blessings in Djenné, see Mommersteeg (2009, chapter 4).

27. *Ala ka dubabu minε.*

28. *Ɛ kεra Bamanan yé!*

29. *Ɛ kεra Malian yé!*

30. Or *ami* (diminutive).

31. In Djenné a *marabout* explained to Mommersteeg that "there are three kinds of events. Firstly, there are things that happen to us; we cannot avoid them. Secondly, there are things that we can get; however, we need to ask God for them through blessing" (2009, 80–81). The same marabout explained that there are other things we request through offerings (*saraka*).

32. Women, including the mother, do not participate directly in the religious baptism. They stay behind and prepare tea and breakfast (e.g., mayonnaise bread), which are distributed when the ceremony ends. However, in the afternoon, women perform the customary baptism. They gather together in the same place for a more festive celebration that includes gift giving, music, and dance.

33. *An bε dubabu kε sisan.*

34. For illustrations of such long series of blessing, see Mommersteeg (2009, 75, 77).

35. During funerals, blessings also ask for granting Heaven to the deceased person.

36. See chapter 5.

37. According to Louis Brenner, this learning system is based on an "esoteric episteme"; it is "a hierarchical conceptualization of knowledge, the highest 'levels' of which are made available to only relatively few specialists. Knowledge is transmitted in an initiatic form and is closely related to devotional praxis. The acquisition of knowledge is progressively transformative: one must be properly prepared to receive any particular form of knowledge, the acquisition of which can provide the basis for a subsequent stage of personal transformation [e.g., the spiritual hierarchies of the Sufi orders]" (2001, 18).

38. In Djenné, a fieldwork assistant of Mommersteeg said, "*Baraka* is for everybody" (2009, 151).

39. For an analysis of *baraka* among Muslims in Djenné through the Songhay figure of "the blessed child," see Mommersteeg (2009, 147–48).

40. *Mɔgɔw bε dubabu di. Ala bε barika kε dubabu fε.*

41. *Dubabu yé sira min bε taa barika yé.*

42. *Même si tu es en règle, un policier qui chercher un petit billet va te prouver le contraire!*

43. "The blessed child" as hereditary principle has been put forward by saint lineages in Africa so as to keep *barika* within the same family by transmitting it from father to son (Rosander and Westerlund 1997). This hereditary principle was questioned by Schmitz (2000) in his study of the transmission of *baraka* (spiritual and charismatic kinship) between Muslim scholars and their non-biological disciples in the valley of Senegal.

44. Non-marital ties between the mother and the father of a child are unspoken in local discourses.

45. "Of course, God appreciates someone who is a hard worker and respectful toward his elders, but if the mother of this individual does not respect her husband, sooner or later her child will collect the consequences of her bad behavior" (Sitafa, entrepreneur in Bougouni).

46. Ablaye's father passed away when he was a child.

47. *Ablaye, c'est un petit qui se débrouille bien.*

48. See the economy of piety in chapter 5.

49. *Toutes ces règles-là, elles sont liées à notre environnement. Ce sont des inventeries. Mais sans ces inventeries la vie sociale seraient difficile ici.*

50. Giuliano Luongo, "Réforme du code de la famille au Mali: le parlement cède aux pressions religieuses," *Contrepoints*, January 27, 2012, http://www.contrepoints. org/2012/01/27/66452-reforme-du-code-de-la-famille-au-mali-le-parlement-cede-aux-pressions-religieuses (retrieved May 31, 2021).

51. *Les femmes doivent obéissance au mari.*

52. *Respect mutuel.*

CHAPTER 7

1. For ethnographic vignettes of "hustlers" in the Gambia, see Gaibazzi (2015, 99–104).

2. Similar to South Africa (Park 2013), the bigger importers of Chinese products are not Chinese; they are local traders. On Chinese in Mali, see Bourdarias (2010).

3. An edited book on consumption in Africa, based on fieldwork undertaken mostly in the 1990s, does not include a single article on Chinese goods (Hahn 2008); the massive arrival of Chinese goods in the African continent started in the early 2000s.

4. Japanese goods have been present in Mali since the 1930s; however, foreign goods have had a significant impact on most people's lives only from 2000. Before, the consumption of foreign products (e.g., clothes, bicycles, hats, sunglasses) "was carried on piecemeal fashion" in southern Mali (Peterson 2011, 193). Locals named these new objects with "neologisms" ("bicycle," *negeso*, literally "iron horse"; "plow," *misidaba*, literally "cattle hoe") because their occasional, limited consumption did not really transform people's ways of life (193–98).

5. Similar processes of "social stratification" based on uneven access to material goods operate to some extent in rural Mali (Koenig 2005).

6. The formerly noble activity of farming (see chapter 6) is increasingly being perceived as unattractive and degrading by the youth.

7. In Bamako markets were overcrowded with hawkers of Chinese goods; this harsh competition tended to turn their import trade from China to "a survival mechanism" (Lyons and Brown 2010).

8. Social housing projects have been supported by all elected presidents of the Third Republic of Mali. Their social aim, however, has often been criticized.

9. This motorbike was previously imported from Indonesia, therefore its denomination "Jakarta." It is imported as spare parts put in wooden crates and assembled in Mali to avoid customs duties called *dédouanement*. This fancy motorbike has become so popular among the urban youth in Bamako that their elders jokingly call them the Génération Jakarta.

10. In the early 2010s, Dubaï also became part of these places of material-based civilization par excellence.

11. The monthly wage (and not *les affaires*) of middle-ranking urban state employees did not exceed 150,000 FCFA (US$300) in 2010 Mali.

12. In South Africa the expression "Fong Kong" means something cheap and fake made in China (Park 2013).

13. Examination for public sector jobs.

14. Numerous civil servants wished to retire in expensive Bamako. High civil servants were therefore more able to fulfil this desire.

15. See chapter 5.

16. See chapter 5.

17. See chapter 6.

CHAPTER 8

1. Matthieu Louis (2014) suggests the notion of *itinerrance* to express the wandering that *aventuriers* encounter in their itinerary. Unfortunately, I discovered this fascinating PhD on *aventure* in West Africa (Burkina Faso) only days before the submission of my manuscript.

2. For an analysis of non-state regional political organization in the Sahara, see Brachet and Scheele (2019).

3. Mostly French, Chadian, and Nigerien forces.

4. On the other Ansar Dine, see Peterson (2012).

5. Mouvement du 5 juin—Rassemblement des Forces Patriotiques.

6. *Ici il n'y a rien. C'est calme. C'est à Bamako que ça chauffe.*

7. How young Muslims across the world seek to make their way in a post-9/11 transformed world, see Masquelier and Soares (2016).

REFERENCES

Agnew, C. T., and A. Chappell. 2000. "Desiccation in the Sahel." In *Linking Climate Change to Land Surface Change*, edited by Sue J. McLaren and Dominic R. Kniveton, 27–48. Dordrecht: Kluwer Academic.

Ahmed, Chanfi. 2015. *West African "ulamā" and Salafism in Mecca and Medina: Jawāb al-Ifrīqī––The Response of the African*. Leiden, Netherlands: Brill.

Alimia, Saana, André Chappatte, Nora Lafi, and Ulrike Freitag. 2018. "In Search of Urbanity." *ZMO Programmatic Texts*, no. 12.

Amselle, Jean-Loup. 1977. *Les Négociants de La Savane: Histoire et Organisation Sociale Des Kooroko, Mali*. Paris: Anthropos.

Amselle, Jean-Loup. 1985. "Le Wahabisme à Bamako (1945–1985)." *Revue Canadienne Des Études Africaines* 19 (2): 345.

Amselle, Jean-Loup. 1987. "L'ethnicité comme volonté et comme représentation: à propos des Peuls du Wasolon." *Annales* 42 (2): 465–89.

Amselle, Jean-Loup. 1988. "Un État Contre l'État: Le Keleyadugu." *Cahiers d'Études Africaines* 28 (111): 463–83.

Anderson, Benedict. 1983. *Imagined Communities: Reflections on the Origin and Spread of Nationalism*. London: Verso.

Archambault, Julie Soleil. 2010. "Cruising through Uncertainty: Mobile Phone Practices, Occulted Economies, and the Politics of Respect in Southern Mozambique." PhD thesis, SOAS, University of London.

Archambault, Julie Soleil. 2011. "Breaking up 'Because of the Phone' and the Transformative Potential of Information in Southern Mozambique." *New Media & Society* 13 (3): 444–56.

Archambault, Julie Soleil. 2017. *Mobile Secrets: Youth, Intimacy, and the Politics of Pretense in Mozambique*. Chicago: University of Chicago Press.

Arnoldi, Mary Jo. 2006. "Youth Festivals and Museums: The Cultural Politics of Public Memory in Postcolonial Mali." *Africa Today* 52 (4): 55–76.

Arnoldi, Mary Jo. 2007. "Bamako, Mali: Monuments and Modernity in the Urban Imagination." *Africa Today* 54: 3–24.

Asad, Talal. 1986. "The Idea of an Anthropology of Islam." Washington, DC: Center for Contemporary Arab Studies, Georgetown University.

Auzias, Dominique, and Jean-Paul Labourdette. 2011. *Le Petit Futé Mali 2012/2013*. Paris: Petit Futé.

Bailleul, Charles. 1996. *Dictionnaire bambara-français*. Bamako, Mali: Editions Donniya.

Bailleul, Charles. 2005. *Sagesse bambara: proverbes et sentences*. Bamako, Mali: Donniya.

Bakhtin, Mikhaïl. 1978. "Formes Du Temps et Du Chronotope Dans Le Roman." In *Esthétique et Théorie Du Roman*, edited by Mikhaïl Bakhtin, 235–398. Paris: Gallimard.

Banerjee, Sheela. 2015. "Interpretation and Reality: Anthropological Hauntings in *The Waste Land*." *Modernism/Modernity* 22 (2): 237–54.

Bardem, Isabelle. 1993. "L'émancipation des jeunes: un facteur négligé des migrations interafricaines." Edited by Véronique Dupont and Christophe Guilmoto. *Cahiers des Sciences Humaines* 29 (2–3): 375–93.

Barley, Nigel. 1984. *Adventures in a Mud Hut: An Innocent Anthropologist Abroad*. New York: Vanguard Press.

Barnes, John Arundel. 1994. *A Pack of Lies: Towards a Sociology of Lying*. Cambridge: Cambridge University Press.

Bastide, Roger. 1960. *Les religions africaines au Brésil; vers une sociologie des interpénétrations de civilisations*. Paris: Presses universitaires de France.

Bateson, Mary Catherine. 1989. *Composing a Life*. New York: Atlantic Monthly Press.

Bayart, Jean-François. 1989. *L'Etat En Afrique: La Politique Du Ventre*. Paris: Fayard.

Bayart, Jean-François, Achille Mbembe, and Comi M. Toulabor, eds. 1992. *Le Politique Par Le Bas En Afrique Noire: Contributions à Une Problématique de La Démocratie*. Paris: Karthala.

Bazin, Jean. 1885. "A chacun son Bambara." In *Au cœur de l'ethnie*, edited by Jean-Loup Amselle and Elikia M'Bokolo, 87–127. Paris: La Découverte.

Bazin, Jean. 1974. "War and Servitude in Segou." *Economy and Society* 3 (2): 104–24.

Bazin, Jean. 1979. "La production d'un récit historique." *Cahiers d'Études Africaines* 19 (73): 435–83.

Bazin, Jean. 1988a. "Genèse de l'État et formation d'un champ politique: le royaume de Segu." *Revue française de science politique* 38 (5): 709–19.

Bazin, Jean. 1988b. "Princes désarmés, corps dangereux. Les «rois-femmes» de la région de Segu." *Cahiers d'Études Africaines* 28 (111): 375–441.

Berger, Laurent. 2010. "La Centralisation d'un Culte Périphérique: Islam, Possession et Sociétés d'initiation Au Bèlèdugu, Mali." *Politique Africaine* 118 (2): 143–64.

Bille, Mikkel, and Tim Flohr Sørensen. 2007. "An Anthropology of Luminosity: The Agency of Light." *Journal of Material Culture* 12 (3): 263–84.

Bird, Charles S. 1999. "The Production and Reproduction of Sunjata." In *In Search of Sunjata: The Mande Oral Epic as History, Literature, and Performance*, edited by Ralph A. Austen, 275–96. Bloomington: Indiana University Press.

Bird, Charles S, and Martha B. Kendall. 1980. "The Mande Hero: Text and Context." In *Explorations in African Systems of Thought*, edited by Charles S. Bird and Isabelle Karp, 20–21. Bloomington: Indiana University Press.

Blunt, Alison. 2007. "Cultural Geographies of Migration: Mobility, Transnationality, and Diaspora." *Progress in Human Geography* 31 (5): 684–94.

Bok, Sissela. 1989. *Secrets: On the Ethics of Concealment and Revelation*. Reissue edition. New York: Vintage.

Bondaz, Julien. 2013. "Le thé des hommes." *Cahiers d'Études Africaines* no. 209–210 (1): 61–85.

Bourdarias, Françoise. 2009. "Mobilités chinoises et dynamiques sociales locales au Mali." *Politique africaine* no. 113 (1): 28–54.

Bourdarias, Françoise. 2010. "Redéfinitions de L'État-Nation et Des Territoires Au Mali En Temps de Crise: Migrants Chinois et Populations Locales." In *La Crise Vue d'ailleurs*, edited by Pascale M. Phélinas and Monique Sélim, 139–69. Paris: L'Harmattan.

Bourdieu, Pierre. 1979. *La Distinction: Critique Sociale Du Jugement*. Le Sens Commun. Paris: Éditions de Minuit.

Bourdieu, Pierre. 2004. *Science of Science and Reflexivity*. Translated by Richard Nice. Chicago: University of Chicago Press.

Bowen, John R. 1998. "What Is 'Universal' and 'Local' in Islam?" *Ethos* 26 (2): 258–61.

Bowen, John R. 2000. "Imputations of Faith and Allegiance: Islamic Prayer and Indonesian Politics Outside the Mosque." In *Islam across the Indian Ocean: Inside and Outside the Mosque*, edited by David J. Parkin and Stephen Headley, 23–38. Richmont, UK: Curzon Press.

Brachet, Julien, and Judith Scheele. 2019. *The Value of Disorder: Autonomy, Prosperity, and Plunder in the Chadian Sahara*. Cambridge: Cambridge University Press.

Bravmann, René A. 2001. "Islamic Ritual and Practice in Bamana Ségou—The 19th Century 'Citadel of Paganism.'" In *Bamana: The Art of Existence in Mali*, edited by Jean-Paul Colleyn, Mary Jo Arnoldi, and Museum Rietberg, 34–43. New York: Museum for African Art.

Bredeloup, Sylvie. 2014. *Migrations d'aventures: terrains africains*. CTHS géographie 11. Paris: CTHS.

Bredeloup, Sylvie, and Brigitte Bertoncello. 2006. "La migration chinoise en Afrique: accélérateur du développement ou «sanglot de l'homme noir»?" *Afrique contemporaine* no. 218 (2): 199–224.

Brenner, Louis. 1984. *West African Sufi: Religious Heritage and Spiritual Search of Cerno Bokar Saalif Taal*. London: Hurst.

Brenner, Louis. 1993a. "Constructing Muslim Identities in Mali." In *Muslim Identity and Social Change in Sub-Saharan Africa*, edited by Louis Brenner, 59–78. London: Hurst.

Brenner, Louis. 1993b. "La culture arabo-islamique au Mali." In *Le Radicalisme islamique au sud du Sahara: Da'wa, arabisation et critique de l'Occident*, edited by René Wadih Otayek, 161–95. Paris: Talence.

Brenner, Louis. 2001. *Controlling Knowledge: Religion, Power, and Schooling in a West African Muslim Society*. Bloomington: Indiana University Press.

Bruijn, Mirjam de, Rijk van Dijk, and Dick Foeken, eds. 2002. *Mobile Africa: Changing Patterns of Movement in Africa and Beyond*. Leiden: Brill.

Bruijn, Mirjam de, and Rijk van Dijk. 2003. "Changing Population Mobility in West Africa: Fulbe Pastoralists in Central and South Mali." *African Affairs* 102 (407): 285–307.

Camara, Sory. 1976. *Gens de La Parole: Essai Sur La Condition et Le Rôle Des Griots Dans La Société Malinké*. The Hague: Mouton.

Chabal, Patrick, and Jean-Pascal Daloz. 1999. *Africa Works: Disorder as Political Instrument*. London: International African Institute in association with James Currey, Oxford.

Chakrabarty, Dipesh. 2000. *Provincializing Europe: Postcolonial Thought and Historical Difference* (new ed.). Princeton: Princeton University Press.

Chappatte, André. 2005. "Chefferie Traditionnelle et Conseillers Communaux: Un Élément de Dialectique: La Parenté: Terrain, Commune Rurale de Fama, Région de Sikasso, Mali, . . ." Genève: Université de genève.

Chappatte, André. 2014a. "Chinese Products, Social Mobility, and Material Modernity in Bougouni, a Small but Fast-Growing Administrative Town of Southwest Mali." *African Studies* 73 (1): 22–40.

Chappatte, André. 2014b. "Night Life in Southern Urban Mali: Being a Muslim Maquisard in Bougouni." *Journal of the Royal Anthropological Institute* 20 (3): 526–44.

Chappatte, André. 2016. "Encounter between Tiredness, Dust, and Ebola at a Border Checkpoint of Northwestern Côte d'Ivoire." *Basel Papers on Political Transformations—Mobilities—In and Out of Africa*, no. 10: 9–23.

Chappatte, André. 2017. "'Texas': An Off-Centre District at the Heart of Nightlife in Odienné." In *Understanding the City through Its Margins. Pluridisciplinary Perspectives from Case Studies in Africa, Asia, and the Middle East*, edited by André Chappatte, Ulrike Freitag, and Nora Lafi, 97–116. New York: Routledge.

Chappatte, André. 2018a. "Crowd, Sensationalism, and Power: The Yearly Ansar Dine 'Pilgrimage' of Maouloud in Bamako." *Journal of Religion in Africa* 48 (1–2): 3–34.

Chappatte, André. 2018b. "Exploring Youth, Media Practices and Religious Affiliations in Contemporary Mali through the Controversy over the Musical Zikiri." In *Religion, Media, and Marginality in Modern Africa*, edited by Felicitas Becker, Joel Cabrita, and Marie Rodet, 229–55. Athens: Ohio University Press.

Chappatte, André. 2018c. "'The Vulture without Fear': Exploring the Noble Muslim in Contemporary Rural Mali." *HAU: Journal of Ethnographic Theory* 8 (3): 686–701.

Chappatte, André. 2021. "When Silence Is 'Yeelen' (Light): Exploring the Corporeality of the Mind in a Nocturnal Solo *Zikr* Practice (Odienné, Ivory Coast)." *Critical Research on Religion* 9 (2): 175–90.

Choplin, Armelle. 2020. *Matière Grise de l'urbain. La Vie Du Ciment En Afrique*. Genève: Métis Presses.

Ciekawy, Diane, and Peter Geschiere. 1998. "Containing Witchcraft: Conflicting Scenarios in Postcolonial Africa." *African Studies Review* 41 (3): 1–14.

Clark, Andrew F. 2000. "From Military Dictatorship to Democracy: The Democratisation Process in Mali." In *Democracy and Development in Mali*, edited by John M.

Staatz, David Robinson, and R. James Bingen, 251–64. East Lansing: Michigan State University Press.

Colleyn, Jean-Paul. 2001. *Bamana: The Art of Existence in Mali*. 1er édition. New York: Museum for African Art.

Colleyn, Jean-Paul. 2009. "Images, signes, fétiches. À propos de l'art bamana (Mali)." *Cahiers d'Études Africaines* no. 195 (3): 733–46.

Colleyn, Jean-Paul. 2010. "Préface." In *La géomancie des Monts Mandingues. L'art de lire l'avenir dans le sable*, edited by Jan Jansen and Namagan Kanté, Editions Yeelen, 9–14. Bamako, Mali: African Books Collective.

Comaroff, Jean, and John Comaroff. 1993. "Introduction." In *Modernity and Its Malcontents*, xi–xxxvii. Chicago: University of Chicago Press.

Comaroff, Jean, and John L. Comaroff. 2000. "Millennial Capitalism: First Thoughts on a Second Coming." In *Millennial Capitalism and the Culture of Neoliberalism*, edited by John L. Comaroff, Jean Comaroff, and Robert P. Weller, 1–56. Durham: Duke University Press.

Conklin, Alice L. 1997. *Mission to Civilize: The Republican Idea of Empire in France & West Africa, 1895–1930*. Stanford: Stanford University Press.

Conrad, David C. 2001. "Pilgrim Fajigi and Basiw from Mecca: Islam and Traditional Religion in the Former French Sudan." In *Bamana: The Art of Existence in Mali*, 25–33. New York: Museum for African Art.

Conrad, David C. 2005. "Foreword." In *Wari Matters: Ethnographic Explorations of Money in the Mande World*, edited by Stephen Wootton, Lit Verlag, 5–10. Münster: Lit.

Conrad, David C., and Barbara E. Frank. 1995. "Introduction: Nyamakala, Contradiction, and Ambiguity in Mande Society." In *Status and Identity in West Africa: Nyamakalaw of Mande*, edited by David C. Conrad and Barbara E. Frank, 1–27. Bloomington: Indiana University Press.

Cook, Joanna, James Laidlaw, and Jonathan Mair. 2009. "What If There Is No Elephant? Towards a Conception of an Un-Sited Field." *Multi-Sited Ethnography: Theory, Praxis, and Locality in Contemporary Research*, 47–72.

Cooper, Elizabeth, and David Pratten, eds. 2015. *Ethnographies of Uncertainty in Africa*. London: Palgrave Macmillan UK.

Cordell, Dennis D., Joel W. Gregory, and Victor Piché. 1996. *Hoe and Wage: A Social History of a Circular Migration System in West Africa*. Boulder: Westview Press.

Cosma, Wilungula B. 1997. *Fizi, 1967–1986: Le Maquis Kabila*. Les Cahiers Du CEDAF 25. Bruxelles: Institut africain CEDAF.

Coulibaly, Amadi, and Thea Hilhorst. 2004. *Implementing Decentralisation in Mali: The Experiences of Two Rural Municipalities in Southern Mali*. London: IIED.

Cox, Peter, Dave Horton, and Paul Rosen. 2007. "Introduction: Cycling and Society." In *Cycling and Society*, 1st ed., 1–24. London: Routledge.

Cruise O'Brien, Donal B. 2003. *Symbolic Confrontations: Muslims Imagining the State in Africa*. London: C Hurst.

Cruise O'Brien, Donal B., and Christian Coulon, eds. 1988. *Charisma and Brotherhood in African Islam*. Oxford: Clarendon Press.

Daniel, Serge. 2014. *Les mafias du Mali: Trafics et terrorisme au Sahel*. Paris: Descartes & Cie.

Darbon, Dominique. 1990. "L'État Prédateur." *Politique Africaine*, no. 39: 37–45.

Das, Veena. 2012. "Ordinary Ethics." In *A Companion to Moral Anthropology*, edited by Didier Fassin, 133–49. Boston: John Wiley and Sons.

Das, Veena. 2015. "What Does Ordinary Ethics Look Like?" In *Four Lectures on Ethics*, edited by Michael Lambek, Veena Das, Didier Fassin, and Webb Keane, 53–125. Chicago: Hau Books.

Das, Veena. 2018. "Ethics, Self-Knowledge, and Life Taken as a Whole." *HAU: Journal of Ethnographic Theory* 8 (3): 537–49.

David, Philippe. 1980. *Les Navétanes: Histoire Des Migrants Saisonniers de l'arachide En Sénégambie Des Origines à Nos Jours*. Dakar: Nouvelles Éditions Africaines.

De Jong, Ferdinand. 2007. *Masquerades of Modernity: Power and Secrecy in Casamance, Senegal*. Bloomington: Indiana University Press.

De Jorio, Rosa. 2006. "Politics of Remembering and Forgetting: The Struggle over Colonial Monuments in Mali." *Africa Today* 52 (4): 79–106.

De Jorio, Rosa. 2016. *Cultural Heritage in Mali in the Neoliberal Era*. Springfield: University of Illinois Press.

Debevec, Liza. 2012. "Postponing Piety in Urban Burkina Faso." In *Ordinary Lives and Grand Schemes*, edited by Liza Debevec and Samuli Schielke, 1st ed., 33–47. New York: Berghahn Books.

Deeb, Lara. 2015. "Thinking Piety and the Everyday Together: A Response to Fadil and Fernando." *HAU: Journal of Ethnographic Theory* 5 (2): 93–96.

Deeb, Lara, and Mona Harb. 2013. *Leisurely Islam: Negotiating Geography and Morality in Shi'ite South Beirut*. Princeton: Princeton University Press.

Defoe, Daniel. 2021. *The Life and Adventures of Robinson Crusoe*. Bristol: Read & Co. Classics. Originally published 1719.

Desjarlais, Robert, and Jason C. Throop. 2011. "Phenomenological Approaches in Anthropology." *Annual Review of Anthropology* 40 (1): 87–102.

Dieterlen, G., and Y. Cissé. 1972. *Les Fondements De La Société D'initiation Du Komo*. Reprint 2018 édition. Berlin: Walter de Gruyter.

Dieterlen, Germaine. 1951. "Essai sur la religion Bambara." Paris: Presses universitaires de France.

Dieterlen, Germaine. 1955. "Mythe et organisation sociale au Soudan français." *Journal des Africanistes* 25 (1): 39–76.

Diggins, Jennifer. 2015. "Economic Runaways: Patronage, Poverty, and the Pursuit of 'Freedom' on Sierra Leone's Maritime Frontier." *Africa* 85 (2): 312–32.

Dilley, Roy. 2004. *Islamic and Caste Knowledge Practices among Haalpulaar'en in Senegal: Between Mosque and Termite Mound*. Edinburgh: Edinburgh University Press.

Doquet, Anne. 2007. "Des sciences humaines à l'islam." *Cahiers d'Études Africaines* 186 (2): 371–89.

Douglas, Mary, and Baron C. Isherwood. 1996. *The World of Goods: Towards an Anthropology of Consumption.* New York: Routledge.

Dubresson, Alain, and Monique Bertrand. 1997. *Petites et Moyennes Villes d'Afrique Noire.* Paris: Karthala.

Ebin, Victoria. 1996. "Making Room versus Creating Space: The Construction of Spatial Categories by Itinerant Mouride Traders." In *Making Muslim Space in North America and Europe,* edited by Barbara Daly Metcalf, 92–109. Berkeley: University of California Press.

Eickelman, Dale F. 1989. "National Identity and Religious Discourse in Contemporary Oman." *International Journal of Islamic and Arabic Studies* 6 (1): 1–20.

Eickelman, Dale F., and Jon W. Anderson, eds. 2003. *New Media in the Muslim World: The Emerging Public Sphere.* 2nd ed. Bloomington: Indiana University Press.

Ellen, Roy F. 1983. "Social Theory, Ethnography, and the Understanding of Practical Islam in South-East Asia." In *Islam in South-East Asia,* edited by M. B. Hooker, 50–91. Leiden: Brill.

Ellis, Stephen. 2007. *The Mask of Anarchy: The Destruction of Liberia and the Religious Dimension of an African Civil War.* London: Hurst & Company.

Eriksen, Thomas Hylland. 2007. *Globalization: The Key Concepts.* Oxford: Berg.

Ewing, Katherine P. 1990. "The Illusion of Wholeness: Culture, Self, and the Experience of Inconsistency." *Ethos* 18 (3): 251–78.

Fadil, Nadia, and Mayanthi Fernando. 2015. "Rediscovering the 'Everyday' Muslim: Notes on an Anthropological Divide." *Journal of Ethnographic Theory* 5 (2): 59–88.

Favret-Saada, Jeanne. 2009. *Désorceler.* Paris: Olivier.

Feld, Steven, and Keith H. Basso, eds. 1996. *Senses of Place.* Santa Fe: School of American Research Press.

Ferguson, James. 1999. *Expectations of Modernity: Myths and Meanings of Urban Life on the Zambian Copperbelt.* Berkeley: University of California Press.

Ferguson, James. 2006. *Global Shadows: Africa in the Neoliberal World Order.* Durham: Duke University Press.

Ferme, Mariane C. 2001. *The Underneath of Things: Violence, History, and the Everyday in Sierra Leone.* Los Angeles: University of California Press.

Ferrarini, Lorenzo. 2014. "Ways of Knowing Donsoya: Environment, Embodiment, and Perception among the Hunters of Burkina Faso." Manchester: University of Manchester.

Fioratta, Susanna. 2020. *Global Nomads: An Ethnography of Migration, Islam, and Politics in West Africa.* New York: Oxford University Press.

Foeken, Dick, Rijk van Dijk, and Kiky van Til. 2001. "Population Mobility in Africa: An Overview." In *Mobile Africa: Changing Patterns of Movement in Africa and Beyond,* edited by Mirjam de Bruijn, Rijk van Dijk, and Dick Foeken. Leiden: Brill.

Foeken, D.W.J, and S. O. Owuor. 2006. "Surviving in the Neighbourhoods of Nakuru Town, Kenya." In *Crisis and Creativity: Exploring the Wealth of the African Neighbourhood*, edited by Piet Konings and D.W.J. Foeken, 22–45. Leiden: Brill.

Fouquet, Thomas. 2007. "Imaginaires migratoires et expériences multiples de l'altérité: une dialectique actuelle du proche et du lointain." *Autrepart* no. 41 (1): 83–98.

Fouquet, Thomas. 2016. "Paysages nocturnes de la ville et politiques de la nuit." *Sociétés politiques comparées*, no. 38: 2–16.

Fouquet, Thomas. 2017. "La nuit urbaine, un «espace potentiel»? Hypothèses dakaroises." *Cultures & Conflits*, no. 105–106: 83–97.

Frank, Barbara E. 2001. "More Than Objects: Bamana Artistry in Iron, Wood, Clay, Leather, and Cloth." In *Bamana: The Art of Existence in Mali*, edited by Jean-Paul Colleyn, 45–51. New York: Museum for African Art.

Friedman, Jonathan. 1994. "Introduction." In *Consumption and Identity*, edited by Jonathan Friedman, 1–22. Chur, Switzerland: Harwood Academic.

Gaibazzi, Paolo. 2015. *Bush Bound: Young Men and Rural Permanence in Migrant West Africa*. 1st ed. New York: Berghahn Books.

Gaibazzi, Paolo. 2018. "West African Strangers and the Politics of Inhumanity in Angola: The Politics of Inhumanity." *American Ethnologist* 45 (4): 470–81.

Galinier, Jacques, Aurore Monod Becquelin, Guy Bordin, Laurent Fontaine, Francine Fourmaux, Juliette Roullet Ponce, Piero Salzarulo, Philippe Simonnot, Michèle Therrien, and Iole Zilli. 2010. "Anthropology of the Night: Cross-Disciplinary Investigations." *Current Anthropology* 51 (6): 819–47.

Galy, Michel, ed. 2013. *La guerre au Mali Comprendre la crise au Sahel et au Sahara: enjeux et zones d'ombre*. Paris: La Découverte.

Gaonkar, Dilip Parameshwar. 2001. "On Alternative Modernities." In *Alternative Modernities*, edited by Dilip Parameshwar Gaonkar, 1–23. Durham: Duke University Press.

Gary-Tounkara, Daouda. 2008. *Migrants Soudanais-Maliens et Conscience Ivoirienne: Les Étrangers En Côte d'Ivoire, 1903–1980*. Paris: Harmattan.

Geurts, Kathryn Linn. 2002. *Culture and the Senses: Bodily Ways of Knowing in an African Community*. Berkeley: University of California Press.

Gilsenan, Michael. 1982. *Recognizing Islam: An Anthropologist's Introduction*. London: Croom Helm.

Gomez-Perez, Muriel, ed. 2005. *L'islam Politique Au Sud Du Sahara: Identités, Discours et Enjeux*. Paris: Karthala.

Goody, Jack. 1971. *Technology, Tradition, and the State in Africa*. London: Oxford University Press.

Gregoire, Emmanuel. 1992. *Alhazai of Maradi: Traditional Hausa Merchants in a Changing Sahelian City*. Boulder: Lynne Rienner.

Gugler, Josef. 2002. "The Son of the Hawk Does Not Remain Abroad: The Urban-Rural Connection in Africa." *African Studies Review* 45 (1): 21–41.

Guyer, Jane I. 1995. "Introduction: The Currency Interface and Its Dynamics." In *Money Matters: Instability, Values, and Social Payments in the Modern History of West African Communities*, edited by Jane I. Guyer, 1–33. London: James Currey.

Haas, Hein de. 2008a. "Irregular Migration from West Africa to the Maghreb and the European Union: An Overview of Recent Trends." Geneva: International Organization for Migration.

Haas, Hein de. 2008b. "The Myth of Invasion: The Inconvenient Realities of African Migration to Europe." *Third World Quarterly* 29 (7): 1305–22.

Haenni, Patrick. 2005. *L'islam de Marché: L'autre Révolution Conservatrice*. Paris: Seuil.

Hage, Ghassan. 2005. "A Not So Multi-Sited Ethnography of a Not So Imagined Community." *Anthropological Theory* 5 (4): 463–75.

Hage, Ghassan, ed. 2009. "Waiting Out the Crisis: On Stuckedness and Governmentality." In *Waiting*, 97–106. Carlton, Victoria: Melbourne University Publishing.

Hahn, Hans Peter, ed. 2008. "Consumption, Identities, and Agency in Africa." In *Consumption in Africa: Anthropological Approaches*, 9–41. Münster: Lit Verlag.

Hahn, Hans Peter, and Ludovic Kibora. 2008. "The Domestication of the Mobile Phone: Oral Society and New ICT in Burkina Faso." *Journal of Modern African Studies* 46 (1): 87–109.

Hall, Bruce S. 2011. *A History of Race in Muslim West Africa, 1600–1960*. Cambridge: Cambridge University Press.

Hamidou, Magassa. 1996. "La Crise de La Société Malienne: Une Alternative." *Afrique et Développement* 21 (2/3): 141–58.

Handelman, Don. 2005. "Epilogue: Dark Soundings—Towards a Phenomenology of Night." *Paideuma* 51: 247–61.

Hashim, Iman, and Dorte Thorsen. 2011. *Child Migration in Africa*. London: Zed Books, in association with the Nordic Africa Institute.

Hatfield, D. J. 2011. "The [Ghost] Object: Haunting and Urban Renewal in a 'Very Traditional Town.'" *Journal of Archeology and Anthropology* 75: 71–112.

Haugen, Heidi Østbø. 2011. "Chinese Exports to Africa: Competition, Complementarity, and Cooperation between Micro-Level Actors." *Forum for Development Studies* 38 (2): 157–76.

Hilgers, Mathieu. 2009. *Une Ethnographie à l'échelle de La Ville. Urbanité, Histoire et Reconnaissance à Koudougou (Burkina Faso)*. Paris: Karthala.

Hilgers, Mathieu. 2012. "Contribution à Une Anthropologie Des Villes Secondaires." *Cahiers d'Études Africaines* 205 (1): 29–55.

Hill, Joseph. 2018. *Wrapping Authority: Women Islamic Leaders in a Sufi Movement in Dakar, Senegal*. Toronto: University of Toronto Press.

Hirschkind, Charles. 1997. "What Is Political Islam?" *Middle East Report*, no. 205: 12–14.

Hirschkind, Charles. 2006. *The Ethical Soundscape: Cassette Sermons and Islamic Counterpublics*. New York: Columbia University Press.

Hiskett, Mervyn. 1994. *The Course of Islam in Africa*. Edinburgh: Edinburgh University Press.

Ho, Engseng. 2006. *The Graves of Tarim: Genealogy and Mobility across the Indian Ocean*. 1st ed. Berkeley: University of California Press.

Hoffman, Barbara. 1995. "Power, Structure, and Mande Jeliw." In *Status and Identity in West Africa: Nyamakalaw of Mande*, edited by David C. Conrad and Barbara E. Frank, 36–46. Bloomington: Indiana University Press.

Hoffman, Barbara G. 2000. *Griots at War: Conflict, Conciliation, and Caste in Mande*. Bloomington: Indiana University Press.

Holder, Gilles. 2009a. "'Maouloud 2006,' de Bamako à Tombouctou: Entre Réislamisation de La Nation et Laïcité de l'état: La Construction d'un Espace Public Religieux Au Mali." In *L'islam: Nouvel Espace Public En Afrique*, edited by Gilles Holder, 237–89. Paris: Karthala.

Holder, Gilles. 2009b. "Vers Un Espace Publique Religieux: Pour Une Lecture Contemporaine Des Enjeux Politiques de l'islam En Afrique." In *L'islam: Nouvel Espace Public En Afrique*, edited by Gilles Holder, 5–20. Paris: Karthala.

Holston, James. 1989. *The Modernist City: An Anthropological Critique of Brasília*. Chicago: University of Chicago Press.

Holten, Lianne. 2013. *Mothers, Medicine, and Morality in Rural Mali: An Ethnographic Study of Therapy Management of Pregnancy and Children's Illness Episodes*. Zürich: Lit.

Horton, Dave. 2013. "The Role of Cycling in the Urban Environment." In *Promoting Walking and Cycling: New Perspectives on Sustainable Travel*, edited by Colin Pooley, 129–50. Bristol: Policy Press.

Horton, Robin. 1961. "Destiny and the Unconscious in West Africa." *Journal of the International African Institute* 31 (2): 110–16.

Howes, David, ed. 1991. *The Varieties of Sensory Experience: A Sourcebook in the Anthropology of the Senses*. Toronto: University of Toronto Press.

Jackson, Michael. 1988. "In the Thrown World: Destiny and Decision in the Thought of Traditional Africa." In *Choice and Morality in Anthropological Perspective: Essays in Honor of Derek Freeman*, edited by Derek Freeman, George N. Appell, and T. N. Madan, 193–210. Albany: State University of New York Press.

Jackson, Michael. 1989. *Paths toward a Clearing: Radical Empiricism and Ethnographic Inquiry*. Bloomington: Indiana University Press.

Jackson, Michael. 1996. "Introduction: Phenomenology, Radical Empiricism, and Anthropological Critique." In *Things as They Are: New Directions in Phenomenological Anthropology*, edited by Michael Jackson, 1–50. Bloomington: Indiana University Press.

Jackson, Michael, and Albert Piette. 2015. "Introduction: What Is Existential Anthropology?" In *What Is Existential Anthropology?*, edited by Michael Jackson and Albert Piette, 1st ed., 1–29. New York: Berghahn Books.

Jansen, Jean. 2009. "Framing Divination: A Mande Divination Expert and the Occult Economy." *Journal of the International African Institute* 79 (1): 110–27.

Jansen, Jean, and Namagan Kanté. 2010. *La géomancie des Monts mandingues: L'art de lire l'avenir dans le sable*. Bamako, Mali: Editions Yeelen.

Janson, Marloes. 2014. *Islam, Youth, and Modernity in the Gambia: The Tablighi Jama'at*. New York: Cambridge University Press.

Jonckers, Danielle. 1990. "La Sacralisation Du Pouvoir Chez Les Minyanka Du Mali." *Systèmes de Pensée En Afrique Noire*, no. 10: 145–67.

Jonckers, Danielle. 1993. "Autels sacrificiels et puissances religieuses. Le Manyan (Bamana—Minyanka, Mali)." *Systèmes de pensée en Afrique noire*, no. 12: 65–101.

Jones, Jim. 2002. *Industrial Labor in the Colonial World: Workers of the Chemin de Fer Dakar-Niger, 1881–1963*. Portsmouth, NH: Heinemann.

Jones, Phil. 2005. "Performing the City: A Body and a Bicycle Take on Birmingham, UK." *Social & Cultural Geography* 6 (6): 813–30.

Jónsson, Gunvor. 2008. "Migration Aspirations and Immobility in a Malian Soninke Village." *IMI Working Paper Series* 10: 1–45.

Kane, Ousmane. 2003. *Muslim Modernity in Postcolonial Nigeria: A Study of the Society for the Removal of Innovation and Reinstatement of Tradition*. Leiden: Brill.

Kassibo, Bréhima. 1992. "La Géomancie Ouest-Africaine. Formes Endogènes et Emprunts Extérieurs." *Cahiers d'Études Africaines* 32 (128): 541–96.

Kassibo, Bréhima, Bréhima Béridogo, Jérôme Coll, Yaouaga Félix Koné, and Soli Koné. 1997. "La Décentralisation au Mali: État des Lieux." Edited by Bréhima Kassibo. *Bulletin de l'APAD*, no. 14.

Kedzierska-Manzon, Agnieszka. 2014. *Chasseurs mandingues: violence, pouvoir et religion en Afrique de l'Ouest*. Paris: Karthala.

Keïta, Cheick Mahamadou Chérif. 1995. *Massa Makan Diabaté: Un Griot Mandingue à La Rencontre de l'écriture*. Paris: L'Harmattan.

Keïta, Naffet, ed. 2012. *L'Esclavage Au Mali*. Paris: L'Harmattan.

Khan Mohammad, Guive. 2016. "Ce Made in China Qui Fait Bouger l'Afrique. Motos Chinoises et Entrepreneuriat Au Burkina Faso." In *Entrepreneurs Africains et Chinois. Les Impacts Sociaux d'une Rencontre Particulière*, edited by Laurence Marfaing and Karsten Giese, 271–303. Paris: Karthala.

Kieffer, Julien. 2006. "Les jeunes des «grins» de thé et la campagne électorale à Ouagadougou." *Politique Africaine* no. 101 (1): 63–82.

Kipnis, Andrew B. 2008. *China and Postsocialist Anthropology: Theorizing Power and Society after Communism*. Norwalk, CT: Tate Publishing and Enterprises.

Klein, Martin A. 1998. *Slavery and Colonial Rule in French West Africa*. Cambridge: Cambridge University Press.

Klein, Martin A. 2005. "The Concept of Honour and the Persistence of Servility in the Western Soudan." *Cahiers d'Études Africaines* 45 (179–180): 831–52.

Klein, Martin A. 2009. "Slave Descent and Social Status in Sahara and Sudan." In *Reconfiguring Slavery: West African Trajectories*, edited by Benedetta Rossi, 26–44. Liverpool: Liverpool University Press.

Kobo, Ousman Murzik. 2012. *Unveiling Modernity in Twentieth-Century West African Islamic Reforms*. Leiden: Brill.

Koenig, D. 2005. "Social Stratification and Access to Wealth in the Rural Hinterland of Kita, Mali." In *Wari Matters: Ethnographic Explorations of Money in the Mande World*, edited by Stephen Wootton, 31–56. Münster: Lit.

Kohlhagen, Dominik. 2006. "Display, Fraud, and Cosmopolitanism. Coupé-Décalé's Success in Africa and Beyond." *Politique Africaine*, no. 100: 92–105.

Konaté, Doulaye. 2003. "Les Migrations 'Dogons' Au Wasulu (Mali Sud) Ou Le Pari de l'intégration Des Populations 'Déplacées' Dans Leur Milieu d'accueil." In *Etre Étranger et Migrant En Afrique Au XXe Siècle: Enjeux Identitaires et Mode d'insertion*. Paris: L'Harmattan.

Kresse, Kai. 2007. *Philosophising in Mombasa: Knowledge, Islam, and Intellectual Practice on the Swahili Coast*. London: Edinburgh University Press.

Kresse, Kai. 2018. *Swahili Muslim Publics and Postcolonial Experience*. Bloomington: Indiana University Press.

Kusenbach, Margarethe. 2003. "Street Phenomenology: The Go-Along as Ethnographic Research Tool." *Ethnography* 4 (3): 455–85.

Labouret, Henri. 1929. "La Parenté à Plaisanteries En Afrique Occidentale." *Africa: Journal of the International African Institute* 2 (3): 244–54.

Laidlaw, James. 2010. "Ethical Traditions in Question: Diaspora Jainism and the Environmental and Animal Liberation Movements." In *Ethical Life in South Asia*, edited by Anand Pandian and Daud Ali, 61–80. Bloomington: Indiana University Press.

Lambek, Michael. 2000. "The Anthropology of Religion and the Quarrel between Poetry and Philosophy." *Current Anthropology* 41 (3): 309–20.

Lambek, Michael. 2010a. "Introduction." In *Ordinary Ethics: Anthropology, Language, and Action*, edited by Michael Lambek, 1–36. New York: Fordham University Press.

Lambek, Michael. 2010b. "Toward an Ethics of the Act." In *Ordinary Ethics: Anthropology, Language, and Action*, edited by Michael Lambek, 39–63. New York: Fordham University Press.

Lambek, Michael. 2012. "Religion and Morality." In *A Companion to Moral Anthropology*, edited by Didier Fassin, 339–58. Chichester: John Wiley and Sons.

Lambek, Michael. 2015a. *The Ethical Condition: Essays on Action, Person and Value*. Chicago: University of Chicago Press.

Lambek, Michael. 2015b. "Living as If It Mattered." In *Four Lectures on Ethics: Anthropological Perspectives*, 5–51. Chicago: HAU Books.

Lambek, Michael. 2018. "On the Immanence of Ethics." In *Moral Engines: Exploring the Ethical Drives in Human Life*, edited by C. Mattingly, Rasmus Dyring, Maria Louw, and Thomas Schwarz Wentzer, 137–54. New York: Berghahn Books.

Lapidus, Ira M. 1997. "Islamic Revival and Modernity: The Contemporary Movements and the Historical Paradigms." *Journal of the Economic and Social History of the Orient* 40 (4): 444–60.

Larsen, Jonas. 2014. "Ethnography and Cycling." *International Journal of Social Research Methodology* 17 (1): 59–71.

Launay, Robert. 1988. "Warriors and Traders: The Political Organization of a West African Chiefdom." *Cahiers d'Études Africaines* 28 (111): 355–73.

Launay, Robert. 1992. *Beyond the Stream: Islam and Society in a West African Town*. Berkeley: University of California Press.

Launay, Robert. 2016. *Islamic Education in Africa: Writing Boards and Blackboards*. Bloomington: Indiana University Press.

Launay, Robert, and Benjamin F. Soares. 1999. "The Formation of an 'Islamic Sphere' in French Colonial West Africa." *Economy and Society* 28 (4): 497–519.

LeBlanc, Marie Nathalie, and Benjamin F. Soares. 2008. "Introduction to Special Issue: Muslim West Africa in the Age of Neoliberalism." *Africa Today* 54 (3): vii–xii.

Lecocq, Baz. 2010. *Disputed Desert: Decolonisation, Competing Nationalisms, and Tuareg Rebellions in Northern Mali*. Leiden: Brill.

Lecocq, Baz. 2015. "Distant Shores: A Historiographic View on Trans-Saharan Space." *Journal of African History* 56 (1): 23–36.

Lecocq, Baz, and Georg Klute. 2018. "Tuareg Separatism in Mali and Niger." In *Secessionism in African Politics: Aspiration, Grievance, Performance, Disenchantment*, edited by Lotje de Vries, Pierre Englebert, and Mareike Schomerus, 23–57. London: Palgrave Macmillan.

Lefebvre, Henri. 2000. *La production de l'espace*. Paris: Éd. Anthropos. Originally published 1974.

Lindholm, Charles. 1985. "Paradigms of Society: A Critique of Theories of Caste among Indian Muslims." *European Journal of Sociology* 26 (1): 131–41.

Loimeier, Roman. 2016. *Islamic Reform in Twentieth-Century Africa*. Edinburgh: Edinburgh University Press.

Long, Susan Orpett, and Scott Clark. 1999. "Introduction." In *Lives in Motion: Composing Circles of Self and Community in Japan*, edited by Susan Orpett Long. Ithaca, NY: East Asia Program, Cornell University.

Louis, Matthieu. 2014. "Ethnologie de l'aventure: pratiques contemporaines de la mobilité masculine et productions identitaires en Afrique de l'Ouest (Burkina Faso)." Université de Strasbourg.

Low, Setha M., and Denise Lawrence-Zúñiga, eds. 2003. *The Anthropology of Space and Place: Locating Culture*. Malden, MA: Blackwell.

Lugo, Adonia E. 2012. "Planning for Diverse Use/Rs: Ethnographic Research on Bikes, Bodies, and Public Space in LA." *Kroeber Anthropological Society* 101 (1): 49–65.

Lydon, Ghislaine. 2005. "Slavery, Exchange, and Islamic Law: A Glimpse from the Archives of Mali and Mauritania." *African Economic History*, no. 33: 117–48.

Lyons, Michal, and Alison Brown. 2010. "Has Mercantilism Reduced Urban Poverty in SSA? Perception of Boom, Bust, and the China–Africa Trade in Lomé and Bamako." *World Development* 38 (5): 771–82.

Mahmood, Saba. 2005. *Politics of Piety: The Islamic Revival and the Feminist Subject*. Princeton: Princeton University Press.

Mamdani, Mahmood. 1996. *Citizen and Subject: Contemporary Africa and the Legacy of Late Colonialism*. Princeton: Princeton University Press.

Mamdani, Mahmood. 2004. *Good Muslim, Bad Muslim: America, the Cold War, and the Roots of Terror*. 1st ed. New York: Pantheon Books.

Manchuelle, François. 1989. "Slavery, Emancipation, and Labour Migration in West Africa: The Case of the Soninke." *Journal of African History* 30 (1): 89–106.

Manchuelle, François. 1997. *Willing Migrants: Soninke Labor Diasporas, 1848–1960*. Athens: Ohio University Press.

Mann, Gregory. 2003. "Old Soldiers, Young Men: Masculinity, Islam, and Military Veterans in Late 1950s Soudan Français (Mali)." In *Men and Masculinities in Modern Africa*, edited by Lisa A. Lindsay and Stephan Miescher, 69–87. Portsmouth, NH: Heinemann.

Manrique, Nathalie. 2015. "Noces gitanes: ostentation et dissimulation." *Cahiers d'anthropologie sociale* no. 12 (2): 95–107.

Marsden, Magnus. 2005. *Living Islam: Muslim Religious Experience in Pakistan's North-West Frontier*. Cambridge: Cambridge University Press.

Marsden, Magnus. 2009. "A Tour Not So Grand: Mobile Muslims in Northern Pakistan." *Journal of the Royal Anthropological Institute* 15: S57–75.

Marsden, Magnus, and Konstantinos Retsikas. 2013. "Introduction." In *Articulating Islam: Anthropological Approaches to Muslim Worlds*, edited by Magnus Marsden and Konstantinos Retsikas, 1–33. Heidelberg: Springer Netherlands.

Marshall-Fratani, Ruth. 2006. "The War of 'Who Is Who': Autochthony, Nationalism, and Citizenship in the Ivoirian Crisis." *African Studies Review* 49 (2): 9–44.

Masquelier, Adeline. 2001. *Prayer Has Spoiled Everything: Possession, Power, and Identity in an Islamic Town of Niger*. Durham: Duke University Press.

Masquelier, Adeline. 2007. "Negotiating Futures: Islam, Youth, and the State in Niger." In *Islam and Muslim Politics in Africa*, edited by Benjamin F. Soares and René Otayek, 243–62. New York: Palgrave Macmillan US.

Masquelier, Adeline Marie. 2009. *Women and Islamic Revival in a West African Town*. Bloomington: Indiana University Press.

Masquelier, Adeline Marie. 2019. *Fada: Boredom and Belonging in Niger*. Chicago: University of Chicago Press.

Masquelier, Adeline Marie, and Benjamin F. Soares, eds. 2016. *Muslim Youth and the 9/11 Generation*. Albuquerque: University of New Mexico Press.

Masuzawa, Tomoko. 2005. *The Invention of World Religions; or, How European Universalism Was Preserved in the Language of Pluralism*. Chicago: University of Chicago Press.

Mbembe, Achille. 2000. *De la postcolonie: essai sur l'imagination politique dans l'Afrique contemporaine*. Paris: Karthala.

McNaughton, Patrick R. 1988. *The Mande Blacksmiths: Knowledge, Power, and Art in West Africa*. Bloomington: Indiana University Press.

McNaughton, Patrick R. 1995. "The Semantics of Jugu: Blacksmiths, Lore, and 'Who's Bad' in Mande." In *Status and Identity in West Africa: Nyamakalaw of Mande*, edited by David C. Conrad and Barbara E. Frank, 46–57. Bloomington: Indiana University Press.

Meillassoux, Claude. 1963. "Histoire et Institutions Du 'Kafo' de Bamako d'après La Tradition Des Niaré." *Cahiers d'Études Africaines* 4 (14): 186–227.

Meillassoux, Claude. 1981. *Maidens, Meal, and Money: Capitalism and the Domestic Community*. Cambridge: Cambridge University Press.

Méker, Maurice. 1980. *Le Temps Colonial: Itinéraire Africain d'un Naïf Du Colonialisme à La Coopération, 1931–1960*. Dakar: Nouvelles Éditions Africaines.

Miles, William F. S. 2004a. "Conclusions." *African Studies Review* 47 (2): 109–17.

Miles, William F. 2004b. "Introduction." *African Studies Review* 47 (2): 55–59.

Mitchell, W.J.T. 2005. *What Do Pictures Want? The Lives and Loves of Images*. Chicago: University of Chicago Press.

Mokhefi, Mansouria, and Alain Antil, eds. 2012. *Le Maghreb et son Sud: vers des liens renouvelés*. Paris: CNRS.

Mommersteeg, Geert, ed. 2009. *Dans la cité des marabouts: Djenné, Mali*. Translated by Mireille Cohendy. Brinon-sur-Sauldre, France: Grandvaux.

Moulard, Sophie. 2008. "'Senegal yewuleen!' Analyse anthropologique du rap à Dakar: liminarité, contestation et culture populaire." PhD thesis, Université Victor Segalen—Bordeaux II.

Newell, Sasha. 2012. *The Modernity Bluff: Crime, Consumption, and Citizenship in Côte d'Ivoire*. Chicago: University of Chicago Press.

Newton, Robert C. 1999. "Out of Print: The Epic Cassette as Intervention, Reinvention, and Commodity." In *In Search of Sunjata: The Mande Oral Epic as History, Literature, and Performance*, edited by Ralph A. Austen, 313–27. Bloomington: Indiana University Press.

N'Guessan, Kouakou F. 1983. "Les Maquis' d'Abidjan: Nourritures Du Terroir et Fraternité Citadine, Ou La Conscience de Classe Autour d'un Foutou d'igname." *Cahiers ORSTOM. Série Sciences Humaines* 19 (4): 545–50.

Niane, Djibril Tamsir. 1960. *Soundjata Ou l'épopée Mandingue*. Paris: Éd. Présence Africaine.

Nyamnjoh, Francis B. 2001. "Delusions of Development and the Enrichment of Witchcraft Discourses in Cameroon." In *Magical Interpretations, Material Realities: Modernity, Witchcraft, and the Occult in Postcolonial Africa*, edited by Henrietta L. Moore and Todd Sanders. London: Routledge.

Olivier de Sardan, Jean-Pierre. 1996. "L'économie morale de la corruption en Afrique." *Politique Africaine*, no. 63: 97–116.

Olivier de Sardan, Jean-Pierre. 1999. "African Corruption in the Context of Globalization." In *Modernity on a Shoestring: Dimensions of Globalization, Consumption, and Development in Africa and Beyond*, edited by R. Fardon, W.M.J. Binsbergen, and R. A. Dijk, 247–69. Leiden: EIDOS.

Omokaro, Françoise Grange. 2009. "Féminités et masculinités bamakoises en temps de globalisation." *Autrepart*, no. 49: 189–204.

Orsi, Robert A. 2012. "Afterword: Everyday Religion and the Contemporary World: The Un-Modern, or What Was Supposed to Have Disappeared but Did Not." In *Ordinary Lives and Grand Schemes: An Anthropology of Everyday Religion*, 146–61. New York: Berghahn Books.

Ortner, Sherry B. 2005. "Subjectivity and Cultural Critique." *Anthropological Theory* 5 (1): 31–52.

Osella, Filippo, and Caroline Osella. 2008. "Islamism and Social Reform in Kerala, South India." *Modern Asian Studies* 42 (2–3): 317–46.

Osella, Filippo, and Caroline Osella. 2009. "Muslim Entrepreneurs in Public Life between India and the Gulf: Making Good and Doing Good." *Journal of the Royal Anthropological Institute* 15 (s1): 202–21.

Osella, Filippo, and Caroline Osella. 2011. "Migration, Neoliberal Capitalism, and Islamic Reform in Kozhikode (Calicut), South India." *International Labor and Working-Class History* 79 (1): 140–60.

Osella, Filippo, and Daromir Rudnyckyj. 2017. "Introduction: Assembling Market and Religious Moralities." In *Religion and the Morality of the Market*, edited by Daromir Rudnyckyj and Filippo Osella, 1–28. Cambridge: Cambridge University Press.

Otayek, René. 1993. *Le radicalisme islamique au Sud du Sahara: Da'wa, arabisation et critique de l'Occident*. Paris: Karthala.

Otayek, René, and Benjamin F. Soares. 2007. "Introduction: Islam and Muslim Politics in Africa." In *Islam and Muslim Politics in Africa*, edited by Benjamin F. Soares and René Otayek, 1–24. New York: Palgrave Macmillan US.

Pandolfo, Stefania. 2007. "'The Burning': Finitude and the Politico-Theological Imagination of Illegal Migration." *Anthropological Theory* 7 (3): 329–63.

Panella, Cristiana. 2012. *Lives in Motion, Indeed. Interdisciplinary Perspectives on Social Change in Honour of Danielle de Lame*. Tervuren, Belgium: Royal Museum for Central Africa.

Park, Yoon Jung. 2013. "The Chinese, the Taiwanese, 'Fong Kong,' and Labor in South Africa." Lecture at Ralph J. Bunche International Affairs Center. September 12. *Cowries and Rice* (blog).

Parkin, David J. 1972. *Palms, Wine, and Witnesses: Public Spirit and Private Gain in an African Farm Community*. 1st ed. London: Intertext Books.

Parkin, David J. 1985. "Introduction." In *The Anthropology of Evil*, edited by David J. Parkin, 1–25. Oxford: Basil Blackwell.

Patel, Reena. 2010. *Working the Night Shift: Women in India's Call Center Industry*. Stanford: Stanford University Press.

Perinbam, B. Marie. 1998. *Family Identity and the State in the Bamako Kafu, c.1800–c.1900*. Boulder: Westview Press.

Perret, Thierry. 2005. "Médias et démocratie au Mali." *Politique africaine* 97 (1): 18–32.

Person, Yves. 1970. *Samori: une révolution dyula*. Vol. 2. Dakar: IFAN.

Peterson, Brian. 2002. "Quantifying Conversion: A Note on the Colonial Census and Religious Change in Postwar Southern Mali." *History in Africa* 29: 381–92.

Peterson, Brian J. 2008. "History, Memory and the Legacy of Samori in Southern Mali, c. 1880–1889." *Journal of African History* 49 (2): 261–79.

Peterson, Brian J. 2011. *Islamization from Below: The Making of Muslim Communities in Rural French Sudan, 1880–1960*. New Haven: Yale University Press.

Peterson, Brian J. 2012. "Mali 'Islamisation' Tackled: The Other Ansar Dine, Popular Islam, and Religious Tolerance." *African Arguments* (blog). 2012.

Prévitali, Stéphane. 1999. *Je Me Souviens de Ruben: Mon Témoignage Sur Les Maquis Du Cameroun, 1953–1970*. Paris: Karthala.

Rain, David. 1999. *Eaters of the Dry Season: Circular Labor Migration in the West African Sahel*. Boulder: Westview Press.

Ram, Kalpana, and Christopher Houston. 2015. "Introduction: Phenomenology's Methodological Invitation." In *Phenomenology in Anthropology: A Sense of Perspective*, edited by Kalpana Ram and Christopher Houston, 1–26. Bloomington: Indiana University Press.

Rappaport, Roy A. 1999. *Ritual and Religion in the Making of Humanity*. Cambridge: Cambridge University Press.

Rasmussen, Susan J. 2000. "Between Several Worlds: Images of Youth and Age in Tuareg Popular Performances." *Anthropological Quarterly* 73 (3): 133–44.

Rawson, David. 2000. "Dimensions of Decentralization in Mali." In *Democracy and Development in Mali*, edited by R. James Bingen, David Robinson, and John M. Staatz, 265–88. East Lansing: Michigan State University Press.

Riccio, Bruno. 2001. "Disaggregating the Transnational Community: Senegalese Migrants on the Coast of Emilia-Romagna." *ESRC Transnational Communities Programme Working Paper Series*, no. 11: 1–29.

Riccio, Bruno. 2005. "Talkin' about Migration: Some Ethnographic Notes on the Ambivalent Representation of Migrants in Contemporary Senegal." *Vienna Journal of African Studies* 5 (8): 99–118.

Riesman, Paul. 1977. *Freedom in Fulani Social Life: An Introspective Ethnography*. Chicago: University of Chicago Press.

Rosander, Eva Evers, and David Westerlund. 1997. *African Islam and Islam in Africa: Encounters between Sufis and Islamists*. London: C Hurst & Co.

Rouch, Jean, dir. 1957. *Moi, un Noir* [I, a Negro]. Icarus Films.

Rouch, Jean, dir. 1967. *Jaguar*. Editions Montparnasse.

Rudnyckyj, Daromir. 2010. *Spiritual Economies: Islam, Globalization, and the Afterlife of Development*. Ithaca: Cornell University Press.

Sah, Léonard. 2008. *Femmes Bamiléké Au Maquis: Cameroun, 1955–1971*. Paris: Harmattan.

Salter, Christopher Lord. 1969. "The Bicycle as Field Aid." *Professional Geographer* 21 (5): 360–62.

Samaké, Maximin. 1988. "Kafo et pouvoir lignager chez les Banmana. L'hégémonie gonkòròbi dans le Cendugu." *Cahiers d'Études Africaines* 28 (111): 331–54.

Sanogo, Abdrahamane. 2008. "Les relations économiques de la Chine et du Mali." Working Paper. Bamako: AERC Scoping Studies on China-Africa Economic Relations.

Sarró, Ramon. 2009. *The Politics of Religious Change on the Upper Guinea Coast: Iconoclasm Done and Undone*. Edinburgh: Edinburgh University Press for the International African Institute.

Schielke, Samuli. 2006. "Mawlids and Modernists: Dangers of Fun." In *ISIM Review* 17: 6–7.

Schielke, Samuli. 2009. "Being Good in Ramadan: Ambivalence, Fragmentation, and the Moral Self in the Lives of Young Egyptians." *Journal of the Royal Anthropological Institute* 15: S24–40.

Schielke, Samuli. 2010. "Second Thoughts about the Anthropology of Islam, or How to Make Sense of Grand Schemes in Everyday Life." ZMO Working Paper Series 2. Berlin: Zentrum Moderner Orient.

Schielke, Samuli. 2015. "Living with Unresolved Differences: A Reply to Fadil and Fernando." *HAU: Journal of Ethnographic Theory* 5 (2): 89–92.

Schielke, Samuli. 2019. "The Power of God: Four Proposals for an Anthropological Engagement." ZMO Programmatic Texts Series. Vol. 13. Berlin: Leibniz-Zentrum Moderner Orient (ZMO).

Schielke, Samuli, and Liza Debevec. 2012. "Introduction." In *Ordinary Lives and Grand Schemes*, edited by Samuli Schielke and Liza Debevec, 1st ed., 1–16. New York: Berghahn Books.

Schimmel, Annemarie. 2011. *Mystical Dimensions of Islam*. Chapel Hill: University of North Carolina Press.

Schmitz, Jean. 2000. "Le souffle de la parenté. Mariage et transmission de la baraka chez les clercs musulmans." *L'Homme*, no. 154–55: 241–78.

Schmitz, Jean. 2006. "Des «aventuriers» Aux «notables» Urbains. Economies Morales et Communautés Transnationales Des Gens Du Fleuve Sénégal." Anthropologie Du Voyage et Migrations Internationales. Fonds d'analyse des sociétés politiques.

Schmitz, Jean. 2008. "Migrants ouest-africains vers l'Europe: historicité et espace moraux." *Politique africaine* 109 (1): 5–15.

Schnepel, Burkhard, and Eyal Ben-Ari. 2005. "Introduction: 'When Darkness Comes . . .': Steps toward an Anthropology of the Night." *Paideuma* 51: 153–63.

Schulz, Dorothea E. 2002. "'The World Is Made by Talk': Female Fans, Popular Music, and New Forms of Public Sociality in Urban Mali." *Cahiers d'Études Africaines* 168 (4): 797–830.

Schulz, Dorothea E. 2003. "'Charisma and Brotherhood' Revisited: Mass-Mediated Forms of Spirituality in Urban Mali." *Journal of Religion in Africa* 33 (2): 146–71.

Schulz, Dorothea E. 2005. "Love Potions and Money Machines: Commercial Occultism and the Reworking of Social Relations in Urban Mali." In *Wari Matters: Ethnographic Explorations of Money in the Mande World*, edited by Stephen Wootton, 93–115. Münster: Lit Verlag.

Schulz, Dorothea E. 2006. "Promises of (Im)Mediate Salvation: Islam, Broadcast Media, and the Remaking of Religious Experience in Mali." *American Ethnologist* 33 (2): 210–19.

Schulz, Dorothea E. 2007. "'Evoking Moral Community, Fragmenting Muslim Discourses: Sermon Audio-Recording and the Reconfiguration of Public Debate in Mali.'" *Journal for Islamic Studies* 27: 39–72.

Schulz, Dorothea E. 2012. *Muslims and New Media in West Africa: Pathways to God.* Bloomington: Indiana University Press.

Seesemann, Rudiger. 2011. *The Divine Flood: Ibrahim Niasse and the Roots of a Twentieth-Century Sufi Revival.* Oxford: Oxford University Press.

Shklar, Judith. 1979. "Let Us Not Be Hypocritical." *Daedalus* 108 (3): 1–25.

Simmel, Georg. 1950. *The Sociology of Georg Simmel.* New York: Free Press.

Simon, Gregory M. 2009. "The Soul Freed of Cares? Islamic Prayer, Subjectivity, and the Contradictions of Moral Selfhood in Minangkabau, Indonesia." *American Ethnologist* 36 (2): 258–75.

Sissoko, Mamadou. 2007. *Odyssée Héroïque, Cinquante Ans d'action de l'homme El Hadji Abdoulaye Koné Ladji-Blen: Belles Lettres, Connaissance Mystique, Morale Politique; La Palme Du Martyr, Aventures, Critiques Sociales et Religieuses: Une Mission Suicide.* Bamako, Mali: Editions Jamana.

Skinner, Ryan Thomas. 2015. *Bamako Sounds: The Afropolitan Ethics of Malian Music.* Minneapolis: University of Minnesota Press.

Sloane-White, Patricia. 2017. *Corporate Islam: Sharia and the Modern Workplace.* Cambridge: Cambridge University Press.

Sneath, David. 2009. "Reading the Signs by Lenin's Light: Development, Divination, and Metonymic Fields in Mongolia." *Ethnos* 74 (1): 72–90.

Soares, Benjamin F. 1997. "The Fulbe Shaykh and the Bambara 'Pagans': Contemporary Campaigns to Spread Islam in Mali." In *Peuls et Mandingues: Dialectique Des Constructions Identitaires*, by M. E. de Bruijn and J.W.M. van Dijk, 267–80. Paris: Karthala.

Soares, Benjamin F. 2004. "Islam and Public Piety in Mali." In *Public Islam and the Common Good*, edited by Armando Salvatore and Dale F. Eickelman, 205–25. Brill.

Soares, Benjamin F. 2005. *Islam and the Prayer Economy: History and Authority in a Malian Town.* London: Edinburgh University Press.

Soares, Benjamin F. 2006. "Islam in Mali in the Neoliberal Era." *African Affairs* 105 (418): 77–95.

Soares, Benjamin F. 2007. "Saint and Sufi in Contemporary Mal." In *Sufism and the "Modern" in Islam*, edited by Julia Howell and Martin van Bruinessen, 76–92. London: I. B. Tauris.

Soares, Benjamin F. 2010. "'Rasta Sufis' and Muslim Youth Culture in Mali." In *Being Young and Muslim*, edited by Asef Bayat and Linda Herrera, 241–57. Oxford: Oxford University Press.

Soares, Benjamin F. 2014. "The Historiography of Islam in West Africa: An Anthropologist's View." *Journal of African History* 55 (1): 27–36.

Soares, Benjamin F. 2017. "'Structural Adjustment Islam' and the Religious Economy in Neoliberal Mali." In *Religion and the Morality of the Market*, edited by Daromir Rudnyckyj and Filippo Osella, 138–59. Cambridge: Cambridge University Press.

Soares, Benjamin F., and Filippo Osella. 2009. "Islam, Politics, Anthropology." *Journal of the Royal Anthropological Institute* 15 (1): 1–23.

Sounaye, Abdoulaye. 2016. *Islam et Modernité: Contribution à l'analyse de La Ré-Islamisation Au Niger*. Paris: L'Harmattan.

Sounaye, Abdoulaye. 2017. *Salafi Revolution in West Africa*. Vol. 19. ZMO Working Papers. Berlin: Leibniz-Zentrum Moderner Orient (ZMO).

Steger, Brigitte, and Lodewijk Brunt. 2003. *Night-Time and Sleep in Asia and the West: Exploring the Dark Side of Life*. London: Routledge.

Stewart, Alexander. 2016. *Chinese Muslims and the Global Ummah: Islamic Revival and Ethnic Identity among the Hui of Qinghai Province*. New York: Routledge.

Stoller, Paul. 2010. *Money Has No Smell: The Africanization of New York City*. Chicago: University of Chicago Press.

Tacoli, Cecilia. 2001. "Urbanisation and Migration in Sub-Saharan Africa: Changing Patterns and Trends." In *Mobile Africa: Changing Patterns of Movement in Africa and Beyond*, edited by Mirjam de Bruijn, Rijk van Dijk, and Dick Foeken, 141–52. Leiden: Brill.

Tamari, Tal. 1991. "The Development of Caste Systems in West Africa." *Journal of African History* 32 (2): 221–50.

Tamari, Tal. 1996. "L'exégèse coranique (tafsîr) en milieu mandingue: rapport préliminaire sur une recherche en cours." *Islam et sociétés au sud du Sahara* 10: 43–79.

Thomassen, Bjørn. 2012. "Anthropology and Its Many Modernities: When Concepts Matter." *Journal of the Royal Anthropological Institute* 18 (1): 160–78.

Thurston, Alexander. 2016. *Salafism in Nigeria: Islam, Preaching, and Politics*. New York: Cambridge University Press.

Toé, Richard. 1997. *Décentralisation Au Mali: Ancrage Historique et Dynamique Socioculturelle*. Bamako, Mali: Imprim Color.

Touré, Abdou, and Yacouba Konaté. 1990. *Sacrifices dans la ville: le citadin chez le devin en Côte d'Ivoire*. Abidjan, Côte d'Ivoire: Editions Douga.

Tripp, Charles. 2006. *Islam and the Moral Economy: The Challenge of Capitalism*. Oxford: Oxford University Press.

Tuan, Yi-fu. 1977. *Space and Place: The Perspective of Experience*. Minneapolis: University of Minnesota Press.

Turco, Angelo. 2007. "Sémantiques de la violence: territoire, guerre et pouvoir en Afrique mandingue." *Cahiers de géographie du Québec* 51 (144): 307–32.

Valentine, Gill, Sarah L Holloway, and Mark Jayne. 2010. "Contemporary Cultures of Abstinence and the Nighttime Economy: Muslim Attitudes towards Alcohol and the Implications for Social Cohesion." *Environment and Planning A: Economy and Space* 42: 8–22.

van Binsbergen, W.M.J. 2005. "Commodification: Things, Agency, and Identities: Introduction." In *Commodification. Things, Agency, and Identities (The Social Life of Things Revisted)*, edited by W.M.J. van Binsbergen and Peter Geschiere, 9–51. Münster: Lit Verlag.

Verne, Jules. 2005. *Voyages et Aventures Du Capitaine Hatteras*. Paris: Gallimard. Originally published 1866.

Villalón, Leonardo A. 1995. *Islamic Society and State Power in Senegal: Disciples and Citizens in Fatick.* Cambridge: Cambridge University Press.

Vincourt, Sarah, and Souleymane Kouyaté. 2012. "Ce que «parler au grin» veut dire: sociabilité urbaine, politique de la rue et reproduction sociale en Côte d'Ivoire." *Politique africaine* 127 (3): 91–108.

Vivanco, Luis Antonio. 2013. *Reconsidering the Bicycle: An Anthropological Perspective on a New (Old) Thing.* New York: Routledge.

Wacquant, Loïc, and Pierre Bourdieu. 2000. "La nouvelle vulgate planétaire." *Le Monde diplomatique*, May 1.

Ware, Rudolph T. 2014. *The Walking Qur'an: Islamic Education, Embodied Knowledge, and History in West Africa.* Chapel Hill: University of North Carolina Press.

Warms, Richard L. 1992. "Merchants, Muslims, and Wahhābiyya: The Elaboration of Islamic Identity in Sikasso, Mali." *Canadian Journal of African Studies* 26 (3): 485–507.

Warms, Richard L. 1994. "Commerce and Community: Paths to Success for Malian Merchants." *African Studies Review* 37 (2): 97–120.

Weber, Max. 2001. *The Protestant Ethic and the Spirit of Capitalism.* London: Routledge.

Werbner, Richard. 2002. "Introduction: Postcolonial Subjectivities: The Personal, the Political, and the Moral." In *Postcolonial Subjectivities in Africa*, edited by Richard Werbner, 1–21. London: Zed Books.

Whitehouse, Bruce. 2012. *Migrants and Strangers in an African City: Exile, Dignity, Belonging.* Bloomington: Indiana University Press.

Williams, Raymond. 2011. *The Long Revolution.* Cardigan, Wales: Parthian Books.

Wooten, Stephen. 2005. "Maidens, Meal, and Money on the Mande Plateau: A Contemporary Perspective on Capitalism and the Domestic Community in West Africa." In *Wari Matters: Ethnographic Explorations of Money in the Mande World*, edited by Stephen Wooten, 14–30. Münster: Lit Verlag.

Zucarelli, François. 1973. "De La Chefferie Traditionnelle Au Canton: Évolution Du Canton Colonial Au Sénégal, 1855–1960." *Cahiers d'Études Africaines* 13 (50): 213–38.

Printed and bound by CPI Group (UK) Ltd, Croydon, CR0 4YY

09/06/2025

14685676-0001